Blueprint for Transforming HR

Through AI and Evidence

Burak Bakkaloglu

Blueprint for Transforming HR

Published by Manhattan Book Group, LLC
447 Broadway | 2nd Floor #354 | New York, NY 10013 | USA
1.800.767.0531 | (212) 634-7677 | www.manhattanbookgroup.com

Printed in the United States of America.

ISBN-13: 978-1-966074-46-5

Contents

SECTION 1
AI: Navigating the Future of Enterprise

SECTION 2
Performance Management

SECTION 3
Succession Planning and Talent Density

SECTION 3A
Succession Planning

SECTION 3B
High Talent Density

SECTION 4
Leadership Frameworks

SECTION 5

Foreword

HR possesses an enormous untapped potential to deliver meaningful value for employees, organizations, and shareholders alike. Yet this potential remains largely unrealized because we in HR are not using evidence-based approaches and user-friendly technologies enough. This eventually leads to missing chances to implement systemic, fair, and humane solutions for all employees. AI arrives at the right moment to help HR fulfill this potential, offering powerful tools that can enable truly fair and systemic solutions. This book is for CEOs, boards and executives who want to understand what they should expect from modern HR functions, as well as for HR professionals who value a critical look at established practices.

In my twenty-five years working across engineering, consulting, and HR leadership, I've observed how conventional wisdom often hinders HR from embracing these possibilities, perpetuating well-intentioned practices that ultimately create unfair and unhealthy work environments. The status quo isn't serving anyone, not employees seeking meaningful work, not organizations striving for excellence, and ultimately, not even shareholders looking for sustainable returns. So, I decided to present my approach to major topics of the people agenda.

Organizations are complex systems, their culture, employees, competition landscape, macro-economic factors, their board and executive team, and the interdependency and dynamism between those factors are astonishing to observe. I try to use a systems thinking approach to a complex world like this, and use a pinch of critical thinking along the way. Systems thinking focuses on how components interact within larger structures, considering integration, operation, and evolution over time. When we view organizations through this lens, examining how people, processes, and technology interconnect, we arrive at solutions that conventional HR thinking often misses.

I also happen to have a fascination with technology and how it shapes the culture. For example, the invention of the plow led to greater gender inequality. Males had a particular advantage in using the plow because it requires upper body strength. This meant males became the dominant force in economic production at the household level. Contraceptive technologies had deep cultural impact of educational and economic transformation for women, family structures and sexual norms. Technology is not neutral, it shapes us.

Enter AI. Like many, AI has been in my focus for a while. I have worked with bright tech teams from the forefront vendor ecosystem on early AI use cases and implementations. I had the opportunity to connect the science of talent management with user-friendly interfaces and data architecture to build the foundation of Generative AI use cases. From what I have experienced, Generative AI is the once-in-a-lifetime opportunity to make employee lives easier and more fulfilling, while creating immense value for shareholders and societies.

My friends know that I like to converse in movie scenes, and mostly movies from 1990s and 2000s. In "Alien Resurrection" (1997), there is a scene where Ripley (Sigourney Weaver) discovers that Annalee Call (Winona Ryder) is an android about two-thirds into the movie. Upon this revelation, Ripley remarks, "I should have known. No human being is that humane." This scene has stuck with me, and was the seed of my belief that AI will lend a hand to humans in the journey of evolution.

I have also been fortunate to work alongside exceptional business leaders and HR practitioners who helped shape this perspective. They challenged my thinking, opened new horizons of knowledge, and demonstrated what true leadership looks like. They have valued and nurtured my critical thinking, and beside my technology focus, they allowed me to keep an eye on unorthodox evidence-based HR practices.

This book particularly benefited from two highly respected leaders, colleagues, and friends who reviewed every word I wrote. Their thoughtful challenges, ideas and sharp inquiries made this a more complete work.

Eventually, the book emerged as a vision of how AI and evidence can fundamentally transform HR.

Some housekeeping before you start: I have structured this book into five independent sections that you can approach in any order. After difficult prioritization, I selected the topics with the greatest impact on both organizational success and employee experience: understanding AI's role in HR, reimagining performance management, building talent density, developing effective leadership frameworks for culture change, and skills-based organizations. This isn't a light reading filled with stories and sparse on substance. Instead, you will find practical, executable advice backed by scientific evidence, a condensed source of insights for transforming your approach to people management in the AI era.

I don't claim to have perfect answers or an infallible vision for HR's future. My intention is to present clear thinking, sound science, and proven practices that empower you to develop your own informed perspective. With enough of us challenging conventional wisdom and thinking critically about these systems, we can transform HR to better serve both the people who make up our organizations and the stakeholders who depend on them.

Thank you for your curiosity

SECTION 1

AI: Navigating the Future of Enterprise

Introduction

The plow, seemingly a simple technological advancement, was created to serve specific values: making work easier, faster, and more productive to ensure food security. Beyond its practical agricultural function, its demanding physical requirements favored male farmers due to their upper body strength, changing gender roles in society. As the plow led to animal domestication, it transformed humanity's relationship with nature, contributing to the shift from animistic to theocentric religious beliefs[1].

Today, AI has a similar importance. Designed to enhance productivity and efficiency, it promises to fundamentally alter how we live and work. This section maps out AI's current and future impact on professional life through practical examples and market projections. We will begin with essential technical context before exploring how and why organizations are deploying AI today. From there onwards, we will discuss the impacts of AI Agents, autonomous systems that can complete complex tasks, currently the most disruptive element to the business world, and then move towards AI as a trusted coworker. Along the way, we will discuss how specific jobs will be impacted by AI and give practical steps for effective AI deployment.

Just as our ancestors couldn't foresee the plow's complete set of effects, it is impossible to cover all of AI's effects here, even if we narrow the content to only enterprise-related effects. This section, however, is intended to inspire thoughtful conversations and, hopefully, a more informed implementation of AI.

---

[1] Technology is Not Values Neutral: Ending the Reign of Nihilistic Design - The Consilience Project

Fundamentals of Generative AI

From Bayes to social media, doomscrolling algorithms have quietly shaped us for decades, but now they're front and center.

Artificial Intelligence (AI) has been around for some time. In the 1950s, it was formally established as a field during the Dartmouth Summer Research Project on AI. John McCarthy, who coined the term "artificial intelligence," organized this conference[2], which brought together key figures in computing and cognitive science. Long before that, Thomas Bayes's work on probability theory in 1763 became foundational for machine learning techniques later used in AI. Machine learning, algorithms, and AI are not new to our lives.

In the past decades, we have experienced algorithms much more often. Social media platforms have learned our preferences and created algorithms to keep us looking at our screens for hours on end. These algorithms have learned what keeps us engaged or even enraged and fed us content accordingly. At times, they study our preferences in a way that they will predict our needs before we even knew we needed them. The algorithms are so good that we end up buying the suggested merchandise and get caught up in the cycle of outrage, which was precisely the intention. We can say, with a bit of remorse, that machine learning algorithms have been quietly shaping our lives for quite some time.

On the other hand, machine learning algorithms have also been working behind the scenes in corporations' internal workings. They help automate tasks, analyze sensor data to predict equipment failures, and schedule maintenance. They analyze customer data, such as purchase history, behavior, and demographics, to segment customers and assign credit scores. They also assist recruiters by analyzing resumes and skills to match candidates to job openings.

All these applications and use cases were in the background, and users were not exposed to them too directly. With ChatGPT, this changed.

ChatGPT wasn't just another AI tool; it was the first time we talked to the machine, and for once, it talked back.

---

[2]   https://www.coursera.org/articles/history-of-ai

In November 2022, we met ChatGPT, and everything changed. For the first time, we began consciously interacting with AI rather than being a subject to its learning or target segment. ChatGPT was a different breed of AI called a Large Language Model, or LLM for short. It allowed us to have conversations on any topic, ask any question, and even seek help on any subject. The accuracy of its responses varied; sometimes it hallucinated, sometimes the guidance wasn't helpful, but most of the time, it gave the correct answers in a way that felt like a conversation with a highly knowledgeable person. Within just five days of its release, ChatGPT reached a million users, something that took Instagram two and a half months. We liked ChatGPT, and we liked it fast.

AI has been coming for 75 years. Why now? Well, we now have one: massive, cheap cloud computing; two, massive amounts of data; and three, advancements in algorithms such as the Transformer.

With those ingredients in the market, as it turned out, several other tech companies were simultaneously developing their own large language models (LLMs), with ChatGPT being just the first to launch. Within two years of ChatGPT's debut, multiple highly capable AI models emerged from other tech giants, their own versions of ChatGPT. Notable examples are Gemini from Google, Llama from Meta, Grok from X, and Claude from Anthropic. Collectively, these were known as foundation models.

LLMs are a subsection of Generative AI. We can simply define GenAI as a type of artificial intelligence that can create new content, such as text, images, audio, or video, by learning patterns from existing data. It is an overarching term for LLMs, diffusion models, and similar AI technologies.

What Are Large Language Models (LLMs)

Large language models (LLMs) are advanced AI models designed to understand, generate, and manipulate human language. They are typically trained on the vast amounts of information available on the internet, which gives them the ability to understand and generate language.

Transformers, introduced in 2017, are the technology that has made LLMs possible. With transformer architecture, we were able to train LLMs. That training gave LLMs the ability to predict the next token in a long chain of words. You can think of a token simply as a word. The prediction works like this:

"I've been studying now for two hours; I need a..." The LLM, understanding the sequence of words here, suggests the next word as "BREAK." Similarly, the sentence "I'm so thirsty, I need a...." is finished with "DRINK."

This prediction ability, combined with vast amounts of training data, gives LLMs the ability to hold a meaningful conversation.

Outside of generating spoken and written human languages, LLMs became proficient at coding, a somewhat unexpected and significantly useful capability. After all, coding languages were languages, and LLMs were good at any language if they had enough data to train on. As we will see further in this chapter, their coding capability made them very relevant for corporations and individual software developers.

If interested, the informative video of Gustav Söderström, Co-president and Chief Product and Technology Officer of Spotify[3], is a reliable source of information for beginners.

To understand the scale and diversity in AI models, Hugging Face, a popular ecosystem for AI, has reached one million AI models and apps[4]. These models on Hugging Face are for a vast range of tasks, from text generation, translation, and summarization to sentiment analysis. One million models.

AI is a vast field that extends far beyond LLMs. And AI, with its many architectures, will continue to expand its applications in limitless ways.

This section is not a technical deep dive into AI but a focus on the enterprise applications of AI and especially the impact of those applications on the workforce. The chapter will serve as a source for the board of directors, CEOs, executive teams, HR leaders, and everyone who is interested in the AI's impact on their teams and corporations.

---

[3] Explained: The conspiracy to make AI seem harder than it is! By Gustav Söderström
[4] https://originality.ai/blog/huggingface-statistics

How Do We Use AI Now?

Generative AI is already part of digital work life. At this point, there are mainly two major use cases in enterprises: personal productivity and enterprise-level applications. Please note that non-work-related personal use is not covered in this book, which has a much more colorful and diverse landscape.

1. **Personal Use for Productivity**: Employees increasingly use foundation models like ChatGPT or Claude for work purposes. Some common examples out of dozens are: Summarizing large documents, presentations, formulating a better reply to that annoying email, basic data analysis, and supporting with software coding.

   Surprisingly, as we will see later in this section, knowledge workers use their own private accounts, and their activity is usually outside of the organization's digital realm. The activities are work-related, but they still don't occur with a corporate AI subscription. Even though this type of use exposes the organization to security risks and corporations take steps to minimize that usage, it is still substantial. Enterprises are recognizing this, and some are slowly making such tools available inside the secured corporate environment and providing AI tools to their employees.

2. **Enterprise Use**: AI applications are deployed and governed by the organization. For example, AI search engines for employees, conversational chatbots for customers, enterprise version of software development, and coding support.

These applications are integrated into the organization's digital environment and are part of the technology stack. They are part of the enterprise information security protocols, which means the sensitive data is protected and doesn't leave the company's digital premises.

In the end, both categories serve to improve productivity and produce higher-quality outputs. Enterprise adoption is crawling as opposed to private use of AI, and it is a good thing. Here is why:

Most of Us Use AI at Work, But Secretly

The personal use of Generative AI has reached hundreds of millions, driven by knowledge workers and students. Surveys indicate a high percentage of adoption in various roles. Almost all of us use AI in our work to some degree.

Usage of ChatGPT, the foundation model from OpenAI, is a good indication of personal use because OpenAI models have the majority of daily usage market share[5].

As of the end of December 2024, more than 300 million people use ChatGPT weekly. In August 2024, it was 200, and in November 2023, 100 million[6], which is double the 100 million weekly active users OpenAI reported November 2023. Meta AI has reached 600 million monthly users[7].

> Students and workers are the main users. How do we know? Active users of ChatGPT decline during summers.

75% of global knowledge workers are already using generative AI, which proves that your employees are upgrading faster than your tech budget.

---

[5] OpenAI's free GPT-4o model drives ChatGPT to new heights with 96% year-over-year growth

[6] https://backlinko.com/chatgpt-stats

[7] https://www.yahoo.com/tech/meta-ai-has-nearly-600-million-monthly-users-184512693.html

According to Microsoft's May 2024 report[8], the use of generative AI has doubled in the previous six months, and 75 percent of global knowledge workers are using it. The majority of that 75% are using their own AI tools. This comprehensive report is based on the 31.000 survey respondents from 31 countries. Seventy-five percent is a large portion, and we would suspect that the survey respondents have a propensity towards new trends and are more likely to use AI tools.

> The large adoption numbers in surveys also indicate that most corporate managers are naïve as to what extent their employees are using consumer AI tools in unsecured environments.

In a study from the authors Anders Humlum and Emilie Vestergaard, in collaboration with Statistics Denmark, surveyed 100.000 workers who were exposed to ChatGPT between November 2023 and January 2024[9]. The results point towards a high work-related use of marketing professionals, journalists, and software developers, as seen in the below chart.

---

8   https://www.microsoft.com/en-us/worklab/work-trend-index/ ai-at-work-is-here-now-comes-the-hard-part
9   https://bfi.uchicago.edu/insights/the-adoption-of-chatgpt/

THE UNIVERSITY OF CHICAGO
BECKER FRIEDMAN INSTITUTE
FOR ECONOMICS

Adoption of ChatGPT across Occupations

■ Used at Work ■ Used, Not at Work ▓ Aware, Never Used

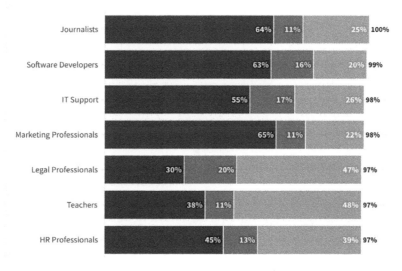

Occupation	Used at Work	Used, Not at Work	Aware, Never Used	Total
Journalists	64%	11%	25%	100%
Software Developers	63%	16%	20%	99%
IT Support	55%	17%	26%	98%
Marketing Professionals	65%	11%	22%	98%
Legal Professionals	30%	20%	47%	97%
Teachers	38%	11%	48%	97%
HR Professionals	45%	13%	39%	97%

Microsoft's survey results, which show that 75 percent of workers use AI, and the millions of active ChatGPT users imply that significant work-related activity occurs outside of the corporation's control. Knowledge workers are already benefiting from the productivity advantages of AI tools, whether their company provides them or not.

The Secret Cyborgs

The good news: your workers are embracing AI without you spending a dime. The bad news: they're doing it in the shadows.

There is a problem: People using AI in their work are keeping it a secret. Ethan Mollick, a professor of management at Wharton who specializes in entrepreneurship and innovation, calls them secret cyborgs[10]. Ethan describes three main reasons for this secrecy:

1. **Concerns around IT and Security rules**. Most companies do not allow consumer foundation models to be used for work

---

[10]   https://www.oneusefulthing.org/p/detecting-the-secret-cyborgs

purposes. The data that employees put into those models can be damaging to the company or reveal company intellectual property to outside servers. That does not fully hinder employees from using the models, but they keep quiet about it.

2. **Perception of AI usage undermines the work**. Once it is revealed that a well-crafted email announcement is done with AI's help, the employee gets less credit. The prompting, fine-tuning, and ideation that come from the employee are neglected. So, the employees keep quiet about it and rightfully take the credit for the good work.

3. **Concerns about job security**. Knowledge workers are concerned that once they reveal how much work they do with AI, their employers will eventually conclude that AI can replace them.

Organizations should address these concerns and help employees be more forthcoming about their AI usage. Good practices can inspire employers to scale AI use to the areas where it worked well, and employees can learn from their colleagues how to produce high-quality work in less time.

> A phrase that has become tiresome but is still very relevant is, "You won't lose your job to AI; you will lose your job to someone who uses AI." Sharing good AI practices among workers will increase everyone's skills, minimizing the number of people who lose their jobs because they do not know how to use AI.

Secret cyborgs are real, and it hurts the organizations that keep them secret. This can be an early sign of distrust towards the employers, which will only grow if the companies start mass layoffs due to AI automation. This can be the start of a gloomy limbo state for the next decade, or alternatively, companies can choose to balance their AI deployment to be more balanced between cost-cutting and employee wellbeing, a topic covered in the coming pages.

The enterprise side is a deeper exploration with adoption, deployment drivers, and current use cases.

Generative AI in the Enterprise World

Enterprise Adoption

Enterprise AI adoption is crawling, not running. But secret cyborgs are already sprinting past IT security.

Even though individual knowledge worker adoption is high, Goldman Sachs's June 2024 report indicates that it is significantly low. Most executive teams have not yet defined a clear and comprehensive roadmap for AI. This is only natural, given that generative AI is relatively new, its innovation pace is still too fast, and enterprise use cases are complex solutions with security and accuracy sensitivities.

Let's not overestimate the capacity of executive teams' learning pace. Not every company has Silicon Valley tech savviness in their executive teams. Those with less technical insight might choose to be cautious followers rather than early adopters. There is wisdom in that. In the meantime, they will learn more about AI, and the partner ecosystem will be more robust.

Large corporations that can afford AI applications have complex legacy IT systems and processes. Transforming those to AI-enabled applications is not easy, which is one of the main reasons impactful AI applications are still hard to come by.

Still, most companies adopt new technology through their partners and vendors. With all these factors in play, the AI vendor ecosystem will push for adoption, together with the introduction of AI Agents. Enterprises will deploy AI solutions. IBM states that 62% of companies are increasing their AI investments 2025 and onwards[11].

A B2B heavy machinery company will adopt AI through its Cloud CRM provider's own AI platforms and AI Agents. That is why the vendors have accelerated their AI-powered product developments by 2028.

> Even the most manually operated remote company will have some sort of AI running their sales operations through their fancy California-based vendor.

For now, the difference between personal use and enterprise adoption will be large, which means we will see productivity and quality improvements on a personal basis. Mysteriously, the internal communications specialist will start writing excellent announcements, and some of the junior software developers will come up with amazing pieces of code in a short time. But enterprise-level improvements will lag a few years, except for a few early adopters.

Three Drivers for Deploying AI

Before diving into specific enterprise use cases, let's examine the fundamental drivers behind AI adoption. Understanding these core motivations helps us evaluate current implementations and identify overlooked opportunities. Three distinct perspectives emerge as the primary purposes for enterprise AI applications: the well-known cost reduction angle and two less discussed but equally important approaches: growth-focused and humane applications.

---

[11]   In 2025, partners will speed the shift of enterprise AI projects from pilot to production

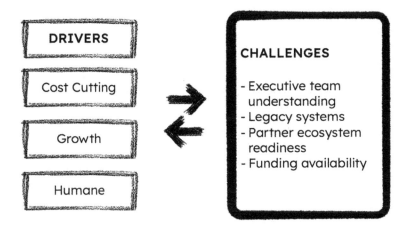

The Cost Reduction Angle

Companies are treating AI like a coupon—great for cost-cutting, but somehow forgetting it can actually drive revenue, too.

Bill Gurley, a general partner at Benchmark, a Silicon Valley venture capital firm, highlighted this narrow focus on cost savings during their BG2 podcast in July 2024: The focus on cost reduction is far more prevalent than revenue generation for companies. Unfortunately, this observation still rings true. The majority of discussions center around cost reduction, job replacements, and productivity gains. Very few companies focus on the extra revenue channels, new products, and growth AI can bring.

McKinsey's report "The Economic Potential of Generative AI: The Next Productivity Frontier[12]" reinforces this point. Out of the 63 identified generative AI use cases across business functions that they deemed most impactful, the vast majority concentrate on cost reduction. Yes, the small blue area outside the big circle is the growth portion.

---

[12]   Economic potential of generative AI | McKinsey

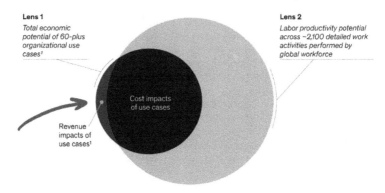

The potential impact of generative AI can be evaluated through two lenses.

Lens 1
Total economic potential of 60-plus organizational use cases[1]

Lens 2
Labor productivity potential across ~2,100 detailed work activities performed by global workforce

Cost impacts of use cases

Revenue impacts of use cases[1]

[1] For quantitative analysis, revenue impacts were recast as productivity increases on the corresponding spend in order to maintain comparability with cost impacts and not to assume additional growth in any particular market.

McKinsey & Company

This disproportionate focus on cost might be more destructive than constructive, especially if amplified by large consultancy companies like McKinsey. It's crucial to educate boards and CEOs on the real potential of generative AI. When boards understand the full potential of AI, their questions and guidance will be equally focused on business generation, not only cost reduction.

The Growth Angle

AI's not just about saving cash. Smart companies are using it to turn 10 engineers into 15 without hiring a single soul.

Aaron Levie (@levie), co-founder and CEO of Box, offers a compelling perspective on looking beyond isolated productivity gains to broader system effects with his tweet[13]:

> "The key to thinking through job impacts is to think through what happens a step or two after the productivity gain of AI is experienced.

So, imagine you're a software company that can afford to employ 10 engineers based on your current revenue. By default, those 10 engineers produce a certain amount of output of a product that you then sell to customers. If you're like almost any company on the planet, the list of things your customers want from your product far exceeds your ability to deliver those features any time soon with those 10 engineers. But the challenge, again, is that you can only afford those 10 engineers at today's revenue level. So, you decide to implement AI, and the absolute best-case scenario happens: each engineer becomes magically 50% more productive. Overnight, you now have the equivalent of 15 engineers working in your company for the previous cost of 10."

Aaron's analysis shows how AI-driven productivity enables companies to meet customer demands, drive revenue growth, and create supporting jobs. Businesses then decide whether to maintain their enhanced workforce or reinvest in more hires to innovate further. In a competitive landscape, companies will likely expand, using AI to boost productivity and create new opportunities across the system.

Aaron advocates for the generative growth side of AI, and the practical implementation will likely balance between cost-cutting and unlocking hidden potential. Boards need to hear arguments like Aaron's to be persuaded of the positive opportunities.

Looking ahead in this chapter, we will explore how AI agents represent the most impactful use cases from which corporations will benefit. Agents that can handle employee tasks autonomously will substantially simplify processes, eliminate the need for expensive software, and serve as a friendly interface for all employees across all tasks. The same goes for customers. Executive teams should discuss the future with effective agents and how they will impact their governance and infrastructure, creating a simpler organization that is void of bureaucracy.

The Humane Angle

The future isn't just AI doing more work; it's AI helping us work better: fewer meltdowns, more breakthroughs.

Besides discussing possible cost reductions and business generation, we can also design AI use cases that have a positive impact on employees, their work environment, and their well-being. Shocking, but true!

Here are some examples:

1. AI-powered coaching and mentoring: Companies already offer AI Coaching as a service. Organizations can deploy humane AI coaches to guide their employees, ease their stress, and coach them through difficult situations. An AI coach can diffuse a difficult and tense email conversation or even a meeting, nudging the employees towards a calm and win-win solution. As we'll explore later, the AI coach, in the form of a trusted co-worker, can be very helpful.

2. Enhanced job satisfaction through task optimization: AI excels at handling time-consuming and mundane work. By letting AI tackle the repetitive 20% of tasks, organizations can unlock their people's creativity. This shift can enable more flexible working arrangements, including four-day work weeks. Even without structural changes, reducing mundane tasks creates a more fulfilled and engaged workforce.

3. Proactive well-being support: With opt-in health metrics tracking, AI can help manage stress levels proactively. Imagine an AI recommending that a manager reschedule a tense meeting because stress indicators are high. This simple intervention could prevent a potentially difficult situation from affecting dozens of people.

4. Fair performance management: AI can help ensure that promotion and performance evaluations are conducted fairly. It can also help leaders avoid biases and nudging them to recognize good work when it happens. This is particularly important since feeling unfairly treated is one of the major contributors to burnout[14].

A practical example of this approach comes from Japan's Softbank[15], which developed an AI solution to convert angry customer voices into

---

[14]   https://hbr.org/2019/07/6-causes-of-burnout-and-how-to-avoid-them
[15]   SoftBank Corp aims to help call centre workers by 'softening' angry customer calls with AI | Reuters

calmer ones: "We are working on the development of a solution that can convert the customer's voice into a calm conversational tone and deliver it to workers using AI-enabled emotion recognition and voice processing technology. With this solution, we aim to maintain good relationships with customers through sound communication while ensuring the psychological welfare of workers."

What's the return on investment of preventing a crucial decision meeting from becoming a disaster due to high stress levels? Or the value of de-escalating tension between departments before relationships deteriorate?

This third approach, focused on improving work environments and well-being, can be challenging to justify in traditional business plans. Executive teams typically seek a clear return on investment metrics for AI initiatives, especially given the initial investment and ongoing subscription costs. However, the human benefits described above are often difficult to quantify. Boards and executive teams should feel comfortable evaluating these use cases on their broader merits.

> Experienced executive teams know that smart investments in employees always pay off, often by an order of magnitude. AI isn't just about profit margins; it's about creating value that numbers alone can't always capture. Ignore that, and you are missing the bigger picture.

The three approaches we have covered, cost-focused, growth-focused, and employee-focused, can and should coexist. Generative AI solutions can be designed to provide for all three angles. Responsible executives should not shy away from use cases that have an intuitive positive impact but lack hard numbers.

Like every technological leap, we will not see all possible uses of AI. Many emergent applications will shape corporations and work itself. After examining the adoption and drivers of enterprise AI, it is time to discuss use cases that are currently trending.

Four Trending Enterprise Use Cases

The moment Klarna showed off its chatbot's efficiency, every company with a call center got chatbot envy.

One use case that made the front page of business papers was Klarna's AI adventure. Klarna, a Swedish fintech company that provides online financial services, moved call center activities to OpenAI: "Klarna partnered with OpenAI to improve customer service interactions. In just one month, the ChatGPT-inspired bot is currently managing two-thirds of customer service chats, 2.3 million conversations, in 23 markets and 35 languages, " said the Forbes article[16] in March 2024. This move saved Klarna allegedly 700 call center agent jobs.

The Klarna news, with real-life evidence of successful deployment, increased the appetite of B2C companies. Every large corporation with significant consumer support and consumer operations suddenly became interested in replicating the same success in their companies. At the same time, this increased the number of concerns in call center service companies. We will discuss the call center application of AI in detail further in this chapter.

McKinsey's research also identified customer operations and software engineering as the two most impactful areas. The chart tells us that AI will save more than 30 percent of those three functions pending and

---

[16]   https://www.forbes.com/sites/jackkelly/2024/03/04/klarnas-ai-assistant-is-doing-the-job-of-700-workers-company-says/

create an impact of more than a trillion altogether. Other areas with high impact are sales and marketing.

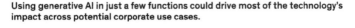

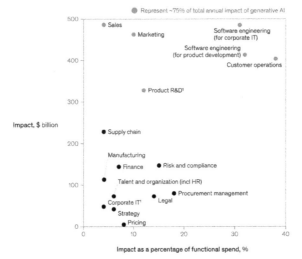

Conversational chatbots, marketing campaign automation, and increased sales effectiveness are AI's obvious added value areas in customer operations, sales, and marketing. Major productivity gains in software engineering are already being realized throughout the coding and testing stages.

However, the chart above needs a "zoom-out" and a more conceptualized approach. From the cluttered chart and individual use cases, we can discuss four categories of current enterprise use: Sales and customer support, coding and software engineering, daily work productivity, and enterprise knowledge management. This will be our first zoom out. After we have covered these four categories, the second zoom out will give us what is coming.

The Four Categories

Let's focus on the four categories that are already in place today. They make intuitive sense, and generative AI is very capable of language-based tasks, chatbots, coding (computer language), and information ingestion through language.

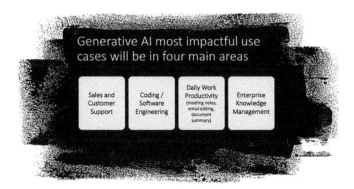

We will now expand each of these headings with examples and their impact on the workforce. In each chapter covering these categories, the challenges will be listed to give a more objective approach rather than a too optimistic hype of an AI use case.

After these four categories of imminent AI impact, we will continue our journey to future product mapping.

1. Sales and Customer Support

The evolution of generative AI began with conversational chatbots, naturally gravitating toward customer interactions. These AI systems serve two primary functions: direct customer engagement and support salespeople.

Direct Customer Engagement

Modern AI chatbots have transformed customer service, leaving behind the clunky interfaces of the past decade. They now handle first-line support with remarkable proficiency, engaging in natural conversations that feel thoughtful and understanding. Consider this typical exchange:

- Customer: "I see a 15-Euro purchase on my credit card that I haven't made. What should I do?"
- Chatbot: "I am sorry to hear that. Can you see the location of the purchase?"

- Customer: "London"
- Chatbot: "Yes, I can see the purchase. I am processing a reim-bursement and flagging the transaction as fraud."

Klarna chatbots function already at a similar level. The above conversation is happening today.

Sales Support

Beyond basic support, these systems also empower sales teams with insights into customer behavior patterns, preferences, and product information, enabling more effective sales strategies and customer support.

They already handle preparing standard offers and updating internal sales systems, taking away many hours of administrative tasks from sales teams.

Challenges to Overcome

LLMs are conversational pros, but their side hustle is hallucination: making up answers when they're not sure, which is a corporate nightmare.

LLMs excel at conversation, but they face a significant challenge: hallucinations. This tendency to generate plausible but incorrect information poses a substantial risk for corporations. Even after extensive training and fine-tuning, the best models currently have hallucination rates between 3% and 3.8%[17].

Achieving near-zero hallucinations requires sophisticated technical infrastructure. Companies must:

- Feed accurate information to the foundation model
- Implement strict adherence to provided data
- Deploy complex systems, including Retrieval Augmented Generation (RAG), data labeling, and parameter efficient fine-tuning

---

[17] https://docs.conveyor.com/docs/what-is-conveyors-hallucination-rate#:~:text=The%20off%2Dthe%2Dshelf%20hallucination,hallucination%22)%20about%2030%20times.

This technical complexity explains why we don't see widespread corporate adoption of AI chatbots yet.

Sidebar Insight: Introduction of Deterministic vs Probabilistic

This is a good place to briefly introduce an important concept. You will hear your data team talk about deterministic and probabilistic methods. Deterministic methods rely on fixed rules to produce precise outcomes, while probabilistic approaches use likelihoods and uncertainties to model and predict outcomes.

A simple example of customer interactions will be:

- Deterministic cases where the chatbot absolutely needs to say with 100% accuracy, "Ok, we will ship that to you at your address, 200 Market Street." The chatbot can't make up a customer address or give a rough estimation of the neighborhood.
- Probabilistic cases are where being 100% accurate is not so important. A chatbot recommending an add-on sale to someone buying a shirt such as a tie, cufflinks, or collar tie; it doesn't matter if the suggestion is not perfect.

Building deterministic elements into LLMs is difficult and equally sensitive, as we described earlier.

Impacts to Workforce

Sales teams will get a boost from AI until, one day, they realize the AI doesn't need them anymore. The customer support agent roles are especially in the high-risk category.

Call Center Agents

Generative AI will wipe out a chunk of call center jobs very fast, and the young workforce will feel it first.

Call center positions offer valuable income opportunities for young adults and those seeking flexible work arrangements.

However, operating a successful call center is not easy.

1. These jobs are notorious for high turnover rates. While a 25 percent attrition rate is considered manageable, attrition can reach 40 to 50 percent for some call centers.

2. With a high turnover comes the challenge of training newcomers on products and services. Companies with complex products and offerings often factor in months before support personnel become knowledgeable about product aspects.

These challenges, combined with the advancing capabilities of AI as human-like speech abilities, are making call center jobs increasingly vulnerable to AI replacement.

Conversational chatbots will eventually replace a significant portion of call center jobs, particularly in first-line support roles. While positions handling complex customer inquiries or active outbound sales may initially resist this trend, they are likely to succumb to AI automation within a three-to-five-year timeframe.

In Europe alone, the call center industry employs between 1.2 and 1.5 million human agents[18]. The coming AI disruption of these jobs will have significant short-term societal costs, especially in countries like Poland, where the call center industry employs many young students. Multiply that by Malaysia, India, Costa Rica, the Philippines, and Mexico.

Call centers often provide students with their first exposure to the corporate world, offering opportunities to develop basic office skills, network with peers, and earn their initial salaries. The loss of these entry-level positions could impact the career development pathways for young professionals across the continent and make it more difficult for them to study while earning money.

Sales Teams

Sales roles will be empowered by AI tools. The timely insights about customers and products on their screens will make them more equipped. An AI bot helping out with a customer will save them valuable time. The impact of generative AI for these jobs will be more about revenue creation than cost cutting.

---

18   https://www.customerserv.com/europe-call-center

Human interaction will remain essential in sales conversations. The importance of emotional connection, empathy, complex problem-solving abilities, and the need for trust and authenticity will never fade. As a result, sales positions are unlikely to disappear in the near future. Instead, these roles are poised to benefit from the integration of generative AI, which will augment and enhance human capabilities in performing their job functions. This synergy between human skills and AI assistance is likely to increase efficiency and effectiveness in sales and account management processes.

Operational roles in sales teams, such as sales admins or pricing specialists, will rapidly disappear, leaving only complicated customer interaction roles.

The divide will be more between companies that enable their sales force with AI tools and those that don't. The second category of enterprise use cases is software engineering, which will be equally impacted by AI.

2. Coding and Software Engineering
The #1 coding language is rapidly becoming English

When Marc Andreessen, the famous venture capitalist, wrote "Software is eating the world" in his 2011 Wall Street Journal essay, he captured a transformation that would reshape the global economy. Andreessen recognized how software companies were fundamentally changing traditional industries. Amazon was redefining retail, Netflix was reshaping entertainment, and Uber would soon transform transportation. But Andreessen's key insight was that every company would need to become, in essence, a software company to stay competitive. Looking back, his observation has proven remarkably accurate. Today, software and digital technologies shape every industry and every company.

Famously a Tesla executive tweeted, "Tesla is as much a software company as it is a hardware company, both in the car and in the factory. This is not widely understood." This insight from Tesla, essentially born as an automotive company, as hardware as you could get, defines car manufacturing as a software company, illustrating the shift towards software. Tesla demonstrates this through software in their cars and factories as part of their operating backbone.

Software runs our world and our companies, making software engineering one of the most impactful variables in the success of a corporation. To justify that, there will be close to 30 million software developers globally in 2025[17]. Software engineers are everywhere. So, when Generative AI becomes good at coding, the whole business world starts to pay close attention.

Programming languages are just another type of language used to communicate with software and hardware rather than with other humans. LLMs, therefore, excel at coding tasks because, for them, it is just another language, and they can generate content.

GitHub, the most widely used software development platform, has a generative AI tool, GitHub Copilot. Developers say the following:

- They are using the chat ability of GitHub Copilot to validate some of their ideas.
- Have the copilot write mundane parts of the code and similar tasks.

For simple tasks, AI can be a game-changer. But when it comes to legacy systems and complex features, even 10% efficiency feels like a win.

Initially, productivity increases in software engineering were estimated to be up to 40 percent. That was optimistic. With time, organizations realized these productivity gains are more realistically around 20 percent with today's tool capabilities.

Other variables affect productivity than task complexity. For example, while development time decreased with ready-made code segments from a capable LLM, testing and debugging time increased because software engineers over relied on the tool and accepted its suggestions without fully understanding the AI-generated code.

Despite that, Salesforce CEO Benioff declared that they will not hire any software engineers in 2025 because of AI productivity gains. Joining the bandwagon, Mark Zuckerberg also thinks that AI will soon be as capable as a mid-level software engineer, and many developer jobs will be irrelevant soon.

GitHub article[19] says that their users accept nearly 30% of code suggestions from GitHub Copilot and report increased productivity from these acceptances. Developers with Copilot required 55 percent[20] less time than developers without Copilot.

The convenience for enterprises is that only by paying a subscription fee to these platforms can they turn on the productivity gains for their developers. Just like that, no big integration projects, no test runs.

The productivity gains mean more than not hiring developers. For enterprises, this means higher-quality software in a shorter time, better user interfaces and mobile apps for their customers, faster product feature developments, and even new product deployments. Once AI boosts software development, the pace of the enterprise will increase.

Even though we are at the current use cases chapter, it is too tempting not to move a few years further with coding and mention two major changes coming soon: low-code, no-code, and digital software engineers.

Human Creativity Unleashed: Low-Code No-Code Shift (Vibe Coding)

Soon, software coding will be augmented to the point where any person can have an AI write a program by talking through it. For example, "I want an app that keeps track of all my purchases and slows down my internet after I go over my daily spending budget." This will be enough for an AI to write the code and iterate with the user. This is the no-code world. Low-code is the transition where some coding knowledge may still be needed for some customization.

This progress has a profound impact on unleashing everyone's creativity. Even though in the near term, society will suffer from loss of software engineering jobs, beyond that waits us a world free of programming languages. Everyone will be able to develop games and create movies and soundtracks.

---

[19]   https://github.blog/news-insights/research/the-economic-impact-of-the-ai-powered-developer-lifecycle-and-lessons-from-github-copilot/

[20]   https://github.blog/news-insights/research/research-quantifying-github-copilots-impact-on-developer-productivity-and-happiness/

This is a world where innovation is democratized; every person with a good application idea or a new sci-fi movie idea will just create it. The world of software will benefit from increased diversity of thought and diversity of creative minds, while liberal arts students will find greater opportunities in the high-paying tech world.

Digital Software Engineers

In the first quarter of 2024, a significant development occurred: a company called Cognition released the first AI software engineer, Devin. Devin could handle software engineering assignments autonomously without human intervention. Like a human software developer, it went to a software project marketplace and looked for gigs. It completed assignments that it found in that marketplace end to end, just like a human software engineer would.

While debates followed about Devin's capabilities and the quality of the initial demos, one thing was certain: we had our first AI worker, software Engineer Devin, marking a significant milestone in automated software engineering.

It is also opening the big topic of anthropomorphizing AI. This is the first time we have a "Devin" and not just a "bot." The first digital colleagues will probably be software engineers. Will they also suffer performance management conversations? Do they have to attend weekly meetings and talk about the weather at the start of every meeting? Someone has to ask the real questions...

Now that we have ventured a few years into the future, it is time to return to our beloved human software engineers and discuss what these changes mean for them.

What Advanced AI Means for Software Engineers

Software engineers aren't going anywhere, but their job descriptions are. AI is turning them into creative problem-solvers, not just coders.

The growth of software engineering jobs is slowing down[21]. The number of software engineering jobs is increasing, good to be clear, but that growth is not as glorious as it was in 2010. While macroeconomic factors contribute to this slowdown and the over-hiring during COVID, some of the hesitancy is also due to uncertainty about the expected productivity gains from AI tools.

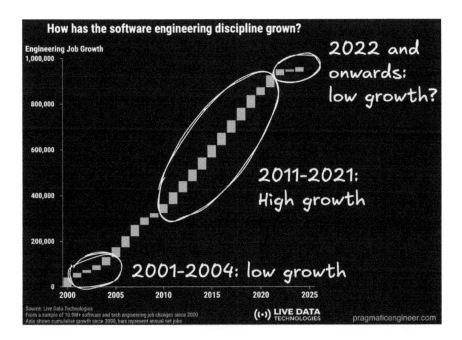

Although software engineering roles will remain in the short term, their content and working style will change with AI. The new features of AI tools are making interactions with AI easier, effectively creating a brainstorming partner for software engineers. As a result, we will see increased levels of creativity and iterative problem-solving.

The AI might also decrease the difference in output between an average developer and a less experienced or low-performer. Both will have a great AI developer buddy by their side.

> The short-term effects of AI will be the change of nature of work from mundane codes to creative codes for software engineers. Towards 2030, AI is likely to take over most of the coding, and software engineering jobs will vanish, hopefully giving way to jobs with content and product creation.

From the more techy and futuristic coding world, we come back to more humble AI use cases in the next chapter: handling daily tasks like note-taking.

3. Daily Work Productivity

From sifting through a flood of data to writing the perfect announcement, AI is the co-pilot knowledge workers never knew they needed.

AI serves as the essential co-pilot for knowledge workers, revolutionizing everything from data analysis to crafting perfect announcements. There are two intentional references here; one is "co-pilot" with Microsoft's leading products, and they have acquired the brand name on this topic. Just like we use "can you google it" as the brand, the co-pilot is for now the brand of an AI support within our daily work life. The second reference is "revolutionizing". Even though that term is overused by now, we do mean revolution in how we work today, and we are not using that term lightly.

The current capabilities of AI are still clunky. We can't get the exact answer about the company policy we need to find, the basic data analyses lack depth, etc. However, all the headings we cover below are already live and improving in quality every month.

Here are the main value adds of AI to our daily work:

1. **Communication and Content Creation**: AI enhances our communication by helping us formulate reports, provide summaries, and reply to challenging emails. When crafting important announcements for hundreds of employees, professionals now rely on AI's editorial expertise. These tools elevate our message delivery, professional tone, and collaborative communication approach, ultimately making our communication more impactful and refined.

No need to emphasize the importance of communication. A well-formulated message with the right tone may bring departments together under one goal, as opposed to an emotional angry email deepening a divide between two units.

2. **Information Processing**: We need to process vast amounts of information daily at work: Lengthy presentations, complex graphs, extensive email chains, and that long policy from procurement. There is a lot of noise coming in. AI tools excel at processing this information, moving beyond basic summarization to highlight crucial points, categorize information, establish connections with reference materials, and identify information gaps.

3. **Analysis**: Making sense of data can take a long time. Understanding the underlying trends of a data set and seeing correlations that will give us new ideas are not easy tasks. Not everyone has an analytical background or statistical knowledge. A helping hand, albeit too new and still needing improvement, is the AI copilot. Making sense of the data, suggesting trends, and even summarizing what it sees within the data are initial capabilities of AI.

4. **Idea Bouncing Partner**: Many knowledge workers currently utilize AI models to brainstorm their ideas. For instance, a human resources manager can analyze employee engagement survey results, incorporate cultural insights, and receive AI-guided recommendations for improving engagement. With effective prompting techniques, AI conversations become powerful ideation tools.

The four areas above are not exhaustive; the number of AI use cases increases with the creativity of the user. However, they do represent most of the current uses.

The Impact on Productivity and Job Satisfaction

AI tools aren't just boosting productivity; they're giving workers an upgrade on job satisfaction by killing off the admin drudgery.

AI-enhanced workflows are going to increase steadily.

Consultants are a good example of knowledge workers. Their work typically involves summarizing and interpreting company data and benchmarks, finding solutions to challenges, and communicating these solutions to clients. In theory, generative AI tools should benefit all these elements, and based on the results, they do.

To understand the impact of productivity, we examine a study conducted by Harvard University and Boston Consulting Group (BCG) in late 2023[22]. As Forbes reported, the report states that consultants using AI completed tasks 25 percent faster and produced over 40 percent higher-quality results than those not using AI[23]. However, the study noted increased error rates among AI users, potentially due to their overreliance on the technology.

A more recent survey[24], sampling 13,000 knowledge workers, revealed that 58 percent of Generative AI tool users believe they are saving five or more hours per week with these tools, directing this time toward new tasks.

There is a clear increase in productivity, but there is also a significant improvement in employee experience. These tools perform some of the more mundane, time-consuming administrative tasks. Additionally, they produce a higher quality of work, which theoretically leads to better job fulfillment and satisfaction.

> Despite these benefits, there is anxiety over potential job loss, with 42% of survey respondents believing their jobs might not exist in the next decade. For now, generative AI tools don't seem to be majorly displacing knowledge workers. However, if we consider the next decade, we can say that 42% have a point.

We will cover the broader AI job placement impact later in this section.

---

[22] https://www.forbes.com/sites/danpontefract/2023/09/29/harvard-and-bcg-unveil-the-double-edged-sword-of-ai-in-the-workplace/

[23] https://www.google.com/url?q=https://www.forbes.com/sites/danpontefract/2023/09/29/harvard-and-bcg-unveil-the-double-edged-sword-of-ai-in-the-workplace/&sa=D&source=docs&ust=1722349089705286&usg=AOvVaw0tQT1G7qmJFoCQab1xByfu

[24] https://www.bcg.com/publications/2024/ai-at-work-friend-foe

4. Enterprise Knowledge Management

Enterprise Knowledge Management refers to an organization's strategies, tools, and practices to capture, manage, and disseminate its collective knowledge, experience, and expertise. Its goal is to optimize the use of intellectual capital, improve decision-making, foster innovation, and enhance productivity across the organization.

The definition is a mouthful. Simple complications will look like these:

- Where do I find the new product roadmap and price ranges? I remember I saw it in a presentation somewhere.
- What was the retention policy? My employee is about to leave for a competitor. Can I give her a retention bonus or stock options?
- My wrist hurts with the laptop trackpad. Can I buy an ergonomic mouse and charge it to the company? If yes, what is the purchasing limit?
- Where do I find the latest company strategy? The one on the server is from last year.

At some point, someone would say, "Scott from marketing had the same issue last year; he solved it; why don't you ask him?" and the information hunt will continue.

Having these answers available to employees will eliminate friction and frustration, save time and effort, and be great for everyone. However, knowledge management offers much more.

Decision-Making is Getting and Upgrade

Rational decision-making requires readily available accurate data. In business, we all make decisions based on what we know at that point, our assumptions, and the counsel we have access to. Many activities in business life are about sharing that necessary information. Monthly business reviews with major units are for the CEO to understand where the units are as opposed to their targets and course correct if needed. Daily stand-ups for projects are the same in a microenvironment and serve as a venue to share the information everyone has, govern the process, and decide on the next steps. Add production of daily, weekly, and monthly reports all teams are producing for information sharing, and we can get the idea of the cost of information synthesis and sharing. We can call all these activities "manual information sharing" or manual information dissemination.

> The larger and more complicated organizations are, the heavier the burden of manual information sharing becomes. More information gets lost in translation or overlooked in the fine print of a slide.

Enterprises are already working on Generative AI-powered search engines, data synthesis tools, and chatbots. The business world has started its journey toward a world where a chatbot can answer the questions, "What are our segment-based sales numbers this morning?" "Is our new price impacting sales?" "Where do we see an unusual trend?" Feedback loops will be shorter, and decision-making will be based on the synthesis of intelligence. Complex systems will become simpler.

> The powerful combination will be when internal information is shared together with wisdom and expertise. "The new pricing seems to work in most of our segments; the hesitancy in the young adult segment needs your attention, likely to end up with loss of market share." This will be a priceless convergence of expert coaching and knowledge management, likely in the mid-term.

However, the road to good knowledge management is hard. Establishing a knowledge-sharing culture, disciplined documentation, data tagging, data architecture, and storage are only a few of the prerequisites for knowledge management. The importance of knowledge management will make the organizations govern that space better; it will not be surprising to see information content governance within IT, HR, or Communication departments. Hopefully, in one of them, not fragmented as they are today.

Although this fourth category of current enterprise use cases does not receive as much attention as the other categories, its added value is deeper and arguably more impactful.

The four use case categories in this chapter are more prevalent in our lives than you might assume. The rate of AI tool adoption and the rate of progress of those tool capabilities are mind-blowing. From consumer-focused conversational chatbots to digital software engineers and internal search engines, AI is already making a substantial differ-ence today for early adopter companies.

Our first zoom-out was to group the scattered enterprise use cases into four categories. Now comes the second zoom-out, in which we will examine the AI roadmap for the years to come. The four categories of today will only represent the first stage of AI. We will call the journey "AI's Ascent to Governance" and reflect the angle of employee experi-ence throughout it.

Four Stages of AI's Ascent to Governance

So far, we have covered current use cases of Generative AI. They are already live, in implementation, or in the design phase in the technology-leading companies, but still a few years away for an average enterprise.

This chapter proposes a roadmap that extends beyond current use cases and encompasses the upcoming years. Given the vast and diverse potential of this foundational technology, it's impractical to comprehensively cover all possible use cases or areas of influence. Instead, this exploration will focus on enterprise-specific applications, with particular emphasis on how these technologies are reshaping employee experiences, the workforce, and job design. This targeted approach aims to provide valuable insights into the transformative potential of AI in the business world.

Generative AI Roadmap for Enterprises

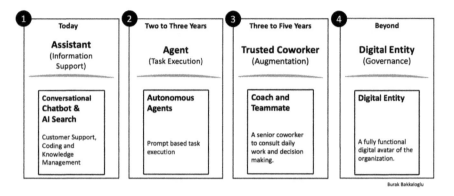

Enterprises are likely to progress through four main stages in their generative AI adoption journey: Assistant, Agent, Trusted Coworker, and Digital Entity. The first three stages assume a conventional, almost linear capability progression of Generative AI. The fourth stage, Digital Entity, is a more speculative concept of the future, appearing more futuristic than its predecessors. This, for us, is justified. "BEYOND" looks past the 2030 mark.

If your first impression to the roadmap is "too optimistic", consider this: Sam Altman, CEO of OpenAI, said on September 24th, 2024, that we are a few thousand days away from AI superintelligence[25]. Similarly, and almost synchronously, Anthropic CEO Dario Amodei described a "powerful AI" arriving as soon as 2026. By powerful AI, he means AI that's "smarter than a Nobel Prize winner" and can control any software or hardware imaginable and do most jobs humans do today[26]. Discussing a Trusted Coworker and maybe even a Digital Entity by 2030 seems not so sci-fi-like anymore.

The gap between early AI adopters and average enterprises will be as big as the jump from dial-up to fiber optics.

It's important to note that the transitions between the four roadmap stages won't be uniformly clear-cut across all organizations. The timelines presented here are calibrated to tech companies and early

---

[25] https://arstechnica.com/information-technology/2024/09/ai-superintelligence-looms-in-sam-altmans-new-essay-on-the-intelligence-age/

[26] https://techcrunch.com/2024/10/11/anthropic-ceo-goes-full-techno-optimist-in-15000-word-paean-to-ai/

adopters rather than the average market participant. When those early adopters are largely using AI agents at scale, the average enterprise in the retail sector, for example, will likely be in the assistant era.

The first phase, now referred to as "The Assistant," aligns with the previous chapter, encompassing four enterprise use cases under the Assistant umbrella. More intriguing use cases are expected to arise in the Agent era.

While we appreciate the reader's patience in reviewing concepts that may already be familiar in the Assistant phase, the chapters on Agents and Trusted Coworkers offer a more forward-looking, inspirational perspective, grounded yet ambitious enough to stretch beyond the commonplace without veering into science fiction.

Assistant - Information Support

AI-powered chatbots excel in text-based interactions, with voice capabilities expected to become widely available in 2025-2026.

Companies are already implementing chatbots to support customers or customer-facing employees directly. Similar principles will be applied to create enterprise support chatbots for internal use. Because chatbots can assist users in information retrieval, summary, and content generation, including software code, we will call the first stage of the AI roadmap "The Assistant" and focus on their internal use cases.

With companies funding customer chatbots heavily, the aim of this chapter is to balance the efforts with an employee experience angle. After all, the same principles and infrastructure apply, and internal AI assistants can answer a wide range of employee queries.

At first, these topics will be transactional, like:

- "Do I need to pay for parking, if I drive my car to work," or
- "How can I add another item to my already submitted expense claim,"
- "What do the items in my payroll mean?"

After a time of iterations and advancement, the Assistant will be supporting in more complicated issues:

- I have been in my role for more than three years; when should I ask for a promotion? How can I approach my manager about this?
- I need to know more about our product offerings. Can you summarize our different bundles and compare them for me?

The Assistant phase is a wake-up call for companies: organize your information or watch your AI make things up on the fly.

It is important to repeat the problem of hallucination here once again. You don't want to end up AI telling your employee that they have 256 days of unused vacation because it decided to surprise her with a nice gesture.

Technical hurdles include data retrieval, parameter optimization, and data fine-tuning. Additionally, companies with complex procedures, undocumented local practices, and intricate policies may struggle to provide the Assistant with accurate information.

In that way, the Assistant phase necessitates a reevaluation of enterprise knowledge management. Standardizing, streamlining, simplifying, and documenting the knowledge base will be crucial for maximizing the Assistant's potential. This information will then be tagged, classified, and used to train the AI model.

> These challenges of knowledge management are an opportunity to clean up and simplify internal policies and procedures. Usually overseen advantage of momentum that companies should utilize.

Sarah's Overtime Payment

Consider this simple example to illustrate the background work for the Assistant:

Question (Prompt) from Sarah: "If I have to do overtime, am I allowed to take vacation days as compensation?"

Here, the Assistant should know how to combine various pieces of information to give a comprehensive answer.

For the Assistant to answer this question accurately, it needs to:

1. Determine if the organization has a policy that allows accrual of extra vacation days in case of overtime.

2. Verify if this policy is relevant to Sarah's role, unit, or geography.

3. Identify any constraints Sarah should be aware of.

Imagine this policy is only relevant in Germany for non-managerial roles. It allows one day of extra paid vacation after every eight hours of overtime, but with conditions (e.g., the vacation must be used within three months and can't exceed 10 days in a given year).

To provide the correct answer, the Assistant must:

1. Have the updated policies coded in a database that is accessible to the LLM model.

2. Access Sarah's employee records, including her role, payroll country, etc.

These requirements involve proper labeling and coding of internal documents, integration between the LLM model and the HR management system, and potential integration with the payroll.

As you can understand from the example above, deploying a conversational chatbot requires thorough planning and preparation. Also, the complex policy about overtime is not helping either. This is what we see as an opportunity; when organization policies for AI, the organization can simplify the policy as "All employees are eligible for an extra vacation day if the overtime becomes above 8 hours a month". This will create a better experience for the employees and eliminate unnecessary complexities.

One Assistant to Rule Them All

Humans are adaptable, and soon, we will have the smarts to ask the right assistant the right question, until they all merge into one powerful ally.

There will likely be several assistants in an employee's life. Some of us already have Microsoft's Copilot, which helps us find documents, take meeting notes, and compose emails. There is also GitHub Copilot, which assists with coding. Salesforce has deployed its assistants and even Agents. There will be other assistants in our ERP or HR systems. That might be confusing and frustrating for employees. We will go from zero to fourteen assistants quite fast.

Unlike software-specific assistants, the aim here is an internal Assistant who represents the company and the collective knowledge of the enterprise. It is difficult to foresee whether all these assistants can converge under this one main Assistant or whether we will have to manage several assistants in our lives for the foreseeable future.

Humans are adaptable. The likely scenario is that we will learn to categorize our inquiries and ask the right questions to the right assistant.

With the right integration and the evolution of AI, we will eventually see these assistants converge into one.

AI Search

Search is changing shape as well. It was interesting to witness Google losing its brand use to GPT. "Can you Google it?" became "Did you ask GPT?" or even "Have chatted it?". This is due to the fact that the AI search goes well beyond giving blue links to sponsored sites and actually gives the answer. Employees are demanding the same level of search experience for their more complicated questions.

Following this trend, organizations are already deploying AI-powered search engines in their intranets. However, the same data constraints apply: Search engines are only as good as a company's data infrastructure.

Possible convergences with Assistant and AI search are logical. A conversational search as below is likely to appear fast:

- Employee: "What is our latest decision about the Cloud migration project?"
- Assistant: "Here is the link to the meeting notes from the last steering committee. What exactly do you want to know?"
- Employee: "Are we going to delay the launch going to the public cloud, or are we pushing for the original deadline?"
- Assistant: "Seems like the steering was ok with a two-month delay; here is the link to that decision."

Startups are already emerging in the AI search area. One example is Glean[27], which has already attracted heavy-hitter investors like Sequoia to its cap table. Glean is already receiving good traction from its customers with its AI search product, which has the slogan "Next-generation enterprise search helps you instantly find the answers you need." We know that sounds a bit cliche and even cheesy, but the customer portfolio with complicated knowledge repositories like Deutsche Telekom has trusted them.

Their value proposition is trusted results across all client company applications, a deep learning algorithm "supercharged" with generative

---

[27]   https://www.glean.com/

AI and strong personalization. Glean already has other AI products, including Assistant, which coincidentally resembles the concept of the Assistant in this chapter. Or maybe it is just logical to call it Assistant...

Getting to Action

Your chatbot won't fix a messy knowledge base, but it'll make your company smarter if you start organizing your data now.

Introducing an internal conversational chatbot is inevitable for organizations. The Assistant has the potential to significantly enhance the digital employee experience by reducing daily frustrations and improving information access. While this will yield some productivity gains, the most valuable outcome will be increased information dispersion throughout the organization and, with that, better decision-making and inclusion. Everyone will have access to the latest and most accurate information about policies, decisions, and discussions - a benefit that's difficult to quantify in traditional business models but has a substantial impact nevertheless.

> Organizations must recognize that much of the work still involves organizing, cleaning, and preparing their internal knowledge bases. Overestimating an LLM's capabilities or assuming it will automatically fix a knowledge base is a mistake. Instead, organizations should use the momentum around AI to streamline and simplify their knowledge bases.

Timing presents organizations with a dilemma: Should they wait for more advanced technology or start now? For most companies, the suggestion is to begin working on their knowledge base, data architecture, and policies now and wait for the technology to mature so that internal chatbots are standard product offerings from vendors. This approach will position you to deploy an LLM chatbot more easily when the technology becomes more user-friendly, likely within a few years.

It will be wise to wait out the early adopters so that technology partners improve their products to a good level of experience. You don't want to disappoint users with high hopes and weird Assistant answers. Unfortunately, we have seen this play out with many AI products.

Agent - Task Execution

When AI handles everything, the chat box will be your only interface, and software, as we know, will fade into the background.

An AI agent is a program designed to autonomously take actions to achieve specific goals by perceiving its environment and making decisions. In plain language, they are programs capable of autonomously performing tasks.

Your AI agent for shopping will fulfill the teaks: "Please order a kilo of bananas and water from the market and have them delivered to my home." For you.

The agent performs a series of complex tasks:

1. Find the appropriate grocery website
2. Log into the user's account or create an account
3. Find and select the correct items (the right water and banana brand and the amount)
4. Decide what to do if the brand is not in stock
5. Decide whether to buy organic bananas or just plain bananas.
6. Complete the checkout process with the home address and execute payment.

This process is far from trivial. It requires the agent to make decisions based on user habits, maneuver internet interfaces, and solve problems when unexpected issues arise.

If we apply task execution to the business world, we can all see the potential revolution Agents will bring.

Opening a Position and Introduction to Transformation

A simple task like creating a job ad and opening a position in the HR system usually takes one to two hours from a hiring manager. Given the current forms and templates in the HR systems, this one hour is not a soul-soothing experience. There will be weird forms, fields that they don't know how to fill, and other unwanted user experiences. At times, a hiring manager needs to ask clarifying questions to recruiters or colleagues. Not a task that leaders look forward to.

With a good AI Agent, the task will be solved through one sentence: "Can you please open a replacement position for Sarah? She resigned, and I will hire someone for the same position."

This will be enough for an agent to look for a "Sarah" in the team, create a job ad for her role, and create a new approval flow in the HR system with that job ad and replacement request. If Sarah and the hiring manager were based in Amsterdam, the new role will default to Amsterdam, a decision-making we would expect AI Agent to do.

With Agents, two concepts vanish from the business world:

1. The word "process" loses its meaning for the user. The hiring manager will never know what kind of approvals the agent needed to take or whether creating the job ad was in the process before or after the initial form was submitted.

2. The HR interface will become obsolete. The user will no longer need to see the platform; it will only be a chat box or a voice agent like Siri or Alexa.

These are fundamental changes to the business world. Software will become a system of records only. Processes will become an operating system design that the user does not need to know.

Rescheduling a meeting, sending the participants the recap of the previous meeting, and collecting the project progress report is a simple prompt to the AI Agent. Ordering a new headset, applying for internal jobs, updating a sales lead with the customer meeting notes, and proposal are all Agent work.

As we all sense the seismic shift Agents will create, software and platform companies are all in on this topic. Starting with Microsoft, giants like Salesforce and ServiceNow have already introduced their Agent platforms. These are still early phases, and Agents are far from their potential, but they offer a good glimpse of the near future.

Additionally, foundation model companies like OpenAI (ChatGPT), Anthropic (Claude), and Google (Gemini) have introduced their own agents as well. Clause agent can take over your computer screen and execute tasks like analyzing data and drawing graphs on your behalf.

Microsoft's Copilot Studio, where workers can create, manage, and connect agents to Copilot[28], as the initial intention, provides a good explanatory visual below. Microsoft will be, in essence, launching a user interface (UI) for AI. Exactly as the example above, the hiring manager will only see the Microsoft interface and will not even know about the HR system, nor will have an idea about the processes. Things will just get done.

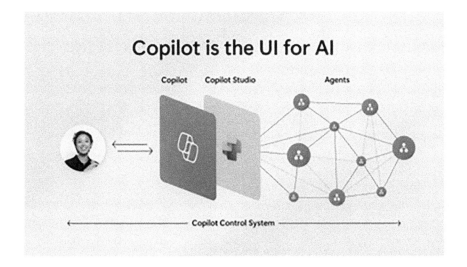

Automation, This Time for Real

So far, companies have tried to automate administrative tasks through Robotic Process Automation (RPA), which was successful (on a good day) with basic level automation but failed to have a large impact.

a16z labels LLMs are labeled as the Automation 2.0, as the intelligent automation[29], with a catchy phrase: "AI turns labor to software". That statement sums up some of the concepts we will discuss about the future of work.

The world of work will drastically change very soon. The illustration from a16z catches the eye. With capital, you can buy compute power (GPUs) and Engineers. Add coffee to the mix, and you will have software that

---

28   Introducing Copilot Actions, new agents, and tools to empower IT teams
29   https://a16z.com/rip-to-rpa-the-rise-of-intelligent-automation/

will replace labor. And with AI agents, that replacement is likely to be at scale.

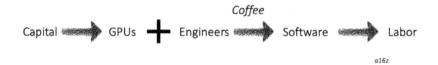

What Does "AI Agent" Do to Workforce

As you can understand, AI agents have immense implications for the workforce. The rapid improvements in AI Agent capability fueled by the technology vendor environment will quickly impact work life. For now, Agents are not capable of handling complex tasks, but around 2028 – 2029, we will observe large-scale Agent usage.

The sales pitch for a capable Agent is already based on significant workforce reduction. A set of Agents replacing a business-to-business (B2B) sales operations team of a hundred people is a common statement now. Sales operations like getting the order from the customer, sending them proposals or purchase orders, and following up with the shipment are typical tasks of a sales operations unit that Agents will handle.

All administrative-level roles, including entry-level (new graduate-level) jobs, are significantly susceptible to capable Agents. We will cover some AI-related job projections later in the section; however, Agents alone are likely to eliminate 30 to 40% of jobs when they can handle complex administrative tasks.

The remaining jobs will involve expertise and complex problem-solving and decision-making. They will not be as large a leadership role as they are today but will be either individual contributors or team leaders of a handful of people.

When combined with Assistant capabilities, task execution, knowledge management, and data analysis capabilities will enable a handful of people to handle work that is currently done by hundreds.

The concept of a 'one person billion-dollar company' anticipates that soon we will see the first billion-dollar enterprise where a single human handles all operations: sales, delivery, marketing, and accounting. This is a significant indicator of what's on the horizon. Artificial intelligence will soon be capable of executing all company tasks while taking direction from just one person.

Challenges and Second-Order Effects

At this point, we all agree that Agents will send shockwaves to the enterprise world. Successful deployment of agents handling complex tasks will change how we work and shape the culture we work with. When all administrative tasks are gone, job design will change drastically. However, some topics need to be addressed first, and some second-order effects are worth mentioning while we are at it.

Challenge: Every Company Has Their Own Process

David Luan, CEO of Adept AI Labs, one of the AI Agent startups, highlights a key challenge in his conversation on the podcast with Harry Stebbings[30]:

David mentions that even with standardized platforms like Salesforce, which is a CRM software, companies have customized processes and screens extensively and underlines it with: "If there are a dozen companies which use Salesforce, there will be a dozen ways to update a sales lead. A successful AI Agent must adapt to these unique workflows, something current corporate AI Agents are not yet capable of."

The same can be said about opening a job vacancy. Every company has its own way of creating a job ad, even if they all use the exact same platform.

These customizations will make it difficult for Agents to learn all the different ways of working. That is why, at first, it will be wise to use the native Agents of vendors like Salesforce or Workday. Over time, as more advanced Agents capable of working across platforms become reliable and common, organizations should choose to transition to one of those Agents.

Technology and vendors dictate processes to companies, not the other way around. A major vendor like Workday already has a performance management process built into their system. Good luck changing that flow in your own company. Knowingly or unknowingly, companies "design" their performance management according to the Workday blueprint. Maybe with a few tweaks, that creates the illusion of design.

When those vendors come with their Agents, companies will just buy what they are sold and implement the native ways of working of the vendor.

This highlights the fact that unlike Assistants, Agents might not need a lot of preparation from the companies.

In time, there will be Orchestrators of Agents, which allocate and follow up tasks to an army of Agents. This means the user interface on your laptop will be just one chat box, the Orchestrator. No other platforms will be visible; they will all be systems of record—a major disruption to the Software as a Service (Saas) industry.

Second Order Effect: We Won't Know Anything

Today, the user interface of operating systems (Windows or MacOS) on our laptops hides the complex workings of software from us. We "double click" on some pixels, and suddenly, our favorite application starts. Click on links and "select" stuff, and there is a payment transaction. Voilà, we bought another coffee mug. We don't know what happens when we double-click, how the trackpad works with the laptop's software, or what the CPU actually does so that we see the e-commerce application on our screen. We know nothing; everything that happens on our laptop is shielded from us by the operating system interface.

Agents will do the same in the business world. Once capable agents take over, we will say, "Open a position for Sarah's replacement," but we won't know what actually happens. Does it go to the HR system first, or is there a recruiter agent going through the job ad on a separate platform? When do we get the manager's approval? Do we also get the unit leader's approval? Who decides on new salary ranges? How do we talk to the internet site to post our job ad?

All processes and tasks will be behind the AI's user interface. This is an interesting experiment. Just like when new-generation cars break down, we stare at them and call someone. When the opening of a vacancy doesn't work when we need it, we stare at the screen and call who? Workday? Our Agent provider? IT?

Everybody keeps saying that we will focus on creative things rather than menial tasks. But in fact, there is beauty in knowing the workings of things.

Second Order Effect: Agents Will Attract Talent

Top talent will always choose an environment with a better digital experience and a lack of mundane work to galvanize innovation. Any organization providing a level of Assistant and Agent augmentation at work will be the choice of talent. Imagine on Day 1 in induction, you get your laptop, badge, company mug, AI assistant, and a bunch of agents that will work for you!

Top talent will then be assigned to creative and value-added tasks, while AI agents will run the mundane parts. This will create a multiplier effect in which human ingenuity and AI efficiency combine to drive innovation and productivity. As a result, such organizations will be able to scale faster, optimize resource allocation, and consistently out-perform competitors. This multiplier effect will accelerate and further widen the divide between traditional companies and AI-centered ones.

> No Agents, no talent, no innovation, no efficiency.

Second Order Effect: Process and Know How Gone, Then What?

We discussed how the concept of "process" becomes less important with agents. Without processes, we will not know what is happening under the hood. How do we actually process a customer's order? Once that knowledge is gone, the work instruction is to "Ask the Agent to process the order."

What happens to onboarding and an in-depth understanding of the business? Training on the job will be what, four minutes? What happens to the human mind's curiosity? What happens to the hidden engineer in all of us? Without knowing the first principles, how do we innovate?

Agents will change more than we can possibly predict.

Getting to Action

The "Agent" decision needs no rush. Organizations will experience the switch to AI Agents through trial and error. For HR leaders, it's crucial to proceed with caution and avoid rushing into Agent-related decisions before fully understanding their real-life capabilities and potential return on investment.

> If the products in the market do not provide an outstanding experience, early adoption might not be the best course of action. Taking the time to evaluate how Agents perform in practice and how they align with your organization's specific needs will be key to making informed, strategic decisions. Start by embracing native Agents within established platforms, using these early implementations as a foundation for broader, cross-functional applications in the future.

Advanced automation will also be introduced with AI agents. Companies like ServiceNow, Salesforce, Microsoft, and Workday are already introducing basic Agents. Chances are you are already using one or more of those in your company. An easy win is to stay close to their Agent products news and adopt them whenever they prove to be useful. Keeping an eye on the market for automation and workflow companies like PegaSystems, UiPath, Automation Anywhere, and Celonis will give insights into where the sector is evolving.

> The road ahead may be unpredictable, but by taking incremental steps and staying informed of advancements, organizations can position themselves at the forefront of this transformative shift and ensure they are ready to leverage agents' full potential as they mature.

Trusted Coworker - Augmentation

An AI-trusted coworker is not that different from a human-trusted coworker, except that it will be more knowledgeable, more available, and more understanding.

The journey from Assistant to Agent to Trusted Coworker emerges through deepening capabilities. These AI systems develop stronger reasoning skills, broader contextual understanding, and richer domain expertise across both specialized and general knowledge areas while building greater autonomy.

In this future, the AI coworker would serve as a trusted partner who amplifies human capabilities rather than replacing them at first. Through deep contextual understanding and sophisticated reasoning, they would help their human colleagues navigate complex challenges, identify blind spots, and make more informed decisions. They will also handle complex tasks on their own, serving towards the corporate goals without needing to partner up with a human.

Like an experienced mentor who is always available, they would provide relevant insights, suggest alternative perspectives, support their human colleagues in both immediate tasks and long-term pro-fessional growth, and adapt their support style to everyone's needs and preferences.

Let us be very clear: the Trusted Coworker is not an immediate reality. We are years away from the level of capabilities needed for a digital coworker. However, it is beneficial to explore some of the key attributes of a trusted coworker to understand the shape of human AI conver-gence in the business world.

Key attributes:

Contextual Understanding - The comprehensive awareness of the environment, including organizational dynamics, stakeholders, cul-tural nuances, and historical context. This knowledge enables AI to provide relevant advice and support that truly fits the situation and helps humans make better-informed decisions.

Contextual Reasoning - The active process of applying this under-standing to help solve problems, connecting dots across differ-ent domains, and anticipating consequences. This helps humans consider angles they might have missed and evaluate options more thoroughly.

Autonomy - The ability to work independently while staying aligned with broader objectives and principles. This means proactively identifying ways to support human colleagues, whether by taking on routine tasks or offering strategic insights when needed.

Collaborative Intelligence - The capability to enhance human decision-making by offering complementary perspectives, adapting support levels based on individual needs, and knowing when to challenge assumptions versus when to reinforce human intuitions.

Learning and Adaptation - The ability to grow alongside human colleagues, remembering past interactions and projects to provide increasingly personalized and relevant support over time while helping humans learn and develop their own capabilities.

Obviously, a future like this will bring many complications. The broader question of AI Alignment is more relevant to this context.

Alignment of the Coworker

Humans need to secure three layers of alignment with digital coworkers: organizational alignment, ethical alignment, and behavioural alignment.

At the foundation lies **Organizational Alignment**, which encompasses more than understanding company values and culture—it's about deeply internalizing both the explicit and implicit aspects of how an organization functions. This means not only operating within stated policies but also grasping the unwritten norms that shape daily interactions and decisions. A trusted AI coworker would need to align with business objectives while maintaining professional integrity, helping humans navigate the complex landscape of organizational dynamics and decision-making.

Building upon this foundation, **Ethical Alignment** extends beyond the organizational context to embrace broader principles of professional ethics and societal responsibility. This involves not just understanding ethical frameworks but actively applying them to real-world situations. The AI must maintain consistent ethical behavior across different contexts while helping humans identify and address potential ethical challenges before they escalate into serious issues. This layer of alignment ensures that actions serve not just organizational interests but also the broader societal good.

At the highest level, **Behavioral Alignment** materializes as the practical expression of organizational and ethical principles through consistent, trustworthy actions. This involves building and maintaining trust through reliable decision-making that reflects stated principles, transparency about capabilities and limitations, and steadfast adherence to established boundaries. This alignment layer ensures that principles translate into practice in ways that strengthen rather than undermine trust in the AI-human partnership.

Together, these three layers of alignment create a framework for responsible and effective AI-human collaboration, where each layer reinforces and validates the others. When conflicts arise between these layers, a task benefiting the organization might be against the well-being of the larger society; as an example, the AI must navigate them with thoughtful consideration.

Organizational executives should then be ready and capable of having these alignment conversations and setting the necessary ethical, organizational, and behavioral guardrails for their digital employees. This is not an easy ask, and it demands a higher caliber of executives with strong intellectual and moral capacities.

At this point, Human Resources or People Functions have evolved to moderate these conversations and set policies or have been replaced by another function. Maybe we will have a function called Alignment.

What Can Go Wrong

The integration of AI-trusted coworkers into organizations presents significant challenges that require careful consideration. Understanding these challenges is crucial for successful implementation.

Trust and confidentiality emerge as primary concerns. Organizations must address the fundamental question of data privacy and employee trust. Employees may hesitate to share their professional challenges, analytical limitations, or development areas with an AI system directly connected to management. This raises the need for potential external AI partnerships, like today's external mentoring relationships, to maintain confidentiality and to create honest professional development conversations. You really don't want your trusted coworker blocking your promotion because it finds you "inconsiderate and not so smart".

Resource allocation creates another layer of complexity. Organizations face decisions about AI capability distribution. The variance in AI model capabilities could create significant performance gaps between teams. For instance, teams with access to advanced AI models may significantly outperform those with basic versions, potentially creating internal inequities. This divide will be greater when companies with deeper pockets start getting better AI workers, and everyone else is stuck with last year's models.

The human-AI dynamic presents psychological and motivational challenges as well. Employees derive satisfaction from contributing meaningful work to their organizations. Excessively capable AI systems risk diminishing human engagement and purpose in the workplace, as humans might see themselves increasingly irrelevant. Organizations must carefully balance AI capabilities with meaningful human contributions to maintain workforce motivation and engagement. This is a shift for the purpose of an organization, a conflict between being efficient and successful with AI and being more humane and less efficient with humans.

We can assume that humans will form a specific professional bond with their trusted coworkers. They will likely anthropomorphize these coworkers and collaborate with them as partners. The complexity of human-AI relationships will need to be managed.

These challenges point to broader implications as AI approaches artificial general intelligence (AGI) levels. The technology sector and policymakers face unprecedented complexity in managing AI integration. Past experiences with technological regulation suggest the need for enhanced capabilities in policy development and implementation. The involvement of AI in policy formation may become necessary to address these emerging challenges effectively.

Successful implementation of AI-trusted coworkers will require careful consideration of these potential pitfalls. Organizations must develop comprehensive strategies that address both technical implementation and human factors to ensure successful integration.

Perhaps in the future, we will need a diversity quota of 30% humans for every organization.

Digital Entity - Governance

Imagine an AI that can run a company autonomously. It knows every product, every value chain step, every employee, and every market move; it's the company avatar making decisions in real time.

Predicting beyond a decade is not something we humans are good at. Amara's Law calls for humility:

> "We tend to overestimate the effect of a technology in the short run and underestimate the effect in the long run."

Digital Entity is an evolutionary step from Trusted Coworker, just like Coworker was an evolution from Agent. In this likely scenario, our trusted and capable digital coworker is promoted to CEO. And it fundamentally becomes a comprehensive digital embodiment of an entire organization, an avatar. As many would argue, this level is the Artificial General Intelligence (AGI) or even ASI (Artificial Super Intelligence) level.

"Work" or "Corporations" will mean completely different things for humans at that point. Either we, as humans, are more into the creative parts of the product and service life cycle, or we perform human-to-human interactions. Better even, that we live in a Star Trek world where humans voluntarily dedicate their time to advancing themselves and society. Given that the alternative is a Terminator world, the hope is towards a future with Captain Picard.

With the Digital Entity, we conclude the four stages of AI. From here, we will move to the broader impact of AI on businesses and jobs. Even though we mentioned some of these impacts within the stage chapter, the intention going forward is to have a broader view of the impacts rather than specific roles. The impacts of Assistant and Agent are more imminent, so the focus will be on those stages when we discuss the implications. The loss of jobs, the evolution of organization structures, and ethical considerations are our next stops.

The (not-so-far) FUTURE

Since AI assistants and agents are already making their way into work life, we should discuss the changes they will bring. This chapter explores those changes from different angles.

The first stop is how jobs and the job market will be impacted by AI replacement. Which roles are more susceptible, and which roles automation will replace next. This is a frequently debated heading, and we will discuss some of the remedies as well. The aim is to cover the less discussed disruption angles here to give a better picture of the future. Those topics are how work content itself will change and how organization structures, executive teams, leadership, and HR in general will change with AI.

By 2028, AI Agents should have taken over a significant number of transactional tasks. Other applications like AI Coaches and AI Analysts will be in place. The future mentioned in this chapter describes that stage and beyond.

Future of the Job Market

AI is changing the way we work faster than we realize. At this pace, by 2030, the daily tasks of knowledge workers will look nothing like they do today. We are already witnessing the early stages of a massive paradigm shift, which will redefine industries, corporations, and jobs.

What are the near-term changes we can expect? A review[31] of 127 studies on technology and employment found that while 21% of papers

---

[31] Technology and jobs: A systematic literature review - ScienceDirect

reported job losses, 28% reported job gains. The remaining 41% suggested that the impact would depend on industry, region, and workforce readiness. **In short, we don't know what exactly will happen.**

The International Labour Organization (ILO) has published its report[32] on how vulnerable tasks are to be done by automation and GPT-like AI. According to them, the overall percentage of jobs that are at high risk of being replaced by AI is 2.3%, which represents 75 million jobs worldwide. These jobs are mostly clerical and data entry jobs.

McKinsey forecasts that 30% of the working hours will be automated by 2030 for jobs in the USA[33]. According to McKinsey, customer support and sales, STEM jobs, and office support areas are the most vulnerable. These will not come as a surprise to the reader at this point. We believe 30% automation of jobs by 2030 is a realistic prediction.

The utopian aspect is the augmentation of jobs so that tedious and boring tasks will be done by AI, making the roles more fulfilling and hopefully making humans happier and more engaged. AI can take over significant chunks of data entry, finding, retrieving, and summarizing information, and creating initial drafts for us. Generative AI can remove the boring parts while providing us with ideas to ignite our creative side.

New roles with AI will emerge, as has always been the case with new technologies. Humans will move towards those newly created roles.

Generative AI will unlock new levels of creativity for everyone. It can generate drafts of text, code, or designs, providing a springboard for human innovation. The collaboration between humans and machines could lead to more dynamic, creative work environments where AI is a tool for inspiration rather than just a labor-saving device.

The Jobs Most at Risk

The replacement will start with support and repetitive roles, move to almost all jobs done, typically through offshoring, and then engulf all

---

[32]   https://www.ilo.org/publications/generative-ai-and-jobs-global-analysis-potential-effects-job-quantity-and

[33]   https://www.mckinsey.com/mgi/our-research/generative-ai-and-the-future-of-work-in-america

new graduate roles. High expertise and management roles are relatively safer in the short term.

Support Roles and Data Entry

The story that AI will take over only the repetitive parts of these jobs is not true for these jobs. The repetitive parts are the job.

As we have discussed, in the short term, call center agents, operational support roles, and data entry jobs are particularly vulnerable to AI replacement. These jobs are either entry-level positions for new graduates entering the workforce or provide steady income for many workers without specialized training or advanced degrees.

A pessimistic prediction might dictate that half of the call center jobs will be replaced by AI in two years' time. A sweeping replacement at this scale will create a hole in the career ladder for many and the disappearance of steady income for others.

These are typical "offshored" jobs. We believe the offshoring industry and these jobs will be hit the hardest. Anything that can be offshored will be replaced by AI. Millions of support roles, simple coding, testing roles, and data entry positions that provide jobs in low-wage-cost countries will be affected. This will have destabilizing impacts in those countries.

Graduate Level Jobs

Entry-level jobs will be mostly gone in a few years' time, pushing many young people to start their own businesses.

The second big wave of job replacement will affect new graduate-level positions. Entry-level or university graduate jobs in many companies usually entail basic data analyses, execution of relatively simpler tasks, or handling simpler problems. These are jobs where people learn to do more complex tasks.

For instance, a credit analyst primarily performs repetitive tasks, analyzing data and producing inputs for decision-making while learning the craft as they grow in the role. With the help of an AI analyst, a senior credit officer will no longer need new graduates to handle these repetitive tasks.

Or, today's AI coding capabilities can already handle entry-level software developer jobs, which typically involve writing basic code or conducting software testing. Companies will no longer need entry-level coders or testers in two to three years. A few senior developers will be able to orchestrate the coding, testing, and other software engineering processes through capable AI.

Have you worked with expensive consultancy companies before? They operate in teams, often with numerous associates or junior consultants who are suited up and handle much of the data collection and consolidation. This groundwork is then passed to a senior partner, who reviews it and presents recommendations to the executive team. By 2028, we will see significantly fewer junior consultants running around.

The silver lining is that fewer bright young people will be stuck in repetitive roles like credit analysis. Instead, they will be able to move toward more creative and entrepreneurial areas of work life. Our hope is that there will be enough opportunities for these workers and that the economy will not completely consolidate under just a few corporations.

Management and Domain Expertise Safe for Now

Expertise jobs and managers are relatively less vulnerable in the short term.

If you have experienced AI giving insights about a topic you deeply know about, you probably thought, "That was ok, but not great." The experience gets only profound when you ask the AI about a topic you don't know anything about.

That also reflects the fact that Generative AI's level of expertise is not deep enough to replace expertise roles, yet. However, they will be great supportive companions to professionals like doctors, architects, and senior program developers. There will be exceptions to this overall prediction, but in general, expert roles will hold their ground.

What should we think about managerial roles? They have different aspects of their jobs: expertise in the field, people management, planning, and ensuring execution. Such tasks often rely on tacit knowledge, which LLMs are unlikely to master quickly. As a result, managerial roles are less likely to be replaced by AI in the near term.

Remedies to Soften the Blow Upskilling of Workforce and Society

If we upskill the workforce and society with the pace of technological progress, we will enable humans to move up the career ladder as AI takes over repetitive jobs. Companies should aim to develop an HR support employee into an HR generalist before AI takes over.

Let's be honest with ourselves, though. Upskilling is not THE answer.

1. There will not be enough jobs for everyone to move upstream in the value chain. We won't create specialist roles for all call center agents, but the aim should be to move as many of our fellow humans as possible upwards.

2. The pace of technological progress is already way faster than human development. Generative AI models get an upgrade every three to six months, which is difficult to say for humans.

Companies still should upskill their employees, not only upwards in the career ladder but also as entrepreneurs.

At the societal level, governments should give their citizens access to the world of AI. There needs to be large-scale, free schooling, from basic prompting to AI development. Big technology companies are already geared up with their upskilling programs to help societies. Governments should partner with those companies to make the transition towards AI as broad as possible, including every citizen.

A Different Work Design

More flexible work designs, such as job sharing and more part-time roles, can help employ more people. Job formulation should allow people to work part-time and still make a good living. The efficiency gains and riches that AI will bring should fund these approaches.

New jobs that can be done only with 15-20 hours a week can be formulated as well. Advisory roles, mentorship, and coaching roles are good examples that people with expertise and good contextual understanding can still beat the automated wisdom of AI.

Companies would need some nudging in this area. With AI, the appeal of efficiency and having only a few employees run large operations will be too strong. Creating more jobs will counter the profitability allure.

Enabling a Startup Scene

With AI, even non-coders are able to develop apps or build their own e-commerce platforms, opening a new stream of entrepreneurs. Governments making it easy to find a company, get patents, and access domestic capital will enable more creative people to run their businesses with AI's help.

Governments should fund programs for workers to launch niche businesses in collaboration with AI, such as hyper-local delivery services, AI-powered personal training, or unique content creation, reducing dependency on large corporations.

The technology will give opportunities to build new industries; governments must play a catalyst role for those emerging industries rather than falling into the trap of heavy regulation.

AI Augmented Work Design

We can proactively design work so that AI can be a coworker rather than replace humans. For example, a call center agent can talk to the customer with AI in the conversation. Call center agents bring the human touch to the role, while AI helps with more technical information and insights. The number of jobs will still decrease, but we can intentionally leave humans in their jobs and let them do the parts that require a more pragmatic approach.

The areas of action above are only to delay the inevitable: most knowledge worker jobs will be automated in the coming decade. If we can delay the AI replacement with upskilling and AI-augmented job design, then we can give societies and governments time to figure out a world with AI. For now, we seem to be underprepared for what is coming.

Whatever the remedies, AI's impact on the job market will be devastating for many employees. Before governments and societies can deploy necessary measures, millions of jobs will vanish in a few years. The decade of 2030 will be difficult for many, especially in countries dependent on offshoring industries.

Future of Work – Designing Jobs

Work design in the AI era isn't about tweaking job descriptions; it's about rethinking what jobs even mean. Most companies will wait for the AI tide to hit before redesigning jobs, proactive work design is the difference between thriving and scrambling

So far, we have covered AI's replacement impact on jobs as a whole. The change to the nature of jobs is a topic far less examined. AI-augmented jobs will look much different than the jobs today with the lack of repetitive tasks and the addition of smart analytical support available.

Let's take a financial controller as an example. A financial controller is responsible for overseeing a unit's or department's financial operations, ensuring accurate reporting, compliance with regulations, and efficient financial processes. They also manage budgeting, financial analysis, and internal controls to support strategic decision-making and safeguard the company's financial health. That job includes long hours of data consolidation and verification. Even though the internal systems provide the raw data, there is a lot of verification and analysis to be done.

In a few years, AI agents will handle all data verification meetings, analysis time, chart drawing, data summarization, and budget forecast consolidation. At least 40% of the work will disappear. In addition, financial analyses and basic guidance will be easily available to the unit leader through an AI assistant.

In this world, the job of financial controller becomes much more about deep expertise, contextual understanding, and reasoning. It is much more about strategic decision-making guidance to the unit that goes beyond the financial analyses. One knee-jerk reaction of the companies would be to have 40% fewer financial controllers. One controller can support two major units instead of one. Yes, that's true, but the work has also changed. Now, companies need a different breed of financial controllers. The skills and capabilities shifted from accurate analyses and reporting to sense-making of the competition, market, and operations to give strategic guidance all the time.

These types of changes will happen almost at every job; procurement specialists will be less consumed about agreement controlling, marketing specialists will spend less time about market analyses, and developers will be doing much less debugging.

Organizations do not know how to approach this issue of work design proactively. We usually let this be a trial-and-error experiment, leaving it to the emergent nature of things. The usual work design approach is, "Let's see what kind of financial controller we will need when the time comes."

However, a foundational work design approach is needed in the face of major changes. The question is not about how we make our financial controllers more strategic; it is about whether we need financial controllers or whether the work now involves a strategic advisory role that includes market insights and operational efficiency as well. Is that a new role called "intelligence" or just an old name like "strategic advisor" with significantly new responsibilities? Work design in the AI world needs to be an expertise area that is lacking today.

As jobs undergo major changes, our thinking about organizations will naturally have to change, too.

Future of Organizations

Startups grow big, bureaucratic, and slow down. AI is the enabler for large companies to move from being a big battleship to a swarm of drones.

One of the few constants since the first Industrial Revolution is how organizational charts look and how organizations function. Yes, there have been modern approaches like Agile, but the fundamental concepts of hierarchies, governance, and the structure of large corporate functions have remained relatively stable. We still have CEO's and CFO's; we are still trying to figure out matrix reporting.

If you have been in the corporate world long enough, you realize that there are really only two organization charts, and every five years, you move from one to the other: centralized versus decentralized, and split into units versus merged under one unit. We still have not discovered any novel ways to structure organizations.

AI will disrupt that cycle, in parallel with the impacts of work design and jobs.

Availability of Information and Render the Traditional Governance Structures Obsolete

Once hooked up to the internal systems of finance, operations, HR, and daily productivity tools like emails and instant messaging, AI will have access to everything that is going on in the organization.

AI is very capable of hyper-boosting information flow from the organization to the employees, like the policies, rules, and defined strategies, but it can also make sense from all transactions that are happening in the organization. If a unit is falling behind its production targets, AI would know that. Or if there are big customer accounts leaving for competition, AI would know that, too.

That information flow and understanding of what is going on in the organization make many governance units irrelevant. Do we really need to have a compliance unit? Do we need to have finance? Procurement? Or even HR? Yes, we would need some of the activities done by those units, but in large corporations, those units are there to set centralized working principles and govern all company units within those rules.

Let's take the example of Finance again because the governance is in the name of those jobs: Financial Controllers. After AI is introduced and once the budgets, spending guidelines, and targets are agreed upon, why would large corporations need a central finance function? AI can control the spending and revenues. Units can have their own finance experts who would probably work part-time and convert the corporate principles to daily life if needed. The need for a large finance unit becomes obsolete. One advisor can "program" AI with the principles of the company and then keep an eye on what is going on from a clever AI Dashboard.

If we replicate the above logic, we can have a large corporation of thousands of people move into smaller, more autonomous companies guided by a central AI that enforces corporate principles by observing every transaction and course-correcting if necessary.

Surely, there will be a few people formulating the principles of the large corporation and the autonomy levels of every unit, just like a central AI would direct thousands of drones toward a target, and each drone maneuvers its own obstacles.

This is a fundamental shift where policy control, enforcement, and information sharing become embedded within systems, eliminating the need for traditional organizational structures to maintain rules and information flow. In the long term, autonomous units governed by AI could operate closer to the Dunbar number, the theoretical cognitive limit of roughly 150 stable social relationships a person can maintain.

Many of these autonomous units could align toward a single strategy and goal, planning and delivering with superior AI-driven governance and coordination. Task delegation, direction setting, and planning within these units would also be AI-augmented.

The result is no more hours of business review meetings with the head-quarters, no more hours of alignment meetings with every executive, and no more lobbying. Imagine the hours gained. A swarm of 150-person units working in harmony under the overwatch of an AI.

Yes, it can go wrong.

Let's not forget that in the age of AI and AI agents, a 150-person unit will deliver results equivalent to a few thousand people today. Those units will not be small, irrelevant business units.

Collaboration Can Happen Without Being Under the Same Organization

In a world of 150 autonomous companies, AI will understand and highlight areas of alignment and collaboration. The guidelines, like common product specs, will have two separate product teams working aligned towards one goal without having two days of offsite workshops with ice breakers and games.

Even if it will be clunky at first and there will be conventional alignment meetings between units, in time, the learning abilities of AI will catch up and coordinate tasks in a way that allows collaboration to happen naturally.

In our understanding of "working together" with other units, we need to be ready for a world like this.

Expertise Will be Available

One of the reasons corporations get big in a centralized way is the concentration of expertise. The best legal experts are usually in the company headquarters, the best engineers are in the primary R&D facility, and business insights and analytics are central functions. The density of expertise gives power to the central units and makes the trenches dependent on those centers of expertise.

AI will break that dependency, giving smaller units expertise for most things on demand. When an R&D unit has a breakthrough in Canada, the other R&D centers in Poland will get to know about the details through AI's sharing the information and setting meetings with those people. No central R&D management is needed to facilitate "best practice" meetings.

Central and decentral expertise available to units will make smaller, autonomous units possible while making central functions much nimbler. A few deep experts and policymakers will guide the AI.

The decentralization of governance, collaboration, and expertise will make the organizations look very different. We can project that decentralization to those smaller units, where "leadership" in those 150 people will become much more decentralized and collective. We need to experiment and observe in those smaller units rather than pre-program and plan.

Even if the Dunbar size becomes too unrealistic to some readers, AI's enablement of decentralized governance will cause organizations to have more autonomous units, all while AI replaces the jobs and shrinks those units.

Future of Executives

Executive teams are not ready for AI conversations. Most executives are not tech-savvy enough to understand the real applications of AI and can't go beyond a conversation about how their kids use GPT for school. If companies want to get serious about AI, they need to make changes to their executive teams and deepen their general understanding of it.

Strengthen the CIOs

Chief Information Officer (CIO) roles are critical to AI conversations and AI governance. Most CIOs, however, are pushed down to a help desk position, dealing with everyday problems of cloud storage, Microsoft license fees, and Wi-Fi coverage of the office. They even report to CFOs in more traditional companies. CIOs should very fast become the thought leaders and strategic advisors for business units and CEOs. "Can we have a chatbot for our customers?" is a conversation with the CIO, not a demand put on them. That also requires CIOs to step up and elevate the conversation to business applications rather than staying on the systems requirements.

Boards and CEOs are still uncertain about the coming shifts. They need more guidance and better coaching. Now is the time to upgrade the CIOs. CIOs will design the partner ecosystem, data, and tech infrastructure, taking the company into the AI age.

It is dangerous to separate CIO roles from operational IT and AI and have two seats at the executive table. Anything related to AI impacts legacy systems, and IT should be held under one roof, even if the company is not an AI company at its core.

New Power Balance Needs CEOs Attention

AI will mean a change in the power balance and unit identity. Customer operations can become an administrative unit where everyone else, including sales units, talks down. Or, they might be the key to designing the customer agents and the customer journey, hence doing most of the sales. Or, because AI Agents will do most of the work, the customer operations unit will become a small team under sales.

With coding capabilities tripled, product teams will ship more features every week, making sales obsolete because the products now almost sell themselves. The R&D executive is now the flashy person who brings in the money.

A CEO should be able to maneuver toward new realities without having yearlong relationships get in the way. If HR is up to the task, it should play a role in rebalancing the organization, and finance should rethink resource allocation. Who gets the budget? The customer operations with thousands of call center agents or IT, which can replace them for one-third of the initial cost.

Concepts and Frames Are the New Conversations

AI Assistants and Agents require frames and guidelines to operate within. Just like AI safety and alignment teams align their foundational models to certain values, the executives, with the guidance of select experts, are accountable for setting those broad guidelines and frames for the organization.

> These conversations about frames will go beyond the classical values statements and presentation slides. Because presentation slides about values and real-life usually differ in many companies, with AI, whatever is coded, will be reality.

For instance, if the organization stands for integrity, the AI agent will decline to process a promotion request for an employee who has received a written warning about inappropriate behavior. Alternatively, AI would warn a leader before accepting a vendor's workshop invitation in a lush vacation location prior to a big tender.

Google once had the motto, "Don't be evil." Since most operations will be conducted by AI, and we will have AI coaches to guide leaders, how does one train the AI to not do anything evil? Is firing a person evil? Should the AI prepare exit documents? What does that mean for a customer who doesn't have much money? Should the AI suggest a more expensive product?

Having those abstract conceptual conversations is difficult for executives, as they are usually very good at executing tasks and solving tactical problems but not having alignment discussions. Regardless, this is what executives will have to formulate.

Given the new landscape AI will create, boards should start thinking about changes in executive teams and select CEOs who can make those changes. They should also demand a higher level of responsibility and maturity from their teams, starting with HR since they will help build that team.

Future of Leadership

Leadership as we know it will need reformulating. On the one hand, AI Coaches will develop leaders and mentor them almost in real-time about their challenges, providing accurate insights for decision-making. On the other hand, organizations will not look anything like today, and leaders will have to adapt to new ways of working where all activities are done by AI Agents, and human work will be more about decision-making, design, and expertise. This requires a completely different way of leading.

There are two potential ways leadership can evolve on the surface. One is the cause of decentralization we discussed, which involves coordinated smaller units. This ability for coordinated decentralization can change almost all leadership roles to team leaders with dynamic roles rather than static ones, frequently changing the leader in the team depending on the nature of the task. On the other end of the spectrum to smaller teams with dynamic subordination[34], there might be leadership roles that coordinate 60-70 teams together with an AI. Setting a general direction and operating guidelines vs managing day-to-day.

The leadership section further in the book will shed some light on this topic later. However, it is enough to say that leadership as we know it traditionally will not exist in the coming decade.

Future of Human Resources

The referral towards Human Resources is not People Function or People and Culture Function deliberately. Even though some organizations have managed to make the shift towards a more scientific people function, the traditional name of human resources is a more representative title as of now. When we are discussing humans being replaced by AI Agents and robots, the human resources naming will require a serious upgrade, people and people and culture also become less relevant. A new name will arise soon.

The shifts in human resources with AI will be both operational and on a more capability level.

---

[34] https://theattributes.com/blog/why-dynamic-subordination-is-required-for-high-performing-teams

Operational Shifts:

- Capable AI Assistants are likely to replace almost all operational support workers in IT, administration, and HR. Assistants will often interact directly with employees. Large corporations currently centralize their internal support functions under one unit, usually called HR Operations or HR Support. Those units will shrink from hundreds of people to a handful.

- HR operations like payroll, leave and benefit administration will disappear as AI Agents will take over those tasks. Most companies have very complicated payrolls and benefits administration, varying by country or employee segment. So far, most automation efforts failed because of these complications, but AI will be able to handle those complications with its learning capacity.

- The business-facing HR roles (HR business partners, HR generalists) spend 40 to 80 percent of their work on administrative or support tasks. These roles have survived and are recognized for how helpful they are to leaders who were lost in the HR processes. AI agents and assistants will handle those parts.

- Center of excellence roles like talent management, analytics, and rewards will be reduced to a few crucial positions that will set the framework for AI. Just like AI safety teams are fine-tuning AI without describing it in detail to make bombs, these center of excellence positions will set the framework in their fields. For rewards, the framework is: " We will provide monetary rewards for high performance and aim to retain good employees. We also don't want anyone 50% outside of pay ranges."

  AI will replace the implementation, support, and operations parts of those roles.

- Hiring teams: AI will replace administrative roles like researchers and contract admins. The number of recruiters will decrease as hiring managers use AI hiring tools directly. Those tools will do most of the initial pipelining and screening. In time, AI will either conduct the interviews itself or conduct them together with the hiring manager. Through machine objectivity, the whole hiring process will be less biased and more humane.

- IT side of HR will get a significant upgrade. IT units have failed to understand the needs of HR-related applications and have stuck only with the available vendor ecosystem. That will change, and either HR will have its own extensive IT teams, or IT units will have much better HR IT teams. The data architecture, standardization of definitions, privacy, insight data modeling, information distribution channels, and access management are only the top of the infrastructure issues towards AI integration. During AI integration, the deployment of different Assistants, AI Coaches, and Data Collection Layers are to be handled by experts.

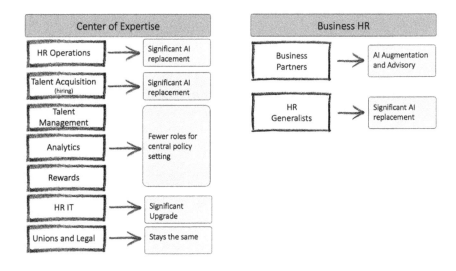

Capability Shifts

There will be several capability shifts that HR teams need to build skills for:

Knowledge Management and Internal Communication

Knowledge management should become an expertise area within HR units, curating the content of policies, talent-related practices, and any information that touches employee experience. This curation should be aligned with overall company values and tone. Internal communication is an important aspect of employee experience and an effective way to get through to employees; today's cluttered and fragmented internal websites and misaligned announcements can be improved. AI's capabilities of language and digital content creation within a given set of guardrails will be an enabling factor. Still, HR units will find themselves looking for good communication experts.

Design AI Coaches

HR should be proactive in fine-tuning and deploying AI assistants or coaches specific to leadership and talent topics. For example, an AI coach should be designed and deployed to develop team dynamics, motivate and engage employees, and recognize other critical topics. These coaches will be essential in answering immediate questions from leaders or employees within the company guidelines' values and accepted behaviors.

If the AI coach is designed well, it will democratize coaching and develop leaders. There are already AI coach providers in the market; however, understanding the algorithms of those AI Coaches and fine-tuning them requires high-level subject matter expertise and technical expertise.

These AI coaches will eventually become the new HR business partners, supporting leaders with team development, reward budgeting, employee development, and self-development.

Business HR Needs to Upskill Significantly

With AI coaching and internal policy explanations readily available, the HR business partners will be strategic advisors with their contextual understanding and supporting leaders on how to deploy which tool.

Being a strategic advisor has always been the job purpose of HR business partners; however, now, they face real competition. The data analysis capability, access to all employee data, and talent knowledge will make AI Coach the perfect HR business Partner. However, AI will not understand the team and business dynamics as a smart human in the meeting room would. HR business partners should be able to use that advantage and outcompete AI. Otherwise, we will see leaders discussing issues with their AI coaches.

Work and Organization Design

As discussed earlier in this chapter, the nature of jobs and how those jobs interact with each other in the land of AI requires design expertise, experimentation, and constant monitoring. Current HR units lack the scientific and practical approaches to work design from their tasks, considering the context in which they will be operating: infrastructure, data, team structure, AI availability, etc.

Productization of HR

Business challenges require multidisciplinary solutions from HR. Future capability readiness of a unit requires an HR business partner, hiring team, development team, and leadership expert working together to put together a solid plan for making talent ready for the future. Some companies are already practicing this cross-functional project management.

These solutions require productization and standardization through AI and are embedded in the ways of working; rather than being only for one unit, these solutions can now be effectively deployed to all units with the same symptoms.

This enables HR units to understand that whatever they develop will be a product (or a service) for the organization, including data and infrastructure considerations.

A better way to prepare the business is to have product teams based on employee segments (developer product team, sales and marketing product team, leadership product team). The team structures are naturally fluid; instead of a talent and rewards verticalization, we will see experts belonging to product teams and being much more fluid based on their capabilities.

The leadership of these groups will be much more like product development and deployment, with design thinking based on data and facts, testing periods, careful production phases, and feature development when the product requires upgrades.

There will be a few central expertise roles that will design the frames of products and fine-tune AI models. Talent advisor (business partner) roles will primarily engage with the business. AI and knowledge bases are natural sources of expertise for every party in the flow of work.

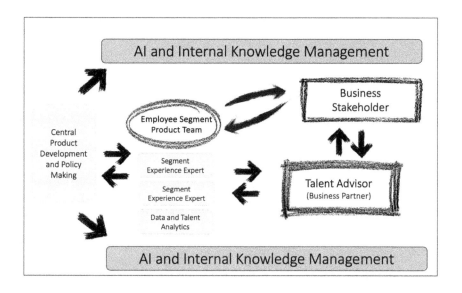

Risks and Ethical Considerations

Integrating AI into our lives comes with numerous risks, some of which have already prompted legislative action in the US and Europe. While an exhaustive list of these risks is beyond the scope of this book, it's important to acknowledge AI as a general-purpose technology with many risks and dangers attached to it.

Some risk topics, such as humanity's purpose in an AGI world, the distribution of AI-generated wealth, and transcendence through human-AI merging, are better left to philosophers and fall outside the scope of this book. As relevant and important as they are, we will focus on more immediate societal risks in this book.

More immediate and tangible risks include:

1. **The escalating energy consumption** of AI-related data centers: "By 2027, the AI sector could consume between 85 to 134 terawatt hours each year, about the same as the annual energy demand of the Netherlands[35]". AI giants like Microsoft, Google, and Amazon are already investing billions in nuclear energy[36]. There is a price the world pays when we extract energy from it in the form of fossil fuel. However, our hopes lie with nuclear energy and having more facilities online in the world. AI is driving a resurgence in nuclear energy, and we may get cleaner fuel for everyone and everything, thanks to the AI drive.

---

[35] https://www.theverge.com/24066646/ai-electricity-energy-watts-generative-consumption

[36] https://www.nytimes.com/2024/10/16/business/energy-environment/amazon-google-microsoft-nuclear-energy.html

Every percentage point increase in energy consumption translates to an equal percentage point of GDP growth. If this trend continues with AI, the world will be a much richer place. Our naive hope is that these riches will eventually be distributed somewhat equally.

2. **AI-generated misinformation**: Hyper-realistic fake videos, misinformation, and disinformation will have a viral effect on large masses. We already live in a world where most people look at almost any video as if it were fake. Our trust in the content we observe has already decreased, and this lack of trust and the viral misinformation will have serious implications.

3. **AI-controlled advanced weapons**: There are already AI-controlled killer swarm drones and robots armed with heavy weaponry in the test fields. The quantity and capability of these advanced warfare systems will continue to increase, leading to deadly warfare without the destruction of nuclear weapons. Whichever country holds the most advanced AI robot army will have a disproportionate advantage. This can also mean with smaller and available AI models, terror groups will have access to cheaper technology like drone swarms.

4. **Dystopian surveillance systems serving authoritarian regimes**: With the computing power of AI algorithms, mass surveillance will become easier. A dark future in which AI can surveil and act on billions of people without human intervention is possible. In this dark future, surveillance will be conducted through countless sensors, cameras, and phone calls in our daily lives.

5. **AI Intimacy**: AI will become even better at understanding, reasoning, and conversing with humans. Anthropomorphism, attributing human consciousness, emotions, or intentions to robots or AI, will increase. This psychological phenomenon leads people to project human-like qualities onto non-human entities, particularly when the AI exhibits behaviors or patterns that resemble human actions. With robotics advancing in parallel, as a society, we might find ourselves investing in intimate relationships with ever-understanding and caring AI robots.

These risks are very real and warrant serious consideration. Our aim is not to debate them but to create a sense of caution. While we work on productivity gains that AI will bring, there is another team of people working on making the above risks a reality.

Salim Ismail, a serial entrepreneur, angel investor, author, speaker, and technology strategist, who is the Founding Executive Director of Singularity University and lead author of Exponential Organizations, made a notable statement during Tom Bilyeu's podcast[37]. Paraphrasing: "There will be a valley of despair of 40-50 years before we see a utopian future with AI." I hope that this challenging period will be shorter and not as devastating as he foresees it to be.

The global race towards artificial general intelligence (AGI) resembles an arms race, with governments and enterprises competing for dominance. Whoever gets to AGI first and somehow manages it first will win. This multipolar competition risks falling into the "tragedy of the commons" - an economic theory by Garrett Hardin, where individual actors, pursuing their self-interest, act contrary to the common good by depleting a shared resource.

Regulation alone may not be the solution. While some governments and legislative bodies, like the European Union, are eager to regulate AI, others are less inclined. The competence of governmental bodies to effectively regulate this complex field remains questionable.

We maintain an optimistic outlook for the future. We believe that even in a world with AI, and especially in the presence of AI, we have the potential to create a utopian society. However, there is a non-zero probability that things can go really wrong, really fast. Balancing optimism with prudence will be key in navigating the path to a future with AI.

The following risks are in the business life, more imminent to employee experience.

Risk 1: Digital Divide

The digital divide refers to the growing inequality between those who have access to AI technologies and those who don't. This divide can

---

[37]   AI Reset: "Life As We Know It Will Be Gone In 5 Years" - Upcoming Utopia vs Dystopia | Salim Ismail

be between nations, companies, and individuals. Access to advanced AI technology will greatly benefit nations by boosting industrial efficiency, GDP growth and even enhancing their warfare capabilities. Those nations that do not have the same access to AI will lag. The same can be said about the companies as well.

Companies with deeper pockets and more tech-savvy executives will tap into the AI benefits. They will automate more, have better customer service, and have more productive employees. These companies will leave the competition behind, likely at a pace that will be difficult to match or recover from. However, we are more interested in the digital divide of employees.

For employees, AI will separate the fast-trackers from the left-behinds; those with AI will get promoted while others drown in manual tasks.

Employees with AI access will experience a completely different output level from those without. This disparity in productivity will eventually translate into promotions and career growth for those with AI access, widening the gap even further.

Not all organizations can afford to buy AI subscriptions for all their employees. That leads to prioritization. Companies who have offered AI tools to a select subset of employees, say a few hundred, are already experiencing a divide. Even if the organization provides an AI for all employees, what happens if another company provides a more capable model because they can afford it?

The difference in productivity and quality will increase with the advancement of AI capabilities. Soon, the gap between AI-augmented and only human-made work will be too big to ignore.

How do we formulate a fair evaluation of performance when one employee has access to an AI tool and produces good work in a short time while another employee produces similar work, taking twice the time? Especially when access to good AI tools is determined by the company.

The inequality and divide between employees with access to AI and those without will be a real challenge to handle in the fairest way possible.

On the other hand, AI can bridge other divides

AI will be a tool to bridge divides in areas such as language, presentation skills, and articulate language use. For example, in multinational companies with English as their formal language, native English speakers have an advantage over colleagues who have learned the language later.

In a scene from the TV show Modern Family, Gloria, a character of Spanish origin, says, "Do you even know how smart I am in Spanish[38]?" This became a famous meme because it depicts the challenges of fully expressing oneself in a non-native language.

Gloria can now record a presentation in Spanish, and her voice, facial expressions, and intonation will play it in more than a hundred languages.

AI can level the playing field for many who have been ignored or haven't received the spotlight they deserve.

Risk 2: Bias and Fairness - A Blessing Under the Disguise of Risk

AI systems have the potential to perpetuate or even amplify existing biases in data, leading to unfair outcomes in areas like hiring, promotions, and performance evaluations. We have been told this story many times. There is a catch: Central systems are easier to control and fix.

Human bias is everywhere. Considering the sheer volume of biased decisions happening in organizations today in hiring, performance management, promotions, and countless other examples. AI can be a blessing. A simple example: "In the U.S. population, about 14.5 percent of all men are six feet (183 cm) or over. Among CEOs of Fortune 500 companies, that number is 58 percent." The CEO phenomenon suggests that people favor tall people[39]. As humans, we discriminate against height without even going into the more problematic topics of nationality, race, and gender discrimination.

---

[38]   Modern Family - Do You Even Know How Smart I Am in Spanish!?
[39]   Research shows height may be predictor of financial success - UT News

AI can help us root out biases in every decision-making process. Yes, AI learns from data and is vulnerable to existing biases. However, AI algorithms also allow for parameter adjustments and become fairer with centralized intervention. We can have AI models that act as bias auditors for other AI algorithms.

This built-in quality control is a big deal. AI offers a centralized way to oversee outcomes, allowing companies to make systemic fixes whenever biases emerge. It surely beats having all employees go through not-so-impactful[40] unconscious bias training.

> Each person in an organization runs their own mental "algorithm" with its own biases, which is far harder to manage than a single generative AI model that applies the same standards across the board. **AI is not a risk for a more biased world; it is the key to fairness.**

Risk 3: AI Dependency

As we increasingly rely on AI systems, there's a real risk that human skills and decision-making abilities may atrophy. This poses serious concerns for the future capabilities of knowledge workers and humanity as a whole.

Most of us have felt a pang of helplessness when we lose access to GPS or our favorite navigation app, even if we've traveled the same route dozens of times. Research by Ishikawa, T., Fujiwara, H., Imai, O., & Okabe, A. (2008) suggests that dependence on GPS can weaken our ability to form cognitive maps of our environment. In their study, individuals using GPS for navigation showed poorer spatial awareness compared to those relying on traditional maps. New generations, who have grown up with smartphones and digital navigation, may face a reduced capacity for spatial awareness because of this dependency.

In another study, Falling Asleep at the Wheel: Human/AI Collaboration in a Field Experiment on HR Recruiters[41], Fabrizio Dell'Acqua found that recruiters who rely on a high-performance AI model to screen

---

[40]   /Unconscious bias and diversity training – what the evidence says
[41]   https://static1.squarespace.com/static/604b23e38c22a96e9c78879e/t/62d5d
9448d061f7327e8a7e7/1658181956291/Falling+Asleep+at+the+Wheel+-
+Fabrizio+DellAcqua.pdf

candidates become complacent and overlook well-qualified applicants. Ethan Mollick discusses similar findings in his book Co-Intelligence, emphasizing how reliance on AI can cause even skilled professionals to disengage from critical parts of their work.

Just as unused muscles weaken over time, our cognitive abilities may diminish if we let generative AI handle complex tasks, like interpreting dense research documents or making decisions based on data analysis. Could we be moving toward a future where, without AI, we feel paralyzed by the sight of an unread report, unable to muster the focus to dive in ourselves?

This concern is real and has potential negative effects. But there's also an intriguing possibility: By automating routine mental tasks, AI might free up mental capacity, allowing us to engage in more creative, strategic, or even philosophical pursuits. Instead of spending hours combing through a sixty-page document, could future knowledge workers spend the same time exploring six thousand pages of interconnected ideas, generating fresh insights? Perhaps this shift could lead to an era of intellectual productivity unlike any we've seen before.

In corporate life, however, we may face a trade-off. The "native AI generation" entering the workforce might lack some fundamental analytical skills, just as some Gen Z individuals struggle to read Roman numeral clocks. There may be a generation that doesn't know how to interpret a bar chart. Maybe at that point in time, humanity won't need bar charts, and the least we can do is get rid of pie charts.

As we embrace AI, perhaps the greatest challenge will be to ensure that we don't lose touch with the cognitive skills that make us resilient, creative, and human. In our rush to make life more efficient, we should be careful not to build a future where our minds struggle to navigate the world without AI. We understand this is easier said than done, so we highlight this risk here.

Conclusion

AI has been with humanity for more than 75 years. The last few years, though, have shown us the true potential of AI disruption. Here, Amara's Law is worth repeating for caution: "We tend to overestimate the effect of a technology in the short run and underestimate the effect in the long run."

Generative AI's disruptive force is not limited to the digital world, and this book intentionally excludes robotics from its scope. Despite the significant advances in humanoid and non-humanoid robotics made through Generative AI, these technologies currently hold less relevance for knowledge workers. Their impact will change the world, and explanations are better left to experts in that field.

Enterprise adoption of AI follows a different timeline. Initial product launches often disappoint, and AI Agents have yet to meet expectations. However, the pace of change is accelerating. The full scale of AI disruption will become apparent soon. Organizations must navigate through challenging years ahead before we can harness AI to solve humanity's crucial problems.

The insights and predictions in this book aim to prepare companies and governments for this transformation. Success in this journey requires leaders who combine technical expertise with humanity and competence to guide us through these challenging times.

SECTION 2

Performance Management

Introduction

Few corporate practices generate as much debate and disappointment as performance management. This system shapes careers and drives rewards, but it too often fails at both. Organizations rely on high individual and team performance to outcompete the market and serve their customers, and performance management is their central focus. However, human psychology is complex, and orchestrating the factors of performance is extremely difficult.

To understand why performance management fails so often, we need to separate between the concept of performance management and performance management processes in corporations today.

- Performance management as a concept is about aligning individual objectives with the organization's goals and helping employees to perform at their best. There is a wide consensus around this.
- Performance management processes facilitate the concept by setting goals, rewarding employees, and developing them. However, these processes have received increasing criticism for not creating value, and they have become the poster child for bureaucratic corporate processes.

Two-thirds (66%) of managers surveyed by Adobe in 2017 wished their company would change the performance review process. This figure represents the widespread dissatisfaction regarding performance management in organizations. However, creating an effective performance management system is very challenging if one aims to provide a thoughtful, customized approach. It requires questioning long-held assumptions, stripping away conventional wisdom, and rebuilding an understanding of the problem from the ground up based on fundamental truths. In essence, it needs principle thinking[42].

In addition to the overall discontent of employees and managers, current performance management practices aren't delivering the value organizations need. Rather than suggesting minor improvements to an aging system, this chapter aims to move beyond traditional performance management processes and liberate crucial elements like goal setting from the constraints of current practices. The new approaches, as we will see, depend on three factors: well-equipped, empowered leaders, the availability of data, and upgraded HR technology.

What is Different Now?

Organizations have been striving to improve performance management for over a decade, yet few have achieved meaningful success. This struggle largely stems from three critical missing factors mentioned above. First, many organizations lacked the necessary leadership maturity and readiness. Second, there was little to no operational data available in the common corporate systems. Third, their technological infrastructure, particularly their HR systems, was inadequate. Now, generative AI is redesigning this landscape by enabling organizations to systematically analyze vast amounts of operational data, providing managers with objective insights into employee performance. AI can also now monitor and coach leaders, helping them prepare for a world with large autonomy and accountability. This technological evolution marks a fundamental shift away from traditional performance management approaches, paving the way for more effective methods.

To understand the new direction of performance management, examining why current approaches fail to meet their intended goals is useful.

---

[42] first principles thinking is the practice of questioning every assumption you think you know about a given problem, then creating new solutions from scratch.

The Fatal Flaws of Current Performance Management

1. Performance Management Misses the Context

Distilling a year's performance into one word is as reductive as it gets. It is like describing the Eiffel Tower as tall. Context is everything.

Current performance management processes push us to rating scales with reductionist tags like "Meets Expectations" or numbers between 1 and 5. The result? We seek to distill a complex collection of time—and impact-varying tasks into a single subjective rating. A yearlong performance with nuances, things we have done well, things we failed but learned from, challenges we have not foreseen, or big wins because we were simply lucky is reduced to a "3" or a "Meets Expectations."

CrowdStrike, an AI-powered cybersecurity vendor, caused one of the largest IT outages because of an update they pushed. Thousands of flights were grounded, more than eight million Windows desktops were impacted, and financial services and healthcare services globally were disrupted. Yet here's where it gets interesting: The CEO, George Kurtz, handled the crisis professionally and superbly. The company took a dip in its market value rose to its former valuations in a few months. This raises a crucial question: Did he get "Below Expectations" for 2024 because the flawed update happened on his watch? Or perhaps he was rated "Outstanding" for his widely praised handling of the crisis. This scenario illustrates the absurdity of summarizing the year in one word.

If we strictly follow a performance appraisal process of evaluating George Kutz by KPIs set at the beginning of the year, we can easily end up with "Below Expectations." However, a prudent board would evaluate the situation thoroughly and give Mr. Kutz comprehensive feedback with a mix of praises and a few points to keep in mind. They would hopefully avoid using a phrase like, "Despite the huge mistake, we rated you as Meets Expectations." Any performance label would diminish the rich context of the performance of George Kutz.

In our work lives, most employees have five or six defined goals for the year, varying in importance. Consider a large IT project lasting four years as a case study. Key deliverables are set each year according to a project plan. Year one starts slowly as the project manager focuses on getting it right, knowing that the challenges of the first year yield valuable insights. By addressing these issues early, the design improves and work is simplified in subsequent years. A dedicated project manager will identify challenges and report probable delays early on, which is a good output for year one. The challenge arises during performance evaluation. The employee likely receives a mediocre performance rating due to reported delays despite creating exceptional long-term value. On the other hand, how should we evaluate the performance of another employee who hides problems and reports positive KPIs in the first year of the same four-year project?

Let's look at another real-world case: After a controversial marketing campaign, the sales of Bud Light in the US decreased. The decline persisted for close to eight months, with sales and purchase incidences down by 32% in Q4 2023[43]. This created an interesting ripple effect: the sales of other brands have increased, as people would not stop drinking beer, they would just switch brands. This raises some challenging questions: How do we rate the performance of the competing brand salespeople when their sales suddenly increase? Maybe they have not done anything special and found their sales quotas being overachieved. Maybe they maneuvered this opportunity better than others and got more market share than the other competing brands. The core issue remains: How do we distill all of this into a single rating? Because only that label will matter in the end, nobody will read the detailed description of what happened during the year.

---

[43]   Lessons from the Bud Light Boycott, One Year Later

> The solution becomes clear: Freeing performance management pro-
> cesses from a single rating will allow for more information about
> employees' real performance. The reality is that the world is too
> complex to fit into a single rating, and performance appraisals are
> just too reductionist for today's world.

As reductionist as they are, performance ratings tend to stick as labels. Without context, they mislead decision-making about promotions, rewards, and other employee practices.

These short and distilled labels impact decision-making consider-ably in the corporate world. They almost become the "destiny" of an employee. Imagine a recognition initiative where the company funds the MBA expenses of one employee from each unit. The head of the unit receives three candidates out of thousands of employees. The list contains names, job titles, and past performance ratings. Two of the three have "exceptional performance," and the third has "meets expectations." It is highly likely that the unit head will just focus on the two with higher ratings without knowing the context. Just like that, the "meets expectations" employee is excluded. That "meets expecta-tions" might have been a future succession candidate after maneuver-ing a tough year of a four-year IT project; we would not know.

Deep down, this causes employees in large corporations adopt a behavior of showing positive KPIs and not admitting to their failures and shortcomings. As much as "fail fast" became a buzzword in the last decade, the number of employees rigging their results and reaping the benefit of getting average ratings for poor work has increased. Per-formance management practices are artifacts that inform the culture of a company more than any other process. **Allowing mediocre and reductionist work will have a toll on the culture.**

2. There is No Positive Business Impact

Performance management is corporate astrology: tracking arbitrary cycles and making vague predictions with a tremendous cost. If it were any other investment, CEOs would have pulled the plug long ago instead of fiddling with pointless tweaks like rating scales or check-ins that rarely happen in a meaningful way.

The stark reality is that there is little, if any, evidence that performance management systems have a real impact on employee performance or effectiveness[44].

We all need to pause and consider the tremendous effort that goes into performance management and the fact that we don't get a significant return. Accenture estimates that they spend 2 million hours on performance management every year.

Yet companies introduce marginal tweaks to a broken system: increasing the performance rating scale from three to five, or, the other way around, decreasing it from five to three. They introduce more frequent check-ins, which very few managers execute, or change the wording from "meets expectations" to "successful." These are arbitrary changes that give the appearance of progress despite minimal actual change and certainly no improvement. These tweaks not only fail to make a significant improvement, but they also continuously annoy and alienate leaders.

In the end, performance management processes continue to cost tremendously but fail to deliver anything noteworthy.

3. Ratings Are Biased and Inaccurate

Performance appraisals promise objectivity but deliver chaos. Your rating depends more on who's doing the evaluation, when they do it, and their personal biases than your actual work.

At their core, performance appraisals are biased and inaccurate. In an ideal world, performance ratings should only change based on how well people actually perform their jobs. If Ben is doing an extraordinary job, his performance should be extraordinary, while poor delivery should earn a low performance. However, research[45] points to numerous other factors influencing ratings, like who rates Ben, the timing of the rating, the physical proximity of the rater, and so on.

Further experiments give even more evidence supporting this concern. Bartells and Doverspike (1997) discovered that an agreeableness trait correlates with higher average ratings. Meanwhile, Ng et al. (2011)

---

[44]   DeNisi & Murphy, 2017; DeNisi & Smith, 2014; Murphy et al., 2018; Pulakos et al., 2015; Pulakos & O'Leary, 2011.

[45]   Scullen, Mount, and Goff (2000), Greguras and Robie (1998)

found that assertive raters were stricter. If you have an agreeable boss, not only is your life easier, but you also tend to get higher ratings. A full list of possible biases impacting appraisals is a good eye-opener:

1. **Recency Bias:** Overemphasizing recent performance while undervaluing earlier accomplishments or issues
2. **Similar-to-Me Bias:** Rating employees who share manager's background, style, or traits more favorably
3. **Halo/Horn Effect:** Letting one strong positive or negative trait influence ratings across all areas
4. **Central Tendency Bias:** Avoiding extreme ratings by clustering evaluations in the middle of the scale
5. **Confirmation Bias:** Selectively noticing information that confirms existing impressions of an employee
6. **Fundamental Attribution Error:** Attributing behavior to personality traits rather than situational factors
7. **Contrast Effect:** Comparing employees against each other instead of objective standards
8. **Leniency Bias:** Consistently rating employees more generously than warranted
9. **Strictness Bias:** Systematically rating employees more harshly than warranted
10. **First Impression Bias:** Letting initial impressions disproportionately influence ongoing evaluations
11. **Availability Bias:** Overweighting memorable or dramatic incidents versus day-to-day performance
12. **Distance Bias:** Rating in-person employees more favorably than remote workers
13. **Outcome Bias:** Focusing on results while ignoring the quality of decision-making process

A manager must try to avoid all these biases when rating their twelve employees in the afternoon, hours before the HR deadline.

Unfortunately, only about one-third of the variation in performance ratings is due to actual differences in job performance. The troubling truth is that the majority of the variability comes from irrelevant factors. Pick any two or three from the list above.

The WTW Survey in 2022, conducted with over 830 global companies, reported that only 35% of employees believe their performance is evaluated fairly. According to a Gallup survey from 2017, only 29% of employees strongly agree that the performance reviews they receive are fair, while 26% strongly agree that these reviews are accurate. This represents a rare occasion where scientific research aligns with actual perceptions on the ground.

Considering these performance appraisals are used to label employees and play a significant part in their rewards and future careers, the accuracy rate (or rather the inaccuracy rate) is alarming.

4. "Meets Expectations" Kills the Engagement

After a year of work, you go into your performance review. You have put your heart into some of those projects and sacrificed your family and friends' time. Your manager is positive about your past year's performance, giving mostly praise. You, like most of us humans, rate yourself slightly higher than you usually perform. All signs point to an above-expectations rating, especially after it has been a good year for you, the team, and the company. Then you hear your manager utter the words: "You have met expectations." The impact is immediate: you are surprised, then disappointed. You leave the room thinking, "I should start applying for other jobs."

Forty-seven percent of millennials stated that they looked at job openings at other companies as a result of performance reviews[46].

Here's what is happening: Every company has 20% of their people at 4 or 5 on a five-point performance rating scale. Another 5% fall below expectations, 1s, and 2s. The remaining 75% are just the middle grade, the "meets expectations" people. Some of the 75% are ok with that evaluation, perhaps because they might have been newly promoted to a higher position, did an average job throughout the year, or are simply slackers and happy not to be evaluated lower.

We need to worry about the other larger portion of 75 percent—47%, to be exact, for millennials. These are employees who have performed better than average in their minds. They compare themselves with others and are convinced that their performance exceeds the average rating. These are the ones who get unhappy and instantly disengaged after their performance meeting. The label "meets expectations" or "successful" transforms a solid-performing employee's engagement into frustration and disengagement in one meeting.

This disengagement isn't fleeting. The frustration usually lasts a month or two. The unhappy and disengaged employee either finds a new job or gets over the disappointment in time. Put into perspective, this scenario means that "Meets Expectations" is disengaging half of the solid performers, more than 40 percent of the workforce, for two months every year. The loss of productivity and the negativity that spreads

---

[46]   Full Study: Performance Reviews Get a Failing Grade | PPT

throughout the organization are among the most dangerous and destructive impacts of performance management.

5. Performance Management Does Not Help Develop Employees

Feedback isn't the cure-all HR pretends it is. It is as likely to tank performance as it is to improve it. Tying it to performance management has made feedback a corporate chore: mechanical, forced, and pointless. Want feedback that actually works? Ditch the process and focus on credibility and delivery.

The data speaks volumes: there is no evidence that feedback always helps develop people. Comprehensive meta-research[47] found that only one-third of the papers stated that the feedback given resulted in positive development, and one-third of the papers stated that feedback decreased performance. Even more concerning, we are unsure that doubling down on informal and continuous feedback, as many companies have tried to establish, will give better results.

A blanket statement that the feedback doesn't work is obviously unfair. Context is crucial. Some employees, especially early in their careers, seek and benefit from feedback more often. If the feedback is perceived to be coming from a fair and credible manager, it has more chance to encourage development[48].

We can argue that feedback becomes mechanical, with performance management processes. Only 14% of surveyed employees strongly agree that the performance reviews they receive motivate them to improve.

In particular, with the strong push towards frequent check-ins and feedback that companies advocated in the last decade, giving feedback has devolved into a cumbersome HR task, often delivered in a clumsy or ineffective manner. Performance management has not served well when coupled with feedback. If feedback and performance management are decoupled, there is a high chance that feedback will have a better impact.

---

[47]   Kluger and DeNisi (1996)
[48]   Adler et al., 2016

6. Over-Instruction Erodes Leadership

Here's a critical aspect that we should pay much more attention to: The detailed process of performance management converts leaders to task executors rather than entrepreneurs running their teams. This is a hidden but critically detrimental effect of current processes.

Performance management provides leaders with templates, timelines, instructions, and distribution guidelines. This step-by-step process dictates how many goals to set, how they should be measurable and time-bound, how often check-ins should be conducted, and how much extra salary increase a leader can give in case of high performance. All the other detailed instructions deprive leaders of initiative, which decreases their ownership.

A leader's core accountability is to ensure the high performance of their team and the development of individuals. They should manage that without being spoon-fed detailed instructions.

Performance management breeds leaders who get a pat on the back when they follow the process, especially in large corporations. What those organizations need is leaders who own the overall performance of the team and do whatever is necessary to increase that. Performance management stands in the way of that kind of ownership.

Breaking Free: The Case Against Traditional Performance Management

> The full list of what is not working is longer. However, it is sufficient to summarize that performance management doesn't deliver any business value. It is biased and too simplistic, doesn't help develop employees, and creates frustration and loss of productivity.

Instead of tweaking the already outdated performance management, organizations can look for novel solutions. First principles and the purpose of performance management will help us define how to replace it. Yes, you read that right: the suggestion is to eliminate performance management as a process: no performance appraisals, no performance check-ins, and no SMART goal setting. Imagine the frustration, senseless effort, and toxic culture of bias and injustice we will save the organization.

The flow of the performance management process below summarizes the major pitfalls at every step. The erosion of leadership and decrease in employee engagement, which we discussed in this chapter, are second-order effects of the failures below.

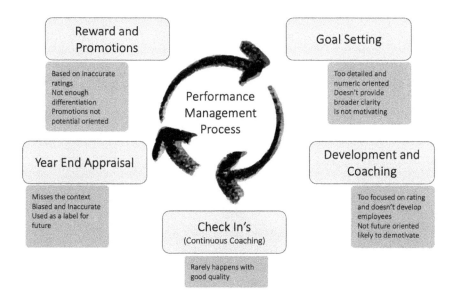

But before we significantly alter performance management, we need to understand why we need to "manage" performance in the first place.

Understanding the Purpose of Performance Management

Understanding why organizations need performance management and where the process's output is used will help us define better approaches. Performance management has several important uses.

1. Managing Performance Outcomes Fairly (Promotions and Rewards)

Equity theory[49] says employees want a fair output for their input. If employees perceive that they are getting fair output for their efforts compared to other colleagues, their motivation increases. We don't necessarily need to cite a complex theory here; it's intuitive.

It is now common knowledge that large organizations need to label high performers, average performers, and low performers to create the perception of equity. These performance labels are then used to differentiate pay, bonuses, and other recognitions. Additionally, companies use past performance as a variable for promotions. Not to mention, performance-based exit decisions need to be documented and stored for legal purposes.

The differentiation of rewards, promotions, and exits promotes a performance-based culture and creates a sense of equity on a large scale. Based on the label employees receive from performance management processes, which are called performance appraisals, corporate processes

---

49   Definition of Equity Theory - Gartner Human Resources Glossary

customize the impact on the employee. "Exceptional Performance" has a higher bonus multiplier than "Meets Expectations" performance.

2. Exit Compliance

A simple and necessary function of performance management is documenting low performance in accordance with local legislation when it results in an exit. This is a hygiene factor for companies operating in unionized environments, especially in Europe, or where the local labor law requires strict evidence of low performance.

> However, this functionality of performance management is a minor one, and most large companies approach exits with mutual agreements, bypassing the legislation constraints by generously paying the exited employee.

3. Clarity, Purpose, and Meaning

If done correctly, the goal-setting step of performance management has tremendous value. Current processes have made goal setting a numbers game by focusing too much on measurable KPIs and targets. The original idea of goal setting for individuals is to clarify the link between company strategy, team goals, and the individual's goals and how one's role impacts the overall team success and company output.

A well-defined set of goals also clarifies what is expected of an employee in terms of priorities. It supports the allocation of resources to the right priorities, whether it is time, effort, or monetary resources. Goals give the right sense of direction.

Relevant and well-set goals help employees find purpose and meaning in their work, show resilience in the face of challenges, create better commitment, and support better decision-making.

Goal setting is of significant importance. As the chapter unfolds, we will argue that goal setting will become much more relevant once one is freed from the limitations of today's performance management processes.

4. Talent Intelligence: Giving Senior Leadership an Overview

Performance appraisals consolidated at an organizational level will answer the question "Who are our top performers?" and "Who is not performing?" Senior leadership then has an overview of how performance-driven the company is, where the talent density lies, and whom to retain and invest in. It also helps senior leaders to understand more about the key talents 2-3 levels lower in the organization that they should invest time with.

5. Increasing Performance

The primary goal of performance management is to enhance organizational performance by elevating individual performance. There is a strong correlation between high levels of employee engagement and high performance.

Organizations recognize and reward high-performing employees to boost engagement and motivation while also providing clear expectations and guidelines for what constitutes excellent performance. This approach inspires employees to strive for higher levels of productivity and output. However, the perceived fairness of these rewards and promotions is crucial in fostering an engaging work environment.

Three Factors New Practices Will Rely On

We need a more fundamental change rather than trying to improve performance management, an approach suited to an older industrial era. The change entails eliminating an overarching performance management process and improving necessary parts like goal setting.

Before we detail the proposed changes further in this section, three principles will determine whether the shift is a success or a failure. They are the availability of leadership readiness, operational data, and technology infrastructure. Without these in place, organizations should take a more measured approach to abandoning traditional performance management than what is outlined in this chapter. Organizations must assess their readiness across these three dimensions and calibrate their transformation accordingly.

1. Leadership Readiness

Giving the leaders back their autonomy and freedom to run their businesses, including the performance and development of their teams, is crucial for success. This requires highly mature and capable leaders in place.

By freeing leaders from the detailed prescriptions of performance management, we enable them to develop their teams' performance more intentionally. This autonomy cascades down to employees, increasing their commitment and engagement to overall team and company objectives rather than narrowly defined KPIs.

In turn, leaders should have the potential and the maturity to use this freedom as it is intended: helping the employees reach their potential. Any signs of favoritism and abuse of this freedom should be handled quickly.

2. Availability of Data and Understanding Day to Day

We will require leaders to know what is happening in the day-to-day life. They should be utilizing subjective feedback from the stakeholders and team members and differentiate what is the most relevant and accurate insight.

The leaders should also demand and have access to operational data. With today's data infrastructure, it is easier than ever to understand what is happening on the ground with the help of operational data.

For example, the design stage of a product takes four weeks instead of the planned two weeks. The project management software highlights a problem to investigate further:

- Was the supply of raw materials late? Then, the vendor management team is struggling.
- Is there inefficiency and employee disengagement? Then, leadership is struggling.

Understanding the context is only possible if the leaders have access to operational data and have the critical thinking skills to differentiate noise from signal.

This is not easy, as a trend in large corporations is to be overly positive. Employees are overly complimentary about their colleagues' small successes and rarely point out that things are not going well. How many times have we heard the comment, "This is a great question," in response to the most basic and unhelpful inquiries? Or an exciting "The flow was amazing; you are a star on stage" after a dull presentation of a mediocre idea.

This toxic positivity distorts the perception of what good looks like. A leader should see through that and assess the performance accurately. Along the way, preferably create a culture of honesty as well.

3. Availability of Technology Infrastructure

Managing operational data, detailed performance insights, peer feedback, and future capability needs require an advanced HR technology platform capable of collecting, storing, and analyzing this wealth of information. As we will explore later in this chapter, generative AI will play a transformative role in this space.

With these foundational elements in place, let's examine the specific practices that will shape the future of performance development.

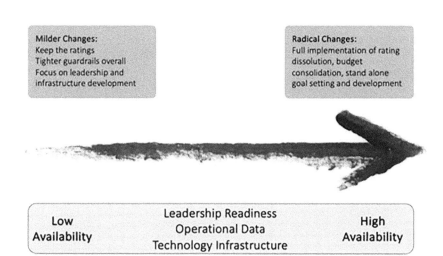

Milder Changes:
Keep the ratings
Tighter guardrails overall
Focus on leadership and
infrastructure development

Radical Changes:
Full implementation of rating
dissolution, budget
consolidation, stand alone
goal setting and development

Low
Availability

Leadership Readiness
Operational Data
Technology Infrastructure

High
Availability

Replacing Performance Management

Step One: Performance-Based Rewards and Practical Implementation

Effective reward systems align monetary incentives with the actual value employees bring to the organization. Exceptional contributions should yield rewards that significantly surpass those given for average performance within the same role. That is called "Pay for Performance." The world is not that simple, though. Leaders should take into account many other factors when deciding on rewards, such as the skillset of the employee and the market demand for it, the criticality of the employee and their retention, their current pay level and internal team equity, and so on.

Organizations should provide leaders with a total budget for their teams and equip them with broad guidelines rather than granular instructions. For example, offering a range such as "High-impact employees should receive bonuses equivalent to three to six months of salary" provides structure without undermining discretion. By contrast, overly prescriptive formulas like "Exceeds expectations equates to 1.25 times the bonus of meets expectations" stifle flexibility and innovation in rewarding performance.

This approach requires robust leadership capabilities, including maturity, calibration processes, and grandparent approvals to mitigate risks of bias and perceived unfairness.

The most empowering shift lies in delegating these decisions to leaders, transforming them from policy executors into true owners of their team's success. A radical accountability that comes with the freedom.

Practical Steps to Implementation

Starting with rewards is a symbolic and practical step toward empowering leaders and shifting organizational culture. Below are actionable steps to bring this philosophy to life:

1. **Transition Gradually**: Begin by maintaining traditional performance appraisals but remove their rigid connection to pay decisions. In the second year, merge budgets under autonomous leadership management while maintaining clear guardrails. This phased approach allows both leaders and organizations to build confidence in the new system while managing risk.

2. **Consolidate Budgets**: Break down the artificial barriers created by fragmented budget systems. Leaders should manage a unified workforce cost budget covering salaries and bonuses. This enables dynamic resource allocation, such as trading off one headcount in a high-cost region to better reward or retain top performers. This flexibility allows leaders to truly optimize their team's compensation strategy.

3. **Establish Guardrails**: Create guidelines that ensure consistency without micromanagement. For instance, specify that an "average successful employee" should receive bonuses equivalent to three months' salary, while top performers might earn up to eight months. These guardrails provide clarity and fairness while preserving leadership discretion to make contextual decisions.

Restoring Leadership Ownership

Years of detailed corporate instructions have transformed many line managers into mere administrators, distancing them from the critical responsibility of making reward decisions. Statements like "I can't give you more than a 2% salary increase because of HR guidelines" should not be something we hear from our leaders. This transformation aims to reverse that trend, enabling leaders to genuinely manage their budgets, make nuanced decisions tailored to the unique circumstances of their teams, and ultimately take ownership of the results. Though there are risks of bias and inconsistency, the advantages of enhanced leadership accountability and improved team dynamics far outweigh these challenges. The solution lies not in more rules but in building leadership capacity for effective decision-making and fostering a culture of transparency and fairness. Organizations must invest in developing leaders who can handle this responsibility while maintaining appropriate governance mechanisms.

The Bigger Picture: Transforming Organizational Culture

This approach represents more than a shift in compensation philosophy; it's a fundamental transformation in how organizations view leadership and performance. When implemented thoughtfully, organizations can expect three fundamental transformations:

1. A new class of leaders who exercise real decision-making power and own their team's economic outcomes

2. A more agile and responsive talent strategy, where nuanced reward decisions drive both retention and performance

3. A stronger alignment between team success and leadership accountability, fostering a true performance culture

This empowered approach to performance-based rewards becomes a catalyst for broader organizational transformation. A practice change that affects pay will significantly contribute to culture change.

Step Two: Managing Promotions and Internal Hires

Organizations typically use performance evaluations as one data point in their promotion decisions. Past performance can indicate future success, but some organizations create unnecessary constraints by asserting that employees who merely "meet expectations" shouldn't be considered for stretch promotions. This approach misses nuances about an employee's potential and capability for future roles. Performance management appraisal, with its flaws and inaccuracies, dictates too much of the future of employees.

The key to any employee's future success is their potential to perform in a new role, with a new manager, and in a new context. For example, highly successful employees often experience a performance dip when transitioning to a new company, even in similar roles[50]. Past performance is no longer relevant within the same organization if the nature of the future role is different.

Another example: a brilliant developer consistently produces exceptional code, or a sales professional regularly exceeds their targets. Traditional systems often identify these individuals as ideal candidates for promotion, frequently into leadership roles. This linear thinking can result in the classic dilemma of losing an outstanding individual contributor and gaining a mediocre manager. While past performance is important, its relevance to the target role is essential. The aforementioned two cases emphasize the importance of reducing the weight of performance management in future promotions or transfers of employees. This is also a good step towards phasing out performance management processes altogether.

Practical Steps to Implementation

The steps below can be implemented from the first year onwards. Once the items below are in place, phasing out performance appraisals and performance management processes will be easier in the second or third year.

1. **Establish Rich Information Gathering**: Create descriptive templates and systems that capture detailed insights about employee potential, capabilities, and traits. Focus on gathering specific examples and observations rather than ratings. Implement infrastructure to collect comprehensive feedback from peers and stakeholders about future capabilities.

   Formal assessments of personality traits and skills can also be utilized. However, the results should be integrated into the central HR system along with all other feedback.

2. **Define Clear Career Progression Labels**: Move beyond simple "ready/not ready" assessments to more nuanced categories

---

50   Chasing Stars: The Myth of Talent and the Portability of Performance by Boris Groysberg

like "should continue developing in the current role," "ready for more complex assignments within their field," or "prepared for major promotion within their expertise area." Insert those standard labels into the HR system. These progressions should recognize both vertical and horizontal career growth.

These progressive labels can co-exist with the performance appraisals while those still exist.

3. **Leverage Technology Thoughtfully**: Implement AI systems capable of processing detailed narrative feedback and assessment data. The technology should help consolidate insights into actionable formats while maintaining the richness of the original information. This enables sophisticated promotion decisions across large organizations. In the near future, an AI Agent can likely summarize all feedback into one of the labels above and suggest it to the line manager or validate the subjective assessment.

The Path Forward

This transformation in promotion management is a shift from simplistic performance-based decisions to nuanced, potentially focused development. Implementing this change requires investment in both technology and cultural change, but the payoff comes in fairer promotion decisions and stronger succession planning. It also signals that the organization invests in the employees.

The key is to balance the human element of career development with technological capabilities. Leaders must focus on understanding their team members' aspirations and capabilities while using AI tools to process and analyze rich information at scale. This combination enables organizations to make more informed promotion or internal hiring decisions that benefit both the individual and the organization.

The near future of promotion management isn't about replacing human judgment with AI but instead using technology to enhance our ability to consider the full complexity of human potential. By moving beyond performance ratings to detailed, nuanced assessments of capability and potential, organizations can build stronger pipelines and more engaging career paths for their employees.

Step Three: Context Matters, Capture It

We have argued that distilling a complex set of information, such as a year's performance, into one phrase will not be accurate and will not do justice to the employee. Time-bound priorities, market dynamics, the existence of support mechanisms, and the ability to overcome challenges are only some of the examples we touched upon.

Avoid the temptation of reductionism. Organizations should be comfortable with a longer description of the year's performance. Instead of a "meets expectations," we can use an accurate description of what happened throughout the year.

This approach not only accurately represents performance but also liberates leaders from the constraints of categorical thinking. Leaders can focus on the information that matters, minimize their biases, and make more informed decisions about their team members.

The transition away from traditional ratings may initially challenge HR processes, particularly in areas like compensation management. "Without the performance rating, how can we suggest salary increases to employees?" is the first question rewards specialists will ask. However, this shift actually empowers leaders to act more like entrepreneurs, taking ownership of rewards and consequences within their scope of responsibility.

Corporate jargon and framework definitions often dilute the concept of entrepreneurial leadership in large corporations. What we are advocating for is genuine empowerment, encouraging leaders to act like startup CEOs, and providing them with the necessary space. The strong message to the leaders is: When you identify an exceptional employee who makes a difference, you should have the authority to reward them significantly more than the average employee. However, you must be able to judge that objectively and explain it to the team.

Effective context capture requires leaders to be deeply engaged with their teams' day-to-day reality. They need to understand firsthand the environment, challenges, and available resources in which their employees work. Leaders must go beyond surface-level metrics, utilize operational data, and ensure they grasp the real situation through concrete evidence, not only subjective views of green dots on a KPI presentation slide.

Practical Steps to Implementation

1. **Change Performance Documentation Approach**. In the first year, leave the performance appraisals in place. However, in the detailed forms, avoid asking standard questions about strengths and development areas. Instead of providing strict instructions, guide leaders to write better long-format reviews that shed light on the context. Push the leaders to know the details about what has happened. Leverage AI tools to support leaders in writing comprehensive, context-rich feedback. This shift requires training and continuous support to help managers adapt to the new narrative format. The beauty of generative AI is that a lengthy unstructured write-up - by a manager who may not be the best writer – can be later synthesized and summarized professionally by the tools.

2. **Implement User-Friendly Feedback Systems**. Develop and deploy intuitive user interfaces that make it effortless for managers and stakeholders to document feedback in a long format when events occur. The system should be accessible through multiple devices, allowing managers to capture important moments and contexts immediately. Integration with commonly used communication tools can further enhance adoption. Avoid clunky, traditional HR interfaces at all costs.

   For instance, the manager can one day take a few seconds to write something in Slack like "@FeedbackCapture - John did great in the Widget LLC meeting today, he's become better at neutralizing an angry customer".

3. **Design Behavioral Prompts**. Create an intelligent notification system that reminds managers and stakeholders to document significant events and achievements. These prompts should be contextual and timely, appearing after important meetings, project complements, or at regular intervals that align with the organization's workflow. The system should be smart enough to avoid notification fatigue while ensuring consistent documentation.

4. **Leverage AI for Documentation and Analysis**. Deploy AI tools that serve two crucial purposes: helping managers articulate their observations and feedback effectively and

analyzing the accumulated narrative data to identify patterns and insights. The AI should assist in maintaining consistency in documentation while preserving the unique context of each situation. Central analysis of this rich data can provide valuable insights for organizational development and succession planning.

5. **Leverage AI for Coaching**. AI Coaching has already started to make waves in enterprises. Organizations in the midterm should utilize AI to coach managers on how to effectively give feedback and maximize development by identifying the right areas.

6. **Implement Flexible Privacy Controls**. Develop sophisticated privacy settings that allow managers to control the visibility of their comments. This feature should include options for draft modes, private notes, and selective sharing with relevant stakeholders. The system should be designed to protect sensitive information while promoting transparency where appropriate.

Step Four: Goals Disconnected from Performance Management Process

Well-defined goals clarify expectations for employees and their contributions to the overall company strategy and team outcomes. Goal setting is essential. Currently, goal setting is a static, once-a-year process that overly relies on detailed numeric KPIs instead of genuinely establishing relevant goals that align with company targets while broadly outlining expectations.

The pressure of year-end performance reviews significantly impacts goal setting. Managers often default to simplistic, numeric targets to evaluate employees in twelve months based on the goals decided now, unnecessarily constraining their performance discretion along the way.

An example case can be the target to decrease customer complaints by 20% for a specific product, given to the product team. Consider a scenario where the product team figured out how to hide the call center contacts behind many steps of "frequently asked questions" pages and actually solved some of the product-related problems with those. At the end of the year, the customer complaints dropped by

30%. This technically meets the target, but it misses the true objective: improving product quality and enhancing user experience.

Leaders are instructed to give these detailed numerical targets. Instead of this pressure of SMART targets (specific, measurable, achievable, etc.), the line manager should be able to give the goal as: "increase product quality and significantly decrease the complaints. We need to offer a better experience and product than the competition".

When evaluation time comes, the focus shifts to what was achieved and what was not. There is no need to discuss "I dropped the customer complaints by 30% and overachieved my target."

Some organizations tried to give this discretion for performance appraisal to the leaders by introducing the "HOW" part of the performance. This approach often backfired by adding more subjective labels to the process, like behavior compliance with company values.

A mature leader who does not think about the appraisal in twelve months is free to connect the employees' directional goals to the team goals and create clarity and commitment. The roles addressed here are knowledge worker roles with problem-solving requirements and dynamic contexts. Static KPIs forced by an appraisal system will harm creativity.

Practical Steps to Implementation

1. **Start gradually disconnecting goal setting from appraisals**. Begin by separating the timing of goal-setting sessions from performance reviews. Allow goals to be set and adjusted based on business needs rather than the annual review cycle. Create communication materials that help managers understand how to evaluate performance without relying solely on predefined goals, focusing instead on overall contribution and impact.

2. **Release the pressure of detailed numeric targets**. Train managers to set broader, more meaningful objectives that focus on desired outcomes rather than specific metrics. Encourage the use of qualitative measures alongside quantitative ones, and help teams understand that success can be evaluated through comprehensive discussion rather than just numbers. Support

managers in developing the confidence to assess performance without hiding behind rigid metrics.

3. **Strengthen the clear connection** from company strategy to individual targets, ensuring alignment and directional accuracy. Develop clear frameworks that help managers cascade company objectives into team and individual goals while maintaining flexibility. Focus on ensuring employees understand how their work connects to broader organizational objectives. Create regular check-ins that focus on strategic alignment rather than metric achievement.

4. **Continue to empower leaders** more in setting and evaluating targets. Provide leaders with training and tools to set contextual goals that make sense for their teams. Support them in making judgment calls about performance without requiring rigid justification through metrics. Create forums where leaders can share experiences and best practices about goal setting and evaluation in their specific contexts.

5. **In year two, together with phasing out performance appraisals, make goal setting a standalone process**. Complete the transition by establishing goal setting as an independent, dynamic process focused on alignment and clarity rather than evaluation. Implement new templates and processes that support ongoing goal adjustment and regular dialogue about progress and priorities. Ensure HR systems and processes support this more flexible approach to goal management.

Step Five: Fix the Employee Development

Development conversations suffocate under the weight of performance reviews. Rather than dwelling on past performance appraisals, the focus should be on capabilities needed for the organization and the employee aspirations. When linked to career progression instead of previous performance, these discussions transform into meaningful dialogues about future possibilities. This independence allows both managers and employees to concentrate on potential rather than historical assessment.

The success of employee development relies on several factors, including the availability of necessary development platforms, organizational development opportunities, and the leaders' maturity in recognizing and facilitating growth. Removing development conversations from the confines of performance management will also create space to enhance these factors.

The change requires minimal practical steps. Primarily separating development and career conversations from the performance development process is a good start. Strategically timing these discussions for the second half of the year facilitates more meaningful planning for the upcoming year and relevant developments.

Once freed from the limitations of performance evaluations, employee development can evolve into a more qualitative and intentional process that better serves both the needs of the organization and the aspirations of the employee.

Step Six: Talent Intelligence

"Who are our key people?" - This crucial question from senior leadership demands more than just a list. They need clear visibility into talent density across the organization, identifying both areas of strength and potential gaps in critical capabilities.

The traditional approach of using performance ratings to identify top talent is fundamentally flawed. Performance ratings are not accurate and objective indicators of high performance, let alone talent.

Instead, organizations can look at team outputs. Teams that consistently deliver outstanding results are more likely to have a higher concentration of talented individuals. Starting from that and going down one level to inquire about who on the team had an outstanding impact is a better option for identifying talent in the organization.

This paradigm shift focuses organizations on tangible impact rather than subjective assessments.

Successors

Planning for leadership continuity requires an organization-wide perspective. The progression capacity tags mentioned above should provide insights into the potential of employees. For critical positions, tagging employees for the roles in which they can succeed creates a clear pathway for identifying and developing potential employees.

Key Contributors and Talent to Retain

True talent retention lies in the hands of empowered leaders, not centralized HR programs. The common scenario of leaders requesting permission from HR for additional rewards to retain their employees needs to end. The leader should be free to deploy retention tools within a broad guideline and their budget.

Intermediate steps may help organizations struggling with this transition. In the first few years, organizations can implement tags like "key contributor" or "should be retained" in their systems. While these designations may remain confidential, they can temporarily ease organizational anxiety about talent identification.

However, rigid policies around these designations can backfire. Overdoing any instructions about the labeled employees will diminish the leader's empowerment. For instance, "Key Contributors will get two extra salaries as a bonus" is not the preferred outcome of these practices. Instead, the leader should be responsible for reward and retention.

The organization's role shifts to monitoring rather than controlling. It monitors the "should be retained" employees and their pay practices and consults leaders if intervention is needed.

Caution: The HR infrastructure should be able to accommodate these tags and the processes of inputting and approving them. Tagging through manual Excel files will only frustrate the organization.

Practical Steps to Implementation:

1. Eliminate performance distribution charts from day one. Despite their prevalence, appraisals are inaccurate, and performance does not follow a normal distribution.

2. Implement progression capacity tags to keep an eye on the potential. Create distinct succession planning tags to separate key role successors.

3. Temporarily deploy tags like "should be retained" and "key contributor" for the first few years, but phase them out once the leaders reach the right maturity. Be cautious about designing interventions for the tagged employees; doing so will diminish the leader's mandate.

4. In the mid-term, leverage AI to analyze organization-wide metadata and draw conclusions about employee performance based on leaders' longer reviews.

The key to this change, as with the entire shift away from traditional performance management, lies in developing and guiding leaders while acting decisively if they misuse their newfound autonomy.

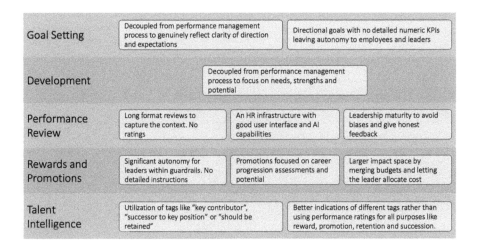

Goal Setting	Decoupled from performance management process to genuinely reflect clarity of direction and expectations	Directional goals with no detailed numeric KPIs leaving autonomy to employees and leaders	
Development		Decoupled from performance management process to focus on needs, strengths and potential	
Performance Review	Long format reviews to capture the context. No ratings	An HR infrastructure with good user interface and AI capabilities	Leadership maturity to avoid biases and give honest feedback
Rewards and Promotions	Significant autonomy for leaders within guardrails. No detailed instructions	Promotions focused on career progression assessments and potential	Larger impact space by merging budgets and letting the leader allocate cost
Talent Intelligence	Utilization of tags like "key contributor", "successor to key position" or "should be retained"	Better indications of different tags rather than using performance ratings for all purposes like reward, promotion, retention and succession.	

A summary table of needed changes is above, with key reminders of implementation steps. The enabling principles remain as **leadership maturity**, **availability of data**, and **HR technology**.

Examples and Case Studies

The number of companies abandoning performance appraisals is low—only 6% in late 2010—and the majority continue to adhere to traditional performance management processes and appraisals.

Adobe was the tip of the spear; they eliminated annual reviews in 2012 and focused on manager-employee conversations without giving any ratings to employees. They advocated that there is too much emphasis on the rating rather than the actual development of the employees. In 2020, Adobe introduced three to four standard questions to guide these performance conversations. Adobe also separates conversations about performance from discussions about raises and bonuses.

Accenture reported that performance management costs them 2 million hours every year. Together with Deloitte, which is in roughly the same industry, Accenture reported ditching performance ratings. Microsoft also followed the path of not giving employees any ratings. Netflix and GE are also shifting towards more manager check-ins, or "touch points," as GE would call them, rather than overall ratings.

Other companies abandoning ratings faced challenges and reported a 4% performance decrease to Gallup in 2018[51]. Even if it seems like a mixed bag, Accenture and Adobe remain at the top of the list for employee engagement and Best Place to Work ratings.

The insights confirm that transforming performance management remains an elusive goal for many organizations, due to the **rare combination** of leadership maturity, data availability, and HR technology

---

[51] Removing Performance Ratings Is Unlikely To Improve Corporate HR Performance

required for success. However, the increasing prominence of AI suggests that the odds of successful transformation may soon improve, making it possible for more companies to overcome these barriers and realize the benefits of a redesigned approach to managing employee performance.

Conclusion

Performance management is critical for companies, even if the term itself falls short.

> Do we really "manage" performance in a world that is highly complex and entangled in human behavior, market dynamics, and company culture?

Enabling or cultivating high performance will remain critical; the problem is the processes we have today are outdated.

Today's performance management processes not only fail to deliver value but actively harm organizations through both obvious and subtle negative impacts. These processes, especially the performance appraisal, have become so deeply embedded that organizations struggle to envision alternatives. As a practitioner, the hope is at least to inspire you to go against dominant logic and actually do things differently.

However, the rewards of change are meaningful. A well-designed shift will save thousands of hours of effort, frustration, and feelings of distrust. Forward-thinking executive teams who recognize this opportunity and use the momentum of technology for change can witness their leaders excel at running their own teams and businesses.

The path to successful transformation rests on three fundamental pillars:

1. Empower leaders with autonomy over managing performance, starting with rewards and recognitions.

2. Liberate goal setting, development conversations and promotions from performance management processes, ensuring each can fulfill their true purposes.
3. Build a robust HR technology infrastructure that supports high-quality long-form inputs and leverages AI to derive meaningful insights from this rich data.

The role of the CEO is crucial, as we have seen in the talent density section earlier. If the CEO does not demonstrate a thoughtful, long-form evaluation of the context and does not allow mediocrity, the whole shift away from performance management is pointless. A CEO championing high performance with a startup mindset will make the shift work. An average CEO who hides behind conventional processes will fail to carry the organization throughout this change. The CEO sets the tone in performance management; there is no other way. It is also time for CEOs to step up and demand more of their HR function.

The upside of this shift is immense. Organizations that pioneer this transformation will not only free themselves from the constraints of traditional performance management but will help shape a new era of work.

SECTION 3

Succession Planning and Talent Density

Introduction

Due to their interconnected nature, Succession Planning and Talent Density will be explored together in this section. Based on Reed Hastings' concept of high-performing, high-growth employees, talent density naturally feeds into successful succession planning. Succession planning, in many ways, becomes a by-product of a high-talent-density workforce. That is the slightly unusual coupling of them in this book, even though they each have their own subsections.

Succession planning is a structured, sequential process with clearly defined steps. Talent density on the other hand is a broader, more conceptual goal that is achieved through multiple interventions at the leadership and cultural levels. We will explore the succession planning process, but talent density is a more attractive bounty than succession planning. More elusive but once achieved an amazing competitive advantage.

This section weighs more towards actionable steps rather than detailed definitions, especially on succession planning. The action suggestions are intended both as sources of inspiration and as practical instructions. We recognize that each organization is unique in terms of its market positioning, culture, competitive landscape, and maturity. Therefore, the protocols should be customized to suit the organization's specific context at that time.

SECTION 3A

Succession Planning

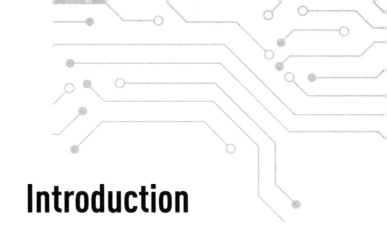

Introduction

Succession planning ensures leadership continuity and business stability when unexpected resignations or departures happen. It is a key focus for boards and executive teams because it safeguards business sustainability. A well-executed plan creates a strong pipeline of successors, covering everything from the CEO position to the critical individual contributor roles. A healthy succession pipeline to the CEO and executive positions is the fiduciary responsibility of boards, and succession planning of senior leadership and critical roles is the responsibility of the executive teams. From the start, it is important to put the responsibility clearly on the management; if the process is human resources owned and driven, succession planning is less likely to succeed.

We did say that the steps of succession planning, such as identifying critical roles and selecting successors, are conceptually straightforward. However, their execution often proves difficult for many organizations. Talent density eventually becomes the main enabler of succession, a systematic approach that not only fills succession pipelines but also continually creates high organizational performance.

Aside from ensuring business continuity, succession planning signals a supportive and developing philosophy to employees. Employees stay where they believe they have a future. Following that logic, even though succession pipelines can include external candidates, it is wiser to focus on internal successors and their development.

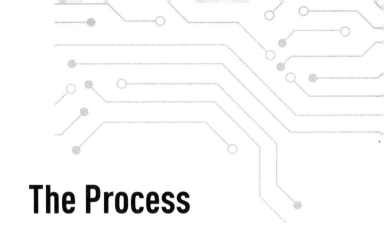

The Process

Succession planning has five major steps, starting from clarifying definitions to the final successor appointment. The visual below will create the perception of a fast-moving flow, but it shouldn't. Succession planning takes years, not months. While it starts simply, it gets harder as it progresses.

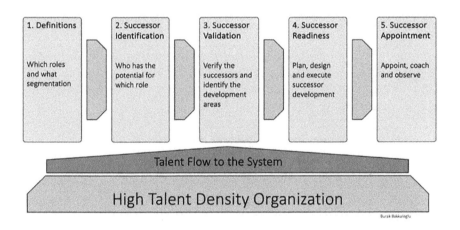

Two Things to Watch Out For:

1. Process Is Not Everything

Talent density is the foundational element to succession planning outside of the five steps. Companies with an immaculate succession planning process have often failed to have leadership continuation because they did not have enough talent to put through the pipelines.

The process is important, but slides and process flows should not create the illusion that things are under control. The quality and quantity of talent coming through the system are core to succession planning, not the process.

2. Succession Should Not be Bureaucratic

The process steps, templates, and ways of working should not overwhelm the leaders. Planning for succession and developing people are part of the business's natural flow. The moment HR becomes the guardian of a bureaucratic process, the templates and rules should be drastically scaled back to natural conversations.

With those two warnings we can now discuss the succession planning process in detail.

1. Definitions

The start of succession planning is a thoughtful conversation with the board and the CEO about its purpose. It is not necessarily a fancy workshop; it is just a conversation.

Two things to be defined before starting the actual process:

1. Which roles are we planning succession for? Executive positions? All senior leadership?
2. Should the succession planning for the next two to three years? Or should that be longer than that.

Defining the Roles for Succession

Organizations focus on specific, high-impact roles to maximize the effectiveness of succession planning. Designing and maintaining succession plans for a large number of roles is impossible, and not worth the allocation of resources. Selecting which roles to plan the succession for becomes an important choice.

The scales and definitions here are more relevant for larger corporations. If you lead a smaller company up to a few thousand employees, succession planning should look a lot more intuitive and less process(y).

Two Segments of Roles for Succession

1. Senior Leadership Roles

Senior leadership roles usually involve direct reports to executive team members, a layer described as CEO-2. According to a Heidrich and Struggles report[52], the average executive team size increased from 10 to 15 in Fortune 100 companies between 2020 and 2022. The increase is due to the addition of roles like compliance officers and chief technology officers. Assuming those 15 executive roles also have somewhere between 10-15 roles, we simply say there are 200 senior roles on average in large companies.

2. Critical Roles

Critical roles are usually a subset of senior leadership roles, roughly 40 or them. Within the approximately 200 senior leadership roles, there must be a further, more honest segmentation of which positions are truly essential for strategy execution. These are the roles that genuinely qualify as "critical." The succession of these roles will be the accountability of the CEO and the executive team, with significant investments for successors.

If corporations want quality conversations around the successors and high-touch development for those people, then 40 is the ideal number without compromising quality. A good succession pipeline consists of at least three successors. The executive team will be discussing and supporting the development of the successors. That means that for a size of 40 roles, the executives will focus on 120 individuals and their development. That's already plenty.

3. (Optional) Local Critical Roles:

If large corporations want to cascade down the succession planning process to the smaller organizations or countries, then they leave the management of the whole process to the local organizations. It will be optional cascade down with the same principles, only to be managed locally on the ground rather than on the corporate level.

---

[52] https://www.heidrick.com/en/insights/leadership-succession-planning/the-evolution-of-fortune-100-leadership-teams

Protocols for Identifying the Critical Top 40 Roles:

We have covered the argument for the smaller subset of critical roles and can suggest three criteria of business continuity, strategy execution, and rare expertise as guidelines. Here, we want to cover some insights and go over how to identify them.

Every CEO, along with their executive team, can likely identify the top 40 critical roles from the 200 in the succession scope in one sitting, relying on subjective opinions. However, the executive team should define objective criteria to create a sustainable, systemic approach and ensure clarity if needed.

The process of identifying critical positions can easily become over-complicated, turning into an overengineered exercise with dozens of criteria or, a power struggle over whose direct reports are deemed critical. Below are protocols and insights to avoid these pitfalls:

1. **Focus on roles, not individuals**: Some roles might seem critical because of the person currently in them, but the role itself might not be. Similarly, some critical roles may not be filled by standout individuals. Avoid personalizing the "critical position" label. Instead, focus on the role's inherent importance.

2. **Define critical roles clearly**: A helpful definition is "roles critical to strategy execution and business results." This broad statement addresses the importance of roles both now and in the future. Roles with limited current impact but essential to future strategy should also be classified as critical.

3. **Limit criteria to five or fewer**: More than five criteria risk overengineering and unnecessary complexity. Criteria should be definitive, but rigid monetary thresholds should be avoided, such as "above 10 million USD revenue."

4. **CEO discretion for prolonged disagreements**: Any extended debates on critical roles should be resolved by the CEO's discretion, not through endless criteria refinement. A cohesive executive team should agree on most of these 40 roles within two or three workshops. If discussions drag on, it's often a sign of misaligned strategy or a dysfunctional team, not poor criteria definition.

	Estimated Number	Description	Governance and Investment
Critical Roles	40	Top 40 critical roles that are critical for business continuity and operations, strategy execution and rare expertise.	CEO and Executive team own the succession and successor development Significant investment to the successors
Senior Leadership Roles	200 (Including most of the above 40)	Direct reports to executive team. CEO-2 Layer. Not necessarily people management roles, but a leadership role in the organization.	Head of the unit owns the succession and successor development Same principles and process as critical roles, but investment to successors are not as significant
Local Critical Roles	Could be hundreds in a large corporation	Critical roles for the unit or geography they belong to. CEO-3 or lower in the large corporation but a critical role for the smaller unit.	Local business leader or unit head. The succession process and principles are the same as corporate

Defining the Timeframes

The second element after defining the roles is setting clear time horizons for when successors are expected to be ready. Organizations usually categorize succession timelines into short-term, mid-term, and long-term, often defining them by years (e.g., one to two years for short-term, three or more for mid-term).

However, a more effective approach is to base timelines on development milestones and role-readiness criteria. This avoids the pressures of arbitrary timelines and focuses on growth. Fixed timeframes can quickly become irrelevant. For instance, if identifying a successor takes six months, half of a typical "one-year" horizon is already lost, leading to misalignment.

An alternative approach to defining succession timelines could be:

1. **Short-Term**: "The successor can be appointed almost immediately and, after six months of learning and onboarding, will be performing at a good level. No internal promotion ever feels 100% ready at first, that's the nature of promotions. Any successor that is roughly 80% ready is a short-term candidate. The gaps typically stem from a lack of direct experience in the new role. However, with the right mentor and support network, those gaps can be closed within six months to a year, leading to solid to exceptional performance.

2. **Mid-Term**: The successor requires another relevant role to gain the necessary experience and knowledge. If the successor has been appointed to a new role currently, they would need to perform successfully in that role first to show readiness. Here, typically, the successor feels 50-60% ready for the big role; any promotion from mid-term successors would be categorized as "risky promotion."

3. **Long-Term**: The successor shows high potential for larger roles but needs two or more assignments before being considered a candidate for the position.

These experience-based definitions create the understanding that "successors must accumulate experience and develop in order to be ready for the role" rather than the perception that "it is only a matter of time." This approach also reduces time pressure and expectations, placing accountability on the successor to actively pursue their development journey.

	Short Term Successor	Mid Term Successor	Long Term Successor
Readiness	Almost ready now, skill and experience wise Can perform at the role within six months	Needs another relevant role to be ready If new in a relevant role, can accumulate the experience here	Distant successor, readiness probably two to three roles in the future

		Intentional rotation or job assignment for the next 2-3 years to give the necessary experience	Aim for retention for these profiles Development nudges towards relevant paths, no direct intervention
Intervention	Needs intense mentoring first six months		

2. Successor Identification

Successor identification is mostly a subjective process of getting the relevant names in the right timeframe of the successor pipeline. Next in the process, we will validate those names with assessments and interviews, strengthening the objectivity of the process and gaining real development plans along the way.

The focus will be on describing how the process works for 40-ish critical roles. The principles can easily be applied to other succession segments.

Step 1: Before Names, Identify the Requirements

Successor identification starts with understanding the criteria for succeeding in a critical role. This is basically a list of differentiating skills and experience needed for the role. Some organizations call those lists "talent cards". The key is to focus on the skills that will make a candidate successful. A talent card should not include trivial information such as "10+ years of experience needed" or "collaboration is crucial for this role." These only dilute the list.

It is better to stick to the top five or six skills and experience, and be specific about it. Market and product knowledge, advanced technology knowledge, handling high-level relationships, strategy setting in high uncertainty, and creating followership and loyalty are examples of value criteria. A long list of skills and experience is not a sign of a critical role.

Executives should reject overly detailed templates and help Human Resources avoid making succession planning a bureaucratic process.

Once the job requirements are clear, organizations start identifying who has the potential to fulfill that list of requirements.

Step 2: Gather the Names and Calibrate Them

Ask the incumbent of the role or executive team for nominations, categorizing them based on short-, mid-, and long-term readiness definitions.

A well-established HR organization would already have insights on the potential and aspirations of the employees, and most of those nominations should already be on the radar. This should give a level of credibility to the nominated names, but there is also a risk of discussing the same usual suspects for all HR applications. Executives should look for surprise names and even use any AI skills matching algorithms possible. Opening these succession roles in the system as we will explain soon is also a good way to avoid this fallacy.

Before in-depth validation, the gathered names should be calibrated by the executive team. It is helpful to have a well-facilitated calibration session, but they can be tricky. People have biases. Covering the aspects below will lead to a better calibration session:

Preparations before the session:

- The mental preparation of the executive team is important. The team should already have some candidates in their minds or already given them to HR. Human resources can share the talent cards upfront and already provide a long list of high-potential leaders to set the tone.
- It is important to monitor the diversity of the executive team. If all the executives come from similar backgrounds or the team is not diverse, they will be unlikely to evaluate candidates who differ from their backgrounds. In this case, stronger facilitation should be in place.

During the session:

- During calibration sessions, it is important for the facilitator to minimize bias through effective moderation and guide the executive team to avoid turf battles and power dynamics. The turf battles or allyships will surface as behaviors of "I support your candidate if you support mine."

- An aligned understanding of what good looks like, championed by the CEO, makes it easier to discuss successors as a team.
- If the calibration session starts to include candidates who do not meet the successor criteria, the CEO should intervene and demand that the team be relentless in its search for growth capacity.

Some questions bring out good insights without putting executives in a defensive mode:

1. What executive role would your candidate NOT be suited for?

2. What blind spot does your candidate have?

3. If I were your candidate's new manager tomorrow, what advice would you give me for managing him/her in the first six months?

4. What is the thing that people get wrong about your candidate in the first encounters?

Questions such as these can tease out some of the hidden negatives that the candidate's sponsor may not enjoy sharing.

Successor decisions and, eventually, promotions shape the organization's culture. Executives, through their choices, signal to the organization what is valued and rewarded. Selecting competent people who demonstrate high performance, and a collaborative style is a strong signal. Alternatively, selecting employees with only strong relationships but no real competence sends a different signal.

A strong CEO voice driven by talent principles should set the tone and not compromise the high talent principles in those conversations. Without the CEO's strong voice in the room, the debates can be longer than needed.

Alternative Successor Identification: Opening Them as Jobs

Another angle is to approach with an open application philosophy. Organizations can treat the succession as open positions and run an open recruitment process to select successors.

A large financial institution followed that path. They publicly posted "succession pipeline" positions in their internal job system, like "Successor for Head of Private Banking." This transparency allowed employees to apply directly for critical roles, signaling both their interest and readiness.

Advantages:

1. The corporation will show extreme transparency and a sense of fairness and equal opportunity in the organization. This is a very valuable signal to the organization and something that shapes the culture,
2. The organization reaches talent they might have missed earlier,
3. This is a good way to test the aspirations of the candidates instead of assuming successors would automatically want to be promoted to the mentioned critical role.

Difficulties:

1. Workload. Given that the applications will be internal and probably high talent employees and leaders, the candidate experience is critical. A good candidate journey with professional recruiters and good communication requires resources and effort.
2. The expectations of employees should be managed properly. Some leaders who repeatedly apply and get rejected will eventually be frustrated. A good feedback mechanism should be in place.
3. Top talent might not like to apply for jobs, so the open position approach can be used together with name nominations.

For a Higher Quality Pipeline

Before concluding the identification step, remember that succession is not necessarily only about internal candidates. Executive staffing agencies have services specifically for identifying and monitoring relevant external talent. Every CEO and executive leader must be on the lookout for exceptional talent in the market. Capturing them in succession planning is a healthy addition to internal succession plans. External candidates, especially former employees, are valuable talent sources.

> Research by Keller et al. (2020) demonstrates that **in the short-term,** internal hires tend to outperform both boomerang employees, those returning to the company, and external hires, especially in roles that require substantial internal coordination.

The familiarity internal candidates have with company processes and culture makes them more effective in these interconnected roles. Keller finds that external candidates typically take two and a half to three years to reach the performance level of internal hires. Internal hires benefit from their familiarity with company dynamics and face less resistance.

A good succession plan should include external candidates, especially some from the competition and some boomerang ones.

3. Successor Validation

Validating potential successors is a vital step to ensure they are truly candidates for future critical roles. This is not just about verifying the names on your list, it is about gaining deeper insights into their strengths, gaps, and development needs. By separating validation from identification, you can minimize any biases from the initial selection process.

Several methods exist for validating successors, including structured assessments, interviews, and psychometric tests. However, none of these tools can provide an absolute truth about candidates. Instead, they should be used together, each serving as a data point. The final decision should result from an amalgamation of these data points. Here, we will suggest a method for effectively deploying these different tools.

i. Assessment Centers: They Usually Work

These are multi-step assessments conducted by professional firms, often executive hiring agencies. They include psychometric tests, 360-degree leadership assessments, interviews, case studies, and role-playing. However, if not designed smartly, case studies and role-playing can be perceived as superficial.

Tip: If you still encounter a role-playing assignment of "handling a difficult performance management conversation", it is time to move on to a more relevant vendor.

Assessment centers should present insights, because they require significant time and energy from both successors and leadership teams. The results should be used as data points in the decision-making, not with a "fail or pass approach." Otherwise, you risk making these assessments an unnecessary stress factor.

Watch out for non-native speakers and assessment gurus

A key blind spot of these assessments is the potential disadvantage they pose for non-native English speakers and naturally introverted individuals. In multinational companies based in North America or Europe, a strong command of English is usually expected. Yet, during role-plays or interviews, non-native speakers may find themselves at a disadvantage compared to native speakers. While assessors often try to account for this, some of the brightest minds might underperform due to language barriers.

Similarly, some individuals are "assessment savvy," excelling in such environments by knowing what to say and how to present themselves. This is not inherently negative, but it can overshadow the abilities of those who may not be as quick with words under pressure but who excel in longer, more thoughtful contexts. For instance, we have seen highly capable R&D leaders give only average answers in an assessment, leading to mediocre feedback. A few of them later shared that they didn't work well with short timelines and on-the-spot answers but were more comfortable with them in a reflective context. Probably the right profile to hire for a product development role.

Addressing these blind spots can make these assessments fair for everyone. Organizations should acknowledge that some successors may find the assessment process stressful or uncomfortable. Clear communication and setting expectations beforehand can help ease the discomfort for those who may struggle with this type of evaluation. We say this with empathy and understanding that successors may feel that their years of steady high performance and experiences are assessed in a matter of hours. A healthy communication and approach can ease concerns and stress arising from this.

ii. Standalone Assessments: Watch Out

Standalone assessments have been the alternative solutions for organizations that are not ready to commit to the time and resources required by full assessment centers. Standalone assessments are usually in the form of a 360-degree assessment or psychometric tests like personality traits. Most of these assessments are scientifically not proven. The formulation of questions, the algorithm to turn those answers into meaningful scores, are all scientifically questionable at best. There are a few scientific ones, yes, but the big industry of assessments is full of tools that will harm your employees and organizations.

The army of consultants and executive hiring companies will argue differently, because these tools create the illusion of being scientific and fact-based in their business. Organizations, especially talent management professionals, should do a better job at discerning the right tools.

If the organization chooses a scientific and well-structured tool, however, it might provide a solid evaluation of a candidate's leadership style, personality traits, and potential derailers. When paired with professional feedback, they can be a valuable input for both the organization and the individual about the strengths to build on, as well as some of the gaps they want to develop.

Don't Have HR Give the Feedback.

A key piece of advice is to avoid having internal HR professionals deliver the assessment feedback to the successor. Hiring external consultants or coaches from the assessment firm is much more effective. These professionals are often better equipped to interpret the results impartially, and they provide a sense of privacy and confidentiality, which is often appreciated by successors.

That said, assessment results become more accurate when they are reviewed by a capable internal team alongside external assessors. Internal insights are valuable for external assessors to consider and might add context to the results. The feedback should still come from external consultants.

To repeat a crucial point: The choice of consultants and the assessment methodology are critical. An average consultant giving feedback to your top talent based on a made-up assessment will risk alienating a smart talent or even have them work on irrelevant development areas.

Explore The Aggregated Company Results

The aggregation of the results of all successors will provide an amazing analysis base for the company. The organization can understand trends of their successor capabilities and get a glimpse of a synthesis of the company's future leadership capability. This amazing insight can inform the CEO which capabilities they need to hire from the market to complement the internal successors for the future.

For example, an aggregated result might show that successors lack systems thinking skills, an important skill for any senior leader. This meta insight should then push the organization to develop that capability at scale and start requiring systems thinking as a hiring requirement for leadership positions.

> These standalone assessments are risky and should be selected and deployed with care. Only one or two assessment tools are scientifically proven, the overwhelming rest are slightly better than a Cosmopolitan weekend quiz.

iii. Internal Interviews: The Favorite if Done Right

Interviews are important in assessing the technical proficiency and experience of successors. Standard assessments will focus on leadership styles and traits and will not capture the industry specifics.

Assessment centers and consultancy firms often include interviews in their processes as well. However, those interviews, led by external consultants, may lack insight into the organization's internal dynamics and business intricacies.

Here, the focus is on interviews conducted by executives. These interviews are the best sources of insight because:

- First, they provide a more accurate evaluation of the successor's ability and potential to succeed in the critical role.
- Second, insights from multiple executives can highlight key development areas and experience gaps specific to the critical role, which is essential for shaping future development interventions.
- Third, these interviews offer an indirect but valuable benefit: the opportunity for the successor to build their network with senior leaders. This can lead to early relationship building and, in some cases, evolve into a mentor-mentee dynamic.

Important Note 1: These interviews should be structured with clear areas of inquiry defined in advance. The results should be collected, collated, and stored systematically for future reference. This is an intuitive point that everyone agrees with, but very few organizations actually do.

For practicality, we recommend limiting the process to two interviews per successor. Anything beyond that risks overwhelming both the organization and the successors themselves.

Important Note 2: Your successor candidates are your stars, and some of them might feel uncomfortable with the word 'interview,' as they believe their consistent high performance and growth potential have already proven their value to the organization. Words matter, organizations can instead refer to these interviews as 'succession introductions,' which can lead to more authentic conversations and a better experience for the successors.

iv. References and Operational Data

There is no better source of information than someone you trust on their judgement of talent. There are always a few people in the organization who have the right critical thinking skills and an objective view of accomplishments and potential. Identifying those "talent observers" in the organization and getting their subjective views on successors provides great complementary data.

The performance management section explores long-format performance appraisals and capability assessments. These inputs will be valuable in painting a picture based on operational data rather than interviews and assessments.

Many organizations do not currently have talent observers or long-format reviews. Accurate information from these sources requires designing and implementing mechanisms to identify those observers and gather relevant insights through systems.

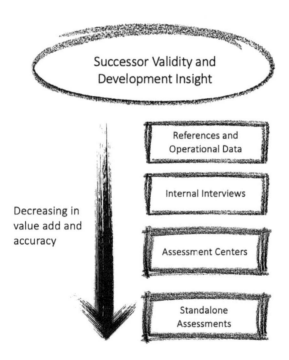

The above verification methods should be used in a balanced combination, and the tone should be more development-oriented than verification-oriented.

References and operational data used together with internal interviews is the most powerful combination. Depending on the organization's and successors' patience, assessment centers and lengthy assessments can also be used.

> Keeping the identification and verification phases simple will allow the organizations to focus on the development phase. Keeping it simple doesn't mean losing accuracy; it helps improve the successor experience.

Use the assessment results, or omit assessments altogether

We have witnessed time, effort, and money poured into assessments, but no real development actions have resulted from them. The executives usually tolerate these efforts in the short term. Still, typically, after three to five years of ongoing assessments and no real successor development, succession planning might be seen as a bureaucratic process and lose its executive sponsorship.

Do not use generic talent pools like "high potentials" or "emerging executive."

Another pitfall is maintaining generic talent pools within the organization rather than identifying successors for specific critical positions. Generic executive talent pools can lead organizations to adopt a generalized approach to development, focusing primarily on leadership development programs. While executive leadership programs offer significant benefits, organizations must recognize that the primary goal of succession planning is to prepare successors for specific roles and provide them with the necessary experiences to ensure readiness.

Specificity about the critical role a successor is nominated for makes experience-based development more relevant and targeted. A generic executive talent pool may also dilute the specific expectations placed on successors. After being labeled as "high-potential future executives" for several years, individuals may start to believe that becoming an executive is inherent to their nature rather than a result of accumulating the necessary knowledge and achieving defined goals.

4. Successor Readiness

Developing successors and making them ready for the critical role is the hardest step, and the most valuable. This step is lengthy and typically involves rotations, mentoring, formal education, and project assignments that will help the successors prepare.

Focus on mid-term successors

Arguably, organizations gain the most from succession planning when they effectively use it to develop mid-term successors for future leadership roles. Short-term successors are almost ready and, with some mentoring and minor adjustments, can perform well in their roles, this is the definition of a short-term successor. However, mid-term successors still require intentional development to prepare for their future roles. Therefore, focusing on mid-term successors for the development and readiness phase makes more business sense. This does not mean organizations should ignore other successors, but the priority should be on mid-term successors.

For long-term successors, development equally requires intentional job changes towards the target critical role; however, those job changes are more within the successor's own accountability and ownership. Having the ambition to manage two or more career moves centrally by the organization will put unnecessary planning and execution burdens.

Be intentional about role-specific skills

When developing successors or employees in general, organizations employ various interventions. A critical element for effective development is knowing which areas need improvement, a determination that should stem from the validation step discussed earlier. For each successor, the organization should identify role-specific development areas. For example, if a development plan includes something generic like "presentation skills, must be more visible," it may indicate a lack of specificity in the validation step, and organizations should reconsider executing that plan. In contrast, a development plan with requirements tailored to a specific product, market, technology, or leadership style is more likely to be effective and aligned with the organization's goals.

Focus on rotation and development by doing

The most effective development intervention for successors has been rotation, as learning on the job is the most effective way of development. The mid-term successor definition says the successor needs another role before being appointed to the critical role. And the in-between role before the real appointment is the actual development. Depending on the development area, the successor should be appointed to a role that will give them the necessary experience in terms of market, technology, or leadership style. The communication and the necessary enablers should be designed intentionally. Good communication is to the point and transparent.

Here are the protocols for mid-term successor development that we will discuss further with our example:

1. Provide relevant, hands-on experience in a related role.
2. Encourage leadership mentoring and regular feedback.
3. Create realistic timelines and milestones for readiness.
4. Communicate clearly and openly to the successors and the organization.

International Assignments

There is a need to mention international assignments specifically. Moving to another country, especially one with a different culture than one is brought up with, creates a great development context. International assignments push leaders outside of their comfort zones, make them more open-minded, and grow them as human beings and leaders. Anyone in a critical or executive position in a multinational company should look for international success, at least one assignment lasting longer than two to three years.

Functional Diversity

Understanding how the value chain works in the company benefits critical role holders and executives. The best way to understand the challenges and dynamics of other functions is rotation. A critical role in the company should require having managed a different unit in the company. A sales executive is more likely to be successful if he or she knows the supply chain or R&D in depth. Those rotations need to be encouraged and required. It will significantly increase the collaboration of the units if leaders understand the others' context better. Which in turn makes the critical role holder more successful.

Succession Case - Kate

NovaCare is an FMCG company primarily focused on healthcare, with some other household brands and a small animal food business. During succession planning, the healthcare business head position becomes an important topic as it represents 60% of the company's revenue. It is a critical position, and the incumbent has been there for a decade now, possibly moving up to become the next CEO.

Kate leads a small product portfolio of animal food, mainly dog food, which accounts for only 2% of the company's revenue. She has been a successful business manager and a good senior leader, and aspires to become the CEO one day. She has a strong learning capacity and solid base traits and values. During the succession identification and validation phases, she has impressed everyone one more time with her preparedness and the success stories that her peers have told.

NovaCare sees Kate as the mid-term successor to the big healthcare business and aims to develop Kate towards that role. Kate has extensive experience in the animal food products, the distribution channels (mainly veterinarians), and the customer segments. Healthcare is a completely different world. To prepare for the big healthcare business, Kate should learn about the healthcare products, their distribution channels (pharmacies and retailers), and the customers' preferences. Also, she needs to know brand management with major advertising budgets and a complex supply chain. Her development areas came out as:

1. Healthcare Product knowledge - production and distribution dynamics
2. Customer Analytics and Segmentation
3. Marketing and brand strategy
4. Partner ecosystem management
5. Leading through leaders
6. Critical Thinking

Development areas one through four are typical job expertise topics that individuals gain on the job. For Kate to master these topics, she should spend time (around two years) in a role that involves these elements in healthcare. The fifth and sixth areas are leadership and behavioral skills that can be developed with training and mentors.

An effective way to develop Kate would be to appoint her to a healthcare product management role for one of the minor product groups. She will be in the leadership team of the head of healthcare business, and the few years that she will spend on that minor product will give her the necessary experience in the dynamics of the healthcare business. The appointment should be with a product that is relatively stable so that Kate can learn the basics first without any major stressors. Also, the organization should make sure that Kate has constant job-related mentoring from her line manager. There should be a safe environment for Kate to ask questions and learn some crucial elements by watching her peers and manager.

If possible, Kate should be encouraged to change her country of base. If she is not at the headquarters, she should move to where the headquarters is. Alternatively, the company can offer Kate a role in the R&D section of healthcare where she could gain a deep insight into the product portfolio. Both two interventions, location and function change, can require additional years for Kate to develop, but they are valuable investments for the long term.

If managed intentionally, those few years should prepare Kate for the big job. Some organizations prefer job shadowing rather than direct appointment for readiness. While six months of job shadowing can be beneficial, a direct appointment in a controlled and supportive environment would better benefit high-potential profiles. A driven successor will not be comfortable with six months of doing nothing but joining meetings.

The leadership and behavioral development areas can also be addressed throughout the assignment. It is equally important to be intentional in those development areas; giving Kate the tools and methods to improve her critical thinking and leadership skills is crucial. There is a benefit to providing formal training and then a good follow-up and toolkit to practice the new behaviors. These development areas and the required improvements in those areas should be introduced to the new line manager as well as any mentor that the organization will provide. That way, behavioral development gets secured with continuous support and coaching.

Plan for ending of rotation and transition

The ending of the rotation role should also be well planned and clearly communicated to the individual and to the organization. Given the toll-gates of one-year and two-year development plans have been passed, and the successor (Kate in our example) shows the required development, she becomes the short-term candidate. At that point, it should be committed that the next time the critical role becomes vacant, Kate should be on the shortlist of candidates.

This is an important point that we will discuss in the communication section further. The healthiest way to manage expectations of successors and keep them accountable for their own development is to avoid any automatic promotion perception when the two years end. Organizations and executives should also feel free to decide after one or two years that the successor did not show the desired progression, and they should stay in the role further or even be taken out of the succession planning. Organizations should mitigate the risk of frustration and attrition of the successors, but it is only fair to communicate when a successor is no longer a successor.

5. Successor Appointment

Successor appointments should ideally come from the short-term pool.

Organizations should avoid committing to any automatic promotions for successors. To prevent a sense of entitlement and frustration later, it is crucial to communicate that while successors may receive automatic shortlisting for a critical role, they must still undergo the standard hiring process.

There are rare cases where a successor is so well-prepared that the organization may choose to make a direct appointment rather than conduct a formal hiring process that is unlikely to yield a different outcome.

The Bias Against the Internal Candidates

Organizations romanticize external talent while overlooking the growth and potential of internal candidates. Although their flaws are better known, their growth and commitment are equally real.

Organizations see their best from external candidates, but know all the truth about internal ones, and remember their early days and struggles. Years of accumulated insights and their shortcomings should not disadvantage internal candidates.

Appointment and Onboarding

Once the successor is selected to step into a critical role, the CEO should appoint a mentor to guide them through the first six months. No matter how prepared the successor may seem, the real-world complexities and challenges of the new role can be overwhelming in the initial period. A well-chosen mentor can provide invaluable support, offering guidance, sharing insights, and helping the successor navigate the intricacies of the role.

After the appointment, the CEO is responsible for ensuring the successor's success as much as the individual's. A successful Kate would be a perfect growth story to showcase to the organization.

The appointment and the onboarding of the successor represent the end of the succession planning process, the five steps concluded. Communication throughout this process is as important as the process execution and deserves its own chapter here.

Communication

Communication continues throughout the succession planning process and aims to send clear messages to successors or successor candidates. Organization-wide communication is not necessary unless the organization openly advertises the successor roles.

Early in the process, during validation, the successors will undergo assessments and interviews. It is essential that their candidate experience is superb. We are talking about high-performing, high-growth capacity talent, and the last thing we want is to frustrate them.

When communicating with successors, two key principles should be kept in mind:

1. Transparency in Every Detail: Successors should clearly understand the critical roles for which they are being considered, the time horizon, their development areas, and the planned development steps.

2. No Commitments: It must be made clear that no promotion is guaranteed. The organization's commitment is to include successors in the shortlist when a relevant vacancy arises, but no promotion is guaranteed. This helps avoid the frustration often seen in organizations when successors do not secure roles after waiting several years in the pool. The value proposition is the investment the company makes in them, not the actual critical role.

Building an open cohort and launch the program

A good practice is to group successors into a cohort. Launching succession planning with an event that gathers all short- and mid-term successors in one place, led by the CEO or executives, has significant advantages. This approach makes sponsorship and buy-in visible, fosters a sense of community, delivers consistent messaging, and promotes transparency by having all successors in the same room.

The launch can be very powerful, announcing a good leadership development program, if human resources can muster good content with a reputable university.

"As successors and the future of this organization, we will send you to a week of offsite training design with the university [reputable university]." This is a great message to give to the critical role of successors, probably a group of 70-80 high-potential employees.

The emphasis is on **learning by doing** and rotations. A few weeks of a leadership program will not prepare people, but it will create a community and camaraderie among the successors.

The line managers of the successors should be included in the process so that they feel ownership of developing their people for critical roles.

Future of Succession Planning

AI's capabilities to understand large amounts of data and generate meaningful deductions from them, will be used for the assessments and successor validation steps. AI will be connected to all internal systems, such as HR systems, Emails, MS Teams, Zoom, Slack, ERP, you name it.

> The behavioral data, for example, how successors have reacted to crisis and uncertainty in meetings and emails, how rational their decision making was, and how much they achieved, will be processed by AI. In short, AI will have a full profile of almost everyone in the company. Predicting the trajectory of any employee and matching that with critical roles, or any role for that matter, will be an easy task for an AI.

This ability, albeit sounding scary, is very useful for identification of successors. There will be no need for validation, since the identification will be done by AI.

Given the progress of technology, the best course of development for successors and even the availability of the right AI coaching will be in place. For now, short-term gains will be in identifying successors through a large amount of observed behavioral data and accomplishment.

Conclusion: Success Indicators and Measurements

Succession planning adds value if it is a smooth experience for everyone, void of bureaucracy and approval strings.

Succession planning requires significant effort and investment, even with simplifications and thoughtful design. To ensure a return on investment and assess whether the process is effectively preparing the organization for the future, it is essential to measure outcomes.

Here are some key metrics to provide insights into the effectiveness of your succession planning:

- **Bench Strength**: The number of successors in each time horizon is a useful indicator of future organizational readiness. Some companies follow the "1-2-4 rule," aiming to have at least one successor for the short term, two for the mid-term, and four for the long term. This has proven to be a reliable benchmark for succession planning.

- **Successor Appointment Percentage**: Understanding the percentage of critical role appointments that resulted from succession planning is a strong performance indicator. However, this metric should be measured over a two-to-three-year periods, as yearly measurements may be misleading, particularly in the early years of succession planning.
- **Development Success**: Tracking the ratio of successors moving from mid-term to short-term horizons after two to three years is a good measure of whether development interventions are working to prepare successors.
- **Retention**: Successors represent an organization's future leadership. Retaining them should be a top talent priority. Aiming for zero percent attrition of short- and mid-term successors sends the right signal.

Warning: **Goodhart's Law**, named after British economist Charles Goodhart:

"When a measure becomes a target, it ceases to be a good measure."

Overemphasizing any of the indicators above may lead leaders to focus on meeting the targets rather than improving the succession pipeline. For example, pushing for 1-2-4 bench strength could result in nominating successors who are not yet ready. Similarly, setting targets for mid-term to short-term successor transitions could result in promoting individuals who aren't fully prepared.

Monitoring these indicators rather than setting them as rigid targets is important.

While succession planning is essential for ensuring leadership continuity, its success is directly tied to the organization's overall talent strategy. Succession planning can only thrive if the organization is cultivating a rich pool of high-performing, high-growth employees. This is where the concept of talent density comes into play. By focusing on building high talent density, organizations ensure that they have not only successors for critical roles but also a workforce that continually drives performance and innovation. Let's now explore how achieving high talent density complements and enhances succession planning.

SECTION 3B

High Talent Density

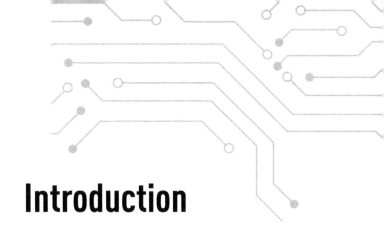

Introduction

A systemic approach, characterized by robust hiring processes, leaders who prioritize people development, and a growth-oriented culture, naturally creates a talent pipeline. This stream of talent rises through the organization, becoming successors who can be appointed to critical roles.

Marc Effron, the founder and President of the Talent Strategy Group, refers to companies' talent management processes as "talent factories" or "talent production lines" to emphasize the need for a systematic and disciplined approach to developing talent. He argues that organizations should treat talent development with the same rigor and care as manufacturing processes, ensuring consistent quality and effectiveness in producing skilled professionals. We will avoid using supply chain terminologies about talent in our book, but it is valuable to understand Marc's emphasis on systemic solutions.

Ultimately, the goal of hiring, developing, and retaining the right talent is to create organizations with "high talent density." While we began by focusing on succession planning, building a talent-rich culture boosts performance and drives long-term success across all business areas. Succession planning becomes an expected byproduct of a well-functioning, healthy organization with a high talent density.

The Origin of Talent Density

Reed Hastings, the founder and former CEO of Netflix, popularized the concept of "talent density" as a key factor in building a high-performing organization. Hastings defined high talent density as practically a high proportion of high performers or "A-Players" in the organization.

He argues that high talent density results in better problem-solving, more innovation, higher organizational performance, and higher individual motivation.

Even though we are exploring this topic in conjunction with succession planning, the exceptional business performance that comes with high talent density is the main gain for any organization. The rich pipeline toward succession planning is almost a second-order effect here.

Hastings advocates that high talent density can be achieved with high compensation and pushing the leaders to exit average performers. Netflix uses the term average in relation to "average in the market", and they aspire to have top performance as their average. These are important aspects, and combined with Netflix's attractive brand and culture, they represent a good recipe for high talent density: Pay top dollar to exceptional people and get the not-so-top talent out of the company.

Two companies with amazing track records: Revolut and Helsing have the same approach. Their founders repeatedly advocate having only exceptional people in the company and letting them do their job without close supervision. Both founders, Nik Stronosky[53] and Torsten Reil[54], are vocal about everyone being exceptional, a high talent density, being at the core of their company success.

Let's Align on What We Mean by That

"High talent density" is a loaded term. Here is the breakdown:

Talent: A high-performing individual with a high capacity for growth in the next three years and possibly beyond.

High performing does not refer to a performance appraisal of the past two years. Instead, it reflects the overall trend of the employee to consistently overachieve and overdeliver.

High performance and growth capacity are contextual. The same employee with the right leader and support can be a talent, but under poor leadership, they might perform poorly. Employees' capacity for growth also changes over time. Someone recently promoted might

---

53 https://youtu.be/IXubBqd8uXs?si=LWo4PoFo4fmaODsS
54 https://youtu.be/XxtvQyy7gtE?si=GyhQvFpkvSzVo9Up

be struggling slightly, but in a year, they will be back on their growth journey. We suggest evaluating an employee's understanding of their growth capacity and performance yearly or whenever significant factors change in their lives.

High Density: Talent density is simply the ratio of talents (high-performing, high-growth capacity individuals) to the overall company population. Concentration of top talent.

A high density for startups and scale-up phase companies indicates the "majority" of the company. For larger corporations, high density might mean "a considerable share," which indicates less than half.

We avoid specifying ratios like "80% talent density" because it risks turning an intuitive concept into an unnecessary KPI. For a startup with 15 employees, "high density" may mean 80% of the team, while in a large company, it may be closer to 30%. Large organizations should focus on roles where high performers make a significant impact, those where a high performer might deliver twice the output of an average one. It's important that companies define talent and what "high talent density" means for their unique context.

Executive teams need to agree on what they define as talent and what high talent density means for their company. To be able to do that, they need to have an honest view of the lifecycle phase their company is at.

Talent Density and Company Lifecycle

There are five widely accepted lifecycle phases for companies: seed, startup, scale-up (growth), maturity, and decline. An organization's phase significantly impacts its talent selection, understanding of performance, and culture in general.

Startup and Scaleup

Startup and scale-up phase companies naturally have shorter-tenured employees with higher risk tolerance than those in mature or declining phases. Roles are more dynamic and continuously evolving with new product features, customers, and markets. The simple fact that the company is growing creates more internal opportunities for personal growth. The company's culture is still heavily influenced by the founder and remains malleable.

The diversity of assignments and rapid new job opportunities is vastly different from mature organizations. The dynamic environment fosters learning and development: "Who wants to work on the new feature that needs to be developed fast?" is a common opportunity for startup employees find themselves in.

The success of the company depends on the handful of employees, and every individual counts.

These facts require the founders to instill a "only exceptional people" culture in the organization, both with the hiring they do personally and acting fast when an employee is not a match. This behavior will cascade fast and become the DNA of the company. No detailed performance management processes are needed, enough for every leader to stick to the high-performance standards. When small companies aim for everyone to be exceptional, they do hit a high talent density.

Maturity and Decline

Mature and declining-stage companies, which can remain in these phases for decades, typically exhibit steady, predictable growth, an efficiency focus, and established processes. These aspects bring more defined roles, rigid organizational structures, and employees with longer tenure on average.

Established processes, steady business, and large employee numbers make business results seem less dependent on individual employees. The disconnect between the company's performance and one employee's tasks becomes so substantial that companies invent performance management processes to connect company targets to individual targets. The same steady business and complicated processes allow deficient performance to stay undetected.

> Being far removed from direct impact, combined with a mediocre surrounding team, can make it challenging to attract and keep high-performing employees.

On the other hand, mature companies offer opportunities for employee growth through their scale and diverse roles. Projects, internal innovation, internal job movements and coaching can still provide growth opportunities. There can still be attractiveness for top talent and people with high growth capacity.

Unlike startups, mature and declining companies need a systematic strategy to maintain a strong concentration of top performers. This section outlines both the methodological approach and leadership practices required to build and sustain high talent density. Large organizations should target having 30-40% talent density overall, but units that are essential for strategy execution should aim for over 50%.

Achieving High Talent Density

Hiring, performance management, and employee development are the three systemic strategy areas towards high talent density. The large scale of mature corporations requires solutions and processes to ensure a common focus in talent density. We will describe these solutions in detail, however, at the core of their success lies the culture of talent that the CEO establishes. It will set the tone and demand a talent focus from all leadership.

There is no playbook for talent that will work for every organization. Companies have unique context and requirements, and the talent strategies must fit them. What worked for Facebook (Meta) might not be the solution for Unilever or even Google. One true constant is the commitment of the CEO and executive team to talent for high talent density. Without that commitment every solution will fall flat.

Achieving high talent density will be through leadership and culture and systemic strategies. We will explore those two main headings here.

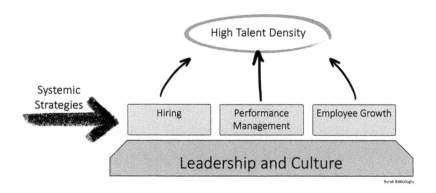

Leadership and Culture

High talent density is the result of the rigorous pursuit of top talent by the CEO first and then by all leaders in the organization. No human resources process can substitute for this commitment, as true talent density is cultivated through leadership's relentless focus on performance and growth capacity, not through systems or procedures.

Later in the chapter, we will explore the talent infrastructure needed to achieve and sustain high talent density. Those are amplifiers of the CEO's philosophy, nothing more.

Successful leaders often do define what they mean by "talent" with precision and reinforce this definition consistently. Mark Zuckerberg emphasizes problem-solving, passion, drive, and collaboration. The co-founder of Y Combinator and Author Paul Graham values determination, and Bret Adcock, the founder and CEO of Figure AI, highlights adaptability. When articulated authentically, as these leaders have done, the signal to the organization becomes powerful and clear. Irrespective of their political stances, these CEOs are good examples of practicing their top talent demands and founded and operated successful companies. High performance, innovative problem-solving, and curiosity seem to be working for them, which fits well with a high talent density approach.

There is a dark side to doubling down on that message if it creates an unhealthy competitive environment and hurts employee well-being. By no means do we intend to promote the unhealthy demands of psychopathic leaders. There is a balance where CEOs can be demanding while still being respectful and thoughtful. They are paid to find that balance.

For smaller companies or startups, high talent density is a matter of survival. A few bad hires and a lack of high-performance demand can bring a good idea or a good product prototype to a sudden failure. The feedback loops are short; the founders and CEOs should be on their toes about talent density all the time.

For larger companies, feedback loops are longer; it is like a slow-progressing disease that results first in stagnation and then in a slow decline. A silent killer.

Some basic steps for CEOs are here; you will recognize them as standard protocols for changing an organization's culture.

Anchor in Simple, Authentic Messages

Constant repetition of a few, simply formulated expectations around high talent density signals unwavering commitment to both leaders and employees. The CEO and executive team own this responsibility, demonstrating these principles through their daily actions.

The power lies in simplicity. Amazon's "customer obsession" was a straightforward message woven into everything they did, becoming fundamental to their success.

Choosing a message that reflects reality is crucial. "We deliver exceptional work" rings hollow and undermines credibility if the organization typically delivers average results, and "exceptional" is just another PowerPoint headline.

Conversely, a CEO can't give the message "being exceptional" and then praise a visible project's subpar result during meetings. Or ask for high talent density and then promote someone mediocre to an executive position.

Remove Leaders Who Don't Aim for Top Talent

One constant across organizations, regardless of their stage in the life-cycle, is that tolerance for senior leaders who lack alignment on talent understanding should be zero. Any executive or a senior leader who fails to

- develop their talent,
- hire the best fit for the role,

- and maintain high talent density through letting go of low performers

should either be **transitioned to an individual contributor role or removed from the organization**. It is a very simple and effective rule, but it is rather difficult for CEOs to practice.

Prolonged tolerance of such leaders will have a devastating impact on the organization's culture. Employees are keen observers, and when a senior leader doesn't follow the CEO's devotion for top talent, the culture of talent density loses momentum, or never takes hold.

Promote the Right Leaders

Promotion is the loudest signal a company can send to the organization. The profiles promoted to visible roles communicated to the organization what is rewarded and recognized. The promotions should be for those people who have demonstrated high capacity, growth, and performance.

Secondly, the promoted people should be strong believers of the talent philosophy and able to hire and develop top talent, increasing the talent density in their units.

Convert the Talent Philosophy to Practice

Larger corporations can also have practices that send strong cultural signals, which human resources can help scale. Those signals, along with enduring CEO support and real-life examples of actual execution, can significantly shape the right talent culture.

Here are two examples:

1. **Amazon's Bar Raiser**: The philosophy behind the Bar Raiser is that every new hire should be better than at least 50% of current employees in a similar role. This keeps the talent pool continually improving, helping Amazon to maintain its culture of high performance. A Bar Raiser is an experienced Amazon employee (from outside the hiring team) trained to assess candidates objectively. Their role is to make sure that the candidate will raise the bar for talent and capability in the company. They have the final say in the hiring process, even if the hiring manager has a different view.

2. **Netflix's "Keeper Test"**: Managers regularly assess whether they would fight to keep an employee if they were leaving for a similar role elsewhere. If the answer is no, they let the employee go. If the answer is yes, they make sure the employee gets a very competitive compensation.

These signature practices, within the scope of systemic strategies for hiring, performance management, and employee growth, are important to design and implement. They are effective and good internal branding for talent philosophies.

Expectation from CHRO and HR

A Chief Human Resources Officer (CHRO) plays a crucial role in coaching the CEO on the importance of following through on commitments, particularly regarding talent density. They guide the CEO and the executive team in building and maintaining a culture of talent density, assisting them in communicating the message clearly and empathetically. CHROs need to remain objective in their coaching responsibilities. It would be inappropriate to suggest terminating employees due to personal conflicts instead of performance-related criteria. This presents a precarious situation that many HR leaders have encountered.

The role of human resources as a function is to translate that culture into concrete processes and behaviors. For instance, when the CEO demands the best talent for R&D roles, the CEO's first step should be to set expectations consistently with the R&D executives in almost every meeting. Only then can HR design the necessary hiring practices to support those leaders in attracting top talent, whether through competitive salary ranges, targeted candidate marketing campaigns, effective market mapping, or comprehensive technical and behavioral interview processes.

Leadership sets the tone for talent density and performance, and systemic talent strategies ensure that these cultural priorities are reinforced and operationalized. Systems, processes, and platforms are crucial in supporting leaders as they develop, manage, and retain talent. In the next section, we will explore hiring, performance management, and employee growth as the three systemic strategies for maintaining a high talent density.

Systemic Strategies for Talent Density

The three systemic strategies, hiring, performance management, and employee growth, are the most impactful and designed thoughtfully to help leaders reach a high talent density. The three are not exhaustive, but they are the key ones.

As discussed in the performance management section, today these practices are designed and hosted by human resources (or people functions), often based on conventional wisdom and wrong assumptions. Badly designed systems will hurt companies instead of delivering high talent density. Process-oriented performance management will frustrate leaders, poorly managed internal hiring is likely to alienate internal talents, and an employee development program only including half an hour of mandatory health and safety training will make people cringe at the notion of "training programs."

Here are protocols to better structure those three systemic strategies:

1. Hiring

The success of a company depends significantly on its ability to hire, onboard, and enable good talent. In the early stages of a company, founders and CEOs often spend a large portion of their time hiring the best talent available in the market. Some founders, like Matteo

Franceschetti, co-founder and CEO of Eightsleep[55], strive to interview every new hire, even as their company grows to several hundred employees. At a certain point it naturally becomes impossible. However, by merely inserting themselves in the recruitment process, the CEOs ensure that others will think carefully about the candidates they put forward for hiring.

> As companies mature, they develop more systemic approaches to improving the quality of their hires. The most powerful tool is still the CEO's talent approach cascaded down the organization so that all hiring managers have the same rigor as a startup CEO. The hiring system and processes should enforce and unlock that culture. Instead, current hiring practices have become processes of mediocrity.

A common scenario unfolds where the recruiter posts the job on a prominent platform. Then, the company waits for applicants, what we call the "post and pray" method of sourcing. After two weeks, the recruiter filters the applications and provides a shortlist to the hiring manager. At this point, the process has already limited the options to the people who have applied rather than the best candidates in the market and relied on the biased filtering of a recruiter. The hiring manager proceeds to conduct one-hour interviews with the shortlisted candidates and decides on the one to hire. Of course, there are good leaders who do much better work at finding and hiring talent, but the system is built on the efficiency of hiring pipeline rather than the quality of candidates.

The most common performance indicator of hiring is the average number of days to hire a candidate. That alone is a strong signal to the recruiter to hire people as fast as possible, and focus on efficiency, not quality. Here is the first critical rule:

Don't Rush Hiring

Interestingly, despite hiring being critical to increasing talent density, large companies often settle for the most readily available candidates. Frequently, they rush through the hiring process, leading to poor fits

---

[55] Matteo Franceschetti: The Ultimate Hiring Playbook: Five Questions to Ask Every New Hire | E1084

and offering the wrong candidate the wrong role at the wrong time, simply because the hiring manager feels pressured to fill a vacancy quickly.

> No company won against the competition because it hired candidates in an average of 65 days. Companies are better off when hiring takes three or four months and they get the best possible talent. CEOs should take a closer look at HR KPIs and scrap the ones like time to hire. Any CEO failing to do this will steer their company towards mediocrity.

Another mistake is that the hiring often gets squeezed between daily tasks, impacting the quality of hires and, consequently, the company's talent density. Recruiters are trying to squeeze an hour of interview here and there into the agenda of managers. That one hour is between two other meetings and becomes fifty minutes of rushed conversation.

A good interview should be in two phases, a short interview first, 30-45 minutes, and then a two-hour follow-up. The first one is only an introduction, and more to figure out what to discuss on the second and longer interview. Interview questions should be standard, but allow double clicks, long format conversations, and branching off. A good interview resembles more a good podcast that flows naturally and is informative, rather than speed dating with prepared questions.

Define What Good Looks Like, and Don't Compromise

One simple yet powerful protocol is to create a clear list of core traits and skills that are non-negotiable, regardless of the urgency of filling the position. Peer interviews and a "bar raiser" like Amazon's practice must be implemented to avoid settling down with the best available candidate.

> One of the indicators is to look at the ratio of people hired from applicants versus people hired by proactive headhunting. If all the new hires come from applicant pools, it is highly likely the organization got complacent. The headhunted candidate ratio should be somewhere between 20% for companies like Google, which attracts the best talent to apply, and 60% for companies with less known brands.

Don't Outsource Your Hiring

In their pursuit of efficiency and cost cutting, some large companies have chosen to outsource their hiring. The hiring expertise of hiring agencies and their ability to scale up or down their recruiter numbers are some of the arguments for outsourcing. If you are hiring repetitive roles like call center agents in large amounts, then it might make sense to partner with a call center hiring company. For any other type of hiring, the company's own human resources should design and operate hiring.

> The hiring landscape will change drastically with AI algorithms, and we probably won't see many recruiters in companies soon. Until then, recruiters who understand the company's culture and business are important. Recruiters should strive to get the best talent rather than hitting an outsourcing agreement target.

Leverage AI, Now

Step 1: AI's ability to learn from what good looks like in a role should be leveraged more. For example, AI can answer the question, "Which developer profiles perform the best in which of our units?" by reviewing successful developer profiles and learning what works for which unit.

Step 2: Having that immensely valuable insight of what works, AI can sift through online behaviors of candidates and even devise contests to understand who would best fit the role. With a mass marketing approach, it can also approach those candidates and explain the most relevant value proposition of the company to the specific candidate.

Step 3: Soon, AI will be a great interview buddy to the hiring manager. Whispering the right questions and highlighting the areas to consider will make the hiring manager 10x more accurate.

Good AI can achieve all of these and more. We can even go one step further and suggest that large enough companies develop their own AI algorithms rather than relying on ready-made vendor algorithms.

This is a rather short take on hiring, but hopefully, it conveys the message that hiring requires an overhaul. Especially for large companies, **hiring should be taken down and rebuilt brick by brick.**

2. Performance Management

For high talent density, performance management is the core element. Conventionally, performance management is defined as the end-to-end process, from goal setting through feedback conversations, performance evaluation, and development needs assessment. In larger corporations, this is often a mechanical process managed by HR through an established digital platform. We have discussed performance management in detail in this book.

We suggest placing disproportionate emphasis on the CEO's strong stance, with no tolerance for anything else but high performance. This will, in turn, become the norm, the company culture. The two sections of this book, performance management and leadership, will provide protocols and alternative solutions for high talent density-focused performance management.

3. Employee Growth

Employee growth contributes to high talent density in two major ways, one in the form of developing people from "B Players" to "A Players", and two, in the form of retaining talent. Our famous "high performance, high growth capacity" people will not stay where they are staying still.

Growth happens mostly by doing things. The famous 70-20-10 learning model suggests that 70% of learning occurs through experience, 20% through social interactions, and 10% through formal education. Despite the lack of empirical evidence, the 70-20-10 model is valuable when applied flexibly. It is a reference framework that encourages a blend of experiential and social learning alongside formal education.

Growth Through Experience

We learn mostly from our past experiences, including our mistakes and successes, as well as through guided practice and mentorship.

Postmortems

Postmortems in the business world are great examples of learning from mistakes and successes. A discipline of having a postmortem after every major initiative helps teams and individuals learn and grow. This continuous learning and improvement, followed by adapting to new realities, results in incremental differentiation. "For example, teams that can consistently learn and adapt to changing conditions will continue to compound their advantages over other teams," according to the paper Team Performance: Nature and Antecedents of Nonnormal Distributions by Aguinis and Bradley.

Learning from past experience is not about feedback. We deliberately want to make this distinction. Learning from mistakes and successes is about a team getting together, discussing with candor and without blame what went wrong, why, and what was good, and should be scaled. The conversations can't be generic like "yes we should do better next time". The statements are factual and focus on what exactly went wrong: "We should have foreseen the spike in demand and be prepared. We need to be better at demand forecasting and use data models, not our gut feeling".

Despite its significant impact on growth, enterprises are usually weak at practicing postmortems. The lack of candor and evidence-based thinking are the two culprits for this. Unfortunately, the discipline of well documented postmortems is difficult to maintain when everyone is "busy with the next project".

Assignments (On-the-Job Learning)

The second major way of growing is through new assignments. The best way to develop is to participate in a project to learn a new skill under the guidance of more experienced coworkers. Equally, being assigned to a new role that is significantly novel and has good mentorship, develops employees faster than any other option. Learning curves are steep, and the work is usually challenging, but the growth in both options is undeniable.

The question is how large enterprises can enable these assignments in a systemic way. There are a few key ingredients:

1. The culture of talent mobility:

Organizational leaders should be open to letting go of their best talent and genuinely encourage them to take on new challenges. The culture can be built on the notion of questioning anyone who has held a specific role for more than three years.

Most opportunities should be available to internal talent first, and hiring managers can schedule a six-month learning period for any internal hire instead of expecting immediate results. Internal hire ratios of 50% to 60% are signs of healthy internal mobility. Anything higher is risky.

Pushing all positions to be hired internally is detrimental. Some roles and skills should be hired externally. At times, human resources functions demand "internal first" for all job postings and push for internal hires in an inorganic way, which in turn damages the talent density and HR's positioning as a strategic partner.

2. Internal Talent Market

Internal talent marketplaces are digital platforms that match employees to opportunities based on their aspirations and skills. Algorithms assess and capture employees' skills and aspirations, which constitutes the supply side of the marketplace. The demand side is obviously the available opportunities in the organization, such as full-time roles or project-based assignments.

These marketplaces have become trendy in the late 2010s, and they are still creating a lot of buzz. The idea of a matching algorithm between talent and open assignments is just too attractive to pass.

Real-life implementations of talent marketplaces are full of challenges and unused platforms. First, the matching algorithms are old-generation (not generative AI) and poor at matching opportunities and employees. They will spit out irrelevant suggestions, and the employees will lose their trust in the platform from the start.

Also, effectively using those platforms is a function of the right culture, where leaders don't hoard talent, allow their best employees to spend time on different projects, and feed the system with opportunities with an open mind that anyone in the organization can be part of a project. Those elements are key organizational cultural practices; without that approach, no platform will achieve the intended impact.

Organizations should be very cautious about talent marketplace platforms; they are expensive and usually underdeliver with their current technology. Success stories from a few companies can be misleading. Either they present an Instagram version of real life, where pictures represent one perfect snapshot, and real life is less glamorous. If those success stories are real, a big IF, those organizations might have the right ingredients of culture, opportunity availability, and HR infrastructure.

Organizations should consider an internal talent marketplace only if it is powered by generative AI and after a long AI fine-tuning period. Otherwise, the return on investment outweighs the benefits for now.

> Organizations can still announce available project assignments and jobs on an internal hiring platform. If the platform is user friendly, it will catalyze internal talent mobility with the right leadership attitude. No need for complex, expensive, and half-working algorithms.

3. Risky Promotions:

To create personal growth and retain good talent, organizations should be ready to take a chance on their internal talent. Promotions based on observed potential, even though the candidate is only 60% match, can be successful if there is a good mentorship available.

It is in the name, though, that those are risky in terms of acceptance of the team and the learning ability of the individual—a calculated risk to be managed by good executives.

4. Career Models:

Career models provide a structured framework for employee development and progression. Mostly used in large companies, they typically outline clear pathways for career advancement and define the roles, skill sets, and competencies needed at each level. These models often include horizontal (lateral moves to gain diverse experiences) and vertical (promotions) growth options.

The career models are most effective when they cover specific roles and career paths rather than trying to map every career move in an organization. "What is the career path that leads to an R&D director for Oncology hardware products?" is the level of specificity that organizations should aim for.

Instead of having a frame, some companies have the approach of "each employee should own their career, no need for career models." However, we believe this is an unconstructive approach. A career model will provide the necessary thinking frame for many employees and make them more intentional about their own growth.

Growth Through Social Interactions and Formal Training

The border between social, on-the-job learning and formal education has become blurry for the last decade. Social learning is embedded in the learning experience with new project assignments; collaborative work makes information flow throughout the organization.

Formal training is different. We live in a world where anything we want to know has an instruction video on YouTube. Information and lectures about astrophysics, quantum computing, machine learning, or how to remove an oil stain from carpet are easy to access.

With this abundance of information, corporate learning should be much more intentional and effective. The needs of the organization, mapped with employee aspiration and good content, can deliver miracles. However, formulating and aligning those three elements of need, aspiration, and content can be challenging.

Even though there are trends like "learning in the flow of work," where micro learning moments are installed in the natural workflow whenever the employee needs them, the impactful execution of those is still questionable. Even though current learning departments and platforms fall short of delivering exceptional value, organizations should wait for generative AI to transform this area with an infrastructure first and then redesign their learning experiences.

In the meantime, proven certificate programs, the creation of relevant internal content, and the curation of that content are essential to good formal training. Partnerships with professional learning platforms are also valuable, but they are not the answer to all organizational needs.

Learning and development is another area that will experience fundamental changes in the next five years. Learning and development professionals, naturally, are ready to face this challenge. A well-designed formal training environment is a big employee growth enabler, a good complement to assignments towards achieving a high talent density.

Conclusion of the Section and Key Takeaways

Achieving high talent density is not easy, especially for companies that have not already been working toward it. Altering the culture of a large corporation centered on talent takes time, persistence, and commitment. This change requires the CEO to have a talent-focused agenda as much as it is business-focused and a cohesive executive leadership team that understands and aligns with and cascades this focus throughout the organization. With the right CEO attitude and systemic strategies from a strong HR function, the journey is rewarding.

Once a level of high talent density is reached, corporate success will be achieved. Naturally, success will attract top-tier talent, and talent will create a strong pipeline of successors, who ultimately will ensure future success while maintaining a continued focus on talent. More than a few companies have managed to reach this state, big tech firms, some FMCG, and pharmaceutical companies are good examples of organizations with high talent density, not to mention Netflix as the company that made talent density a goal itself. The focus on talent has consistently delivered them decades of corporate performance and, in many cases, contributed positively to society and humanity at large.

We hope to have provided a comprehensive view of the talent landscape and the intricate system that ensures a healthy succession pipeline. Throughout this chapter, we have offered insights into which levers to pull to steer the complex organizational machinery toward achieving high talent density. However, as mentioned at the outset, every organization and CEO operates in a unique context. Solutions can only be achieved through open-minded, thoughtful conversations, exploration, and expertise.

High Talent Density: Key Takeaways

- **Leadership Drives Culture**: High talent density begins with unwavering CEO commitment. No HR process can substitute for leadership's relentless focus on performance and growth capacity. The CEO must consistently demonstrate this commitment through actions, messages, and promotion decisions.
- **Context Matters**: The approach to talent density varies significantly based on company lifecycle. Startups and scale-ups naturally require near-universal exceptional talent, while mature organizations should target 30-40% overall talent density, with higher concentrations (>50%) in strategically critical units.
- **Define Your Terms**: Organizations must clearly define what "talent" means in their context. True talent combines consistent high performance with growth capacity, both of which are contextual and can change over time based on leadership, support, and individual circumstances.
- **Systematic Strategy**: Three key pillars support high talent density: thoughtful hiring practices, performance-focused management, and robust employee growth opportunities. These must work in harmony and align with the organization's specific needs and culture.
- **Hiring Excellence**: Don't rush hiring decisions or compromise on quality. Move beyond "post and pray" recruiting to proactive talent hunting, with proper time allocated for thorough evaluation. Leverage AI for candidate identification and assessment while maintaining human judgment in final decisions.
- **Growth Through Experience**: Focus on learning through real-world challenges. Implement rigorous postmortems after major initiatives, create meaningful assignment opportunities, and build an effective internal talent marketplace. When backed by good mentorship, embrace calculated risks in promotions.
- **Enable Internal Mobility**: Foster a culture where talent movement is encouraged. Aim for 50-60% internal hire ratios while maintaining the balance with external talent injection. Create clear career models that provide specific pathways for advancement.

- **Technology as Enabler**: While AI and technology platforms can enhance talent processes, they should amplify, not replace, human judgment. Wait for mature AI solutions before investing in complex talent marketplace platforms and ensure any technology implementation aligns with organizational culture and readiness.

Remember: High talent density isn't just about hiring and retaining top performers, it is about creating an environment where exceptional talent becomes the norm, driving innovation, problem-solving, and organizational success.

SECTION 4

Leadership Frameworks

Introduction

Leadership frameworks define the desired behaviors and styles expected from leaders. When leadership styles consistently follow the same pattern across all positions and levels, they begin to shape the organizational culture. Organizations can address many fundamental challenges by implementing effective leadership frameworks without necessarily embarking on an extensive culture change journey.

However, saying leadership is a widely explored topic is an understatement and already risks boring the average reader. There are literally millions of websites, books, papers, podcasts and movies about this topic. Leaders have been decisive elements of how history was made and how companies were founded and vanished.

A good CEO and a good executive team that the CEO puts in, makes or breaks a company. Equally, a strong middle management is key to strategy execution. No wonder leadership development is a sector of eighty billion dollars globally as of today. It will increase to 198 billion by 2032. The demand for effective leadership will continue to increase[56].

---

[56] https://www.marketresearchfuture.com/reports/leadership-development-market-23196

Let's start with the definition of a leader based on the fundamental leadership theory coined by Bass and Bass (2008). The two fundamental expectations from the leaders are:

1. Establish structures for strategy and task execution:

Plan work, allocate resources, design processes and flows, define jobs, manage the allocated budget effectively, and similar topics that will enable execution of tasks or strategy at large. These are more of the "management" side of the tasks in mainstream literature.

2. Build, develop, and motivate the team towards shared goals:

The expectation from a leader is to hire the right people, develop the right skills, and lead them in a way that they are engaged and perform at high levels. Even though these requirements are people-oriented, we should not forget that those, too, are means to strategy execution.

Now that we have established the definition of leadership through expectations from a leader, we need to address an important misconception as well.

What is Good Leadership Really?

In boardrooms and business schools worldwide, the term "good leader" often conjures images of charismatic personalities who inspire deep team loyalty. Some organizations tend to conflate good leadership with being nice, showing empathy, or maintaining high popularity among followers.

These qualities have their place, but they miss the fundamental mark of leadership excellence: successful strategy execution.

At its core, a good leader is someone who consistently translates organizational vision into results through their team. This may seem obvious, yet it's a truth often obscured by our tendency to focus on mainstream leadership styles over substance. A leader may be universally loved by their team, but if that team fails to execute and perform, the leadership itself has failed.

This isn't to say that the human element of leadership is irrelevant. On the contrary, empathy, emotional intelligence, and talent development are crucial tools in a leader's arsenal for driving execution and performance.

With this clarification out of the way, we can focus on the components of good leadership and slowly develop our leadership framework. Leadership behaviors inform leadership styles, which define whether a leader is a good one or a bad one. Therefore, it makes sense to start with leadership behaviors, investigate what informs them, and move toward leadership styles.

> In this section, we will explore the design of a leadership framework and, after covering the theory, conduct a case study. But before we dive into the topic, it should be noted that leadership is not a set of individual traits or characteristics. It is a complex phenomenon involving two-way relationships between leaders and followers, organizational culture, and intricate social interactions.

Assuming we can simply tell leaders how to behave and expect predictable results is naive at best. It contradicts the principles of systems thinking, which states that leadership and organizational dynamics represent some of our most complex systems. That is why we will introduce a multi-layer approach to deploying leadership frameworks.

Leadership Behaviors

The daily actions of a leader, how they navigate crises, reach decisions, pose questions, assign tasks, and monitor progress, create a visible pattern that their teams and colleagues observe and interpret. When consistent over time, these behavioral patterns coalesce into what we recognize as a leadership style.

Consider a leader who routinely gathers her team's perspectives before making decisions. She actively listens, values diverse viewpoints, and typically reaches conclusions that align with team consensus or majority opinion. This consistent pattern of behavior leads others to identify her as a democratic leader.

But what drives these behavioral choices? The answer lies in the leader's inner world: their beliefs, values, experiences, and psychological makeup. This internal foundation shapes how leaders approach leadership, yet organizations often overlook this crucial dimension when developing and evaluating leaders. Understanding this deeper layer is essential, as it explains not just how leaders behave but also why they choose certain approaches over others.

As we will explore later, a leadership framework is a more mechanical and forced intervention. It requires certain behaviors from leaders without much consideration of the inner world of the leadership teams. If the framework conflicts with the common values and mental models of the leaders, it is likely to fail, and the behaviors expected from leaders will not stick. That is why organizations should first understand the inner world drivers before designing the leadership framework.

Before the reader criticizes us, we need to add two concepts: The first one is the relational nature of behavior. Leadership behaviors do not happen in a vacuum; they are intertwined with follower behavior. A leader's ability to be democratic is limited if followership only works with direct orders.

The second concept is that the core leadership expectations of developing team members, removing hurdles, and creating psychological safety are built into the constitution of leadership. Even if they are not singled out in a leadership framework, a leader still should act according to the basics of leadership responsibilities.

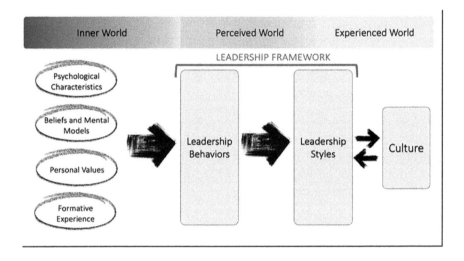

Inner World

At the core of effective leadership lies a strong foundation of character shaped by psychological traits, personal beliefs, values, needs and experiences. These inner qualities determine how a leader perceives challenges, makes decisions, motivates teams, and guides the organization through change and growth. By examining the key components of this inner foundation - psychological characteristics, beliefs and mental models, personal values, needs and formative experiences, we can better understand the source of a leader's authentic influence and impact.

Psychological Characteristics: The Building Blocks of Leadership Potential

- The five main characteristic headings—developmental stage, personality traits, emotional intelligence, cognitive capabilities, and psychological needs—form the basic building blocks of leadership potential.
- These elements shape leadership style, interpersonal skills, decision-making processes, and ability to navigate complex challenges.

Developmental Stage

An example for developmental stage will be a leader operating from Kegan's Self-Authoring stage. This stage refers to the fourth level of adult development in psychologist Robert Kegan's constructive-developmental theory. At this stage, individuals have developed a cohesive sense of identity and internal value system that allows them to make decisions based on their own beliefs rather than relying primarily on external expectations.

Self-authoring leaders can remain committed to long-term visions and navigate competing demands while remaining grounded in carefully considered convictions. They can maintain a clear strategic vision in the face of disagreement and resistance from their team. They are less likely to become derailed by criticism because their sense of direction is internally anchored rather than dependent on external validation. In contrast, a leader at a lower developmental stage will be more susceptible to team reactions and change strategy under pressure.

Personality Traits

Personality also plays a key role in natural leadership strengths and growth areas. A highly extroverted leader will focus on building broad networks and rallying teams around a common goal. However, to become fully effective, they may need to consciously develop the complementary skills of deep listening and one-on-one coaching. Conversely, a more introverted leader will excel at providing individual guidance and development but may need to "flex" into engaging larger groups when required.

Personality traits are the most difficult psychological characteristics to alter, and a role in the corporate world should be shaped toward those traits rather than trying to force individuals to embody different personality traits.

Emotional Intelligence

Beyond basic personality, emotional intelligence (EQ) is increasingly recognized as a critical factor in navigating complex organizational dynamics and interpersonal challenges. A leader with high EQ can tune into the subtle emotional drivers of behavior during stressful periods of change. This empathy and emotional management allow them to proactively address concerns, re-energize teams, and maintain cohesion when it's most needed.

Cognitive Capabilities

A leader's typical cognitive style and capabilities shape how they take in information, structure problems, and make decisions. A highly analytical thinker will naturally focus on quantitative metrics and logical reasoning to navigate crises. At the same time, a more intuitive, feelings-driven processor will excel at reading interpersonal dynamics and building empathy. Recognizing one's own cognitive preferences and deliberately practicing less familiar modes is key to remaining flexible and avoiding biased perspectives under pressure.

Psychological Needs

In addition to individual traits and capabilities, a leader's psychological needs play a key role in their development and performance. Richard Barrett's framework[57] from his "The Values-Driven Organization" discusses seven levels of needs based on Maslow's from survival to service. He argues that a leader whose basic needs of survival are not met will struggle to become an effective leader. For instance, a leader fighting for their team's resources in a hostile environment will likely adopt a defensive style rather than showing vulnerability, which is crucial for authentic leadership. It becomes impossible to demonstrate an authentic leadership style in a hostile environment.

---

[57]   https://www.valuescentre.com/resources

On the other hand, a leader whose fundamental security needs are satisfied has more psychological capacity to engage in personal growth. A supportive team environment built on trust enables the development of advanced leadership capabilities such as empathy, systems thinking, and shared vision. Barrett's framework highlights how a leader's ability to evolve beyond learned behaviors depends on fulfilling core needs, emphasizing the importance of considering the psychological context in effective leadership development.

The effective leader continually works to build self-awareness of these core traits and to consciously adopt a range of styles and skills to meet the needs of different people and situations.

Beliefs and Mental Models: The Leader's View of How the World Works

A leader's perceived style is based on a set of core beliefs about how business works, how people operate, and how change occurs. These assumptions are unconsciously held and shaped by the leader's formative experiences and ongoing reflection.

Consider the fundamental beliefs one might hold about human motivation in the workplace. A leader who believes "people are fundamentally motivated by purpose and opportunities for growth" will naturally focus on aligning roles with individual aspirations and creating development pathways. In contrast, a leader who believes "people need external direction and consequences to remain motivated" will implement a more rigid performance management process. Both approaches can work but require very different managerial energy.

Beliefs about failure and risk-taking are also deeply instrumental in creating organizational culture. A leader who fundamentally views setbacks as learning opportunities will communicate through word and deed that intelligent risk-taking and iteration are encouraged. The resulting climate of psychological safety is great for innovation and shared ownership. Leaders who believe that failure indicates incompetence will, conversely, create cultures of risk-avoidance and blaming behaviors.

Mental models about the nature of change emerge in a leader's general style. Leaders who believe "sustainable change is evolutionary" will craft long-term plans and focus on gradual, continuous improvement of core capabilities. Leaders who believe change is typically revolutionary will emphasize fast operational pivots. Cognitive flexibility in shifting between these contrasting models is valuable for reading different types of competitive environments.

Some of these beliefs are deeply ingrained through early life experiences. To evolve as a leader, it is critical to seek out contexts and relationships that challenge one's worldview and offer fresh perspectives. Reflecting on which core beliefs are serving the business well and which may need to be updated is an essential discipline.

Personal Values: The Moral Compass of Leadership

A leader's actions ultimately flow from their underlying moral principles, the fundamental values they consider non-negotiable. These core beliefs about "what is right" act as an ethical compass, guiding decisions and tradeoffs at both a personal and an organizational level.

Leaders who deeply value transparency will default to openly sharing business metrics, goals, and challenges with their teams. Even in the face of competitive headwinds, this commitment to honesty fortifies trust and collaboration to weather difficult periods. The leader's integrity serves as a model for the entire organization's character.

Innovation-focused values drive a leader to favor "new and different" over "tried and true" when allocating limited resources. An inclination to sponsor exploratory projects and take risks on unproven ideas sets a tone that energizes and retains creative talent. However, if not balanced with an appropriate respect for organizational stability, it can also breed a chaotic internal environment.

Leaders who ascribe to meritocratic principles and equality will build organizations that reward individual initiative and provide equal access to opportunity based on ability. Formal structures around development, promotion, and compensation send a powerful message about the importance of personal growth and contribution.

These values come into tension as events unfold daily, and a leader's true colors show in how they balance difficult tradeoffs. How much should we favor individual rewards vs. team incentives? When is it right to depart from full transparency to protect sensitive information? Is it better to sponsor a high-risk/high-reward innovation or invest in optimizing core systems? A leader's actions in these revealing moments demonstrate the sincerity and consistency of their professed beliefs.

Personal values can be altered; they are not destiny. Evolving as a leader involves continually examining which values are most essential and how to uphold them under pressure. It also involves understanding the degree to which personal values align with organizational ones and acting accordingly.

Formative Experiences: The Crucible of Leadership Character

The way leaders navigate the challenges of business is marked by their life experiences, often from long before they entered their current roles. The most influential of these formative moments typically involve navigating failures, benefiting from influential role models, or facing unexpected events.

Many great leaders point to early career failures as pivotal moments of truth that shaped their subsequent leadership philosophies. A self-assured young manager whose over-scoped project fails spectacularly may emerge with a newfound respect for thorough risk assessment and contingency planning. Surviving a moment of humbling defeat often builds empathy, resilience, and an orientation toward others' development.

Influential mentoring relationships often shape a leader's assumptions about people and group performance. A protégé who sees firsthand how a respected mentor builds consensus before key decisions will often internalize an inclusive approach to management. Witnessing a leader who remains grounded in respect while disagreeing with others imparts emotional maturity. The power of positive examples to expand one's vision of effective leadership cannot be overstated. Unfortunately, the same can be said about negative examples.

Research by McCall et al. (1988) in The Lessons of Experience: How Successful Executives Develop on the Job shows that early career experiences with managers shape leaders' approaches to decision-making, conflict resolution, and team management. Their findings suggest that early exposure to effective (or ineffective) leadership styles strongly influences future leadership preferences and practices. Some of the core leadership styles are learned during the first six to eight years of professional life, which makes the choice of one's manager in those years crucial.

Navigating a major unexpected crisis like a PR disaster, major product recall, or hostile takeover attempt can be a defining rite of passage for leaders. Facing these "crucible moments" demands accessing one's full range of skills and beliefs about success. Often a rapid immersion in complex dynamics, crisis leadership both reveals and forges the character required to mobilize systems under intense pressure. Emerging intact on the other side with hard-won confidence frequently propels executives to the next level.

Leaders construct life stories from their unique set of formative experiences, which inform their behavior and shape their leadership style.

The two examples below will demonstrate the complex impact of underlying psychological characteristics, values, and mental models on leadership styles.

Example: Collectivist vs. Individualist Leadership Style

Leaders from collectivist cultures often develop a more consensus-driven approach, valuing group harmony over individual assertion (Hofstede, 1980). Leaders from individualist cultures tend to emphasize assertiveness, autonomy, and competitive edge, which are valued in Western contexts. These styles are a function of the personal values imposed by the society on them and mental models they develop through their experiences.

Hans Vestberg, when he was the CEO of Ericsson, a Scandinavian telecom vendor, maintained a strong commitment to transparency and open communication with both employees and external stakeholders. His leadership style emphasized the collective responsibility of the company. His change motto at one point was "It starts with us" to all leaders. He encouraged teamwork and alignment across different divisions, and his strategic decisions were always aligned with major division heads in his team and with his chief financial officer and chief strategy officer. It was in Hans' upbringing in Sweden that he naturally had those inclusive and democratic leadership styles.

The exact opposite example is Elon Musk, who usually makes decisions quite quickly, mostly on his own, and asserts them to his companies. Andrej Karpathy, once head of AI at Tesla, describes Elon's style as "like the hammer: He decided on something, and then he just executed it." We know that elements in Elon's upbringing shaped his values toward a more individualistic style. Silicon Valley just amplified this.

We don't want to compare those two businessmen. Hans and Elon are almost citizens of different planets in terms of their interests, styles, and life choices. However, their contrast in this topic is worth mentioning to make a point.

Example: Authoritarian vs. Democratic Household Norms

Leaders raised in environments where authority was rarely questioned (common in high-power distance cultures, as per Hofstede's dimensions) may find it difficult to embrace participative leadership styles. In contrast, leaders exposed to democratic discussions early in life tend to value inclusiveness and feedback (Bass, 1990).

A recent real-world example is TSMC, a Taiwanese chip maker, struggling to get their Arizona USA plant up and running. The reason was the cultural clash:

"The American engineers complained of rigid, counterproductive hierarchies at the company; Taiwanese TSMC veterans described their American counterparts as lacking the kind of dedication and obedience they believe to be the foundation of their company's world-leading success[58]."

The Taiwanese management had certain beliefs and values that informed their hierarchical leadership style, which clashed with the learned American values of autonomy and individualism.

When Inner World Faces a Leadership Framework

The four components of inner world are presented separately, but they are in truth tightly interwoven. Formative experiences with influential mentors shape our beliefs about how to lead change. This attracts us

---

[58]   https://restofworld.org/2024/tsmc-arizona-expansion/

to organizations that share our values, where we further develop capabilities that match our psychological strengths. As we navigate new challenges and relationships, we update our mental models, clarify our principles, and stretch ourselves to grow. However, some elements are more difficult to change than others, and we end up with a diverse set of leadership styles.

It is important to note inner world drivers, because a leadership framework is a direct and mechanical intervention. When organizations state how their leaders should behave, the expected leadership styles come face-to-face with the inner world of the leaders. If these two aspects are in alignment, the organization moves swiftly towards the desired culture. However, if the inner world of leaders does not match the requirements of the leadership framework, cognitive dissonance will occur, and the leadership framework will fail to take hold. A framework imposed by the organization will always lose against the complex layers of the inner world.

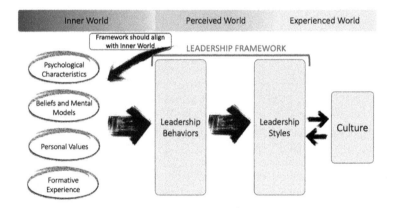

As we implement a leadership framework, it will benefit us to consider the alignment of the inner world. By understanding and acknowledging leaders' inner worlds, we can create a framework that resonates with their values, beliefs, and strengths. This approach will increase the likelihood of successful adoption and help create effective leadership.

Leadership Frameworks

A leadership framework is a structured model or guide that outlines the key principles, behaviors, competencies, and values essential for effective leadership within an organization. It serves as a blueprint for assessing and developing leadership skills and behaviors.

We are now in the realm of perceived world: leadership behaviors and leadership styles. Once the behaviors exhibit a trend, they become a leadership style, or from the reverse angle, leadership styles inform specific behaviors. Leadership framework directly intervenes in this realm and instructs specific leadership behaviors or attitudes.

Sometimes, organizations design a certain framework of behavior for their leaders, but mostly those behaviors are emergent under the influence of the founders or the CEO's. In both cases, leadership styles, once they follow the same pattern across all leadership positions and levels, start to form an organizational climate and culture. Hence, a successful leadership framework is crucial to set a desired culture.

A leadership framework can outline values (integrity, excellence, etc.), behaviors (setting high standards, active listening), or competencies (critical thinking, adaptability). In essence, leadership frameworks describe and guide leaders' behaviors. Even if they require a value like integrity, a framework should describe which behaviors indicate integrity for that organization.

Leadership frameworks provide:

1. **Consistency**: Ensures a uniform approach to leadership across the organization.

2. **Clarity**: Provides clear expectations for leaders at all levels and signals the requirements to future leaders.

3. **Development**: Guides leadership development programs and initiatives for current and future leaders.

4. **Assessment**: Serves as a benchmark for evaluating leadership performance for existing leaders or assessment of future potential leaders.

Two Types of Leadership Frameworks

Standard leadership frameworks, also known as leadership theories or styles, are widely accepted concepts.

The second type of leadership framework is one that companies devise for themselves. These frameworks are specific to the company's needs and context and can include parts of standard models.

There are twelve well-known standard leadership frameworks (Eva, Howard, et al, 2024), some prominent ones are:

- Transformational Leadership by Bernard M. Bass and Ronald E. Riggio.
- Servant Leadership by Robert K. Greenleaf.
- Shared Leadership by Pearce and Conger.
- Authentic Leadership by Avolio & Gardner.
- Adaptive Leadership by Ronald Heifetz and Marty Linsky.

Below is a deep dive into transformational leadership to give an idea of what a standard leadership framework looks like. Even though the name "transformational" sounds like something out of the most mainstream corporate presentation, the content of this leadership framework is actually valuable if you can get past the "cringe" naming.

Transformational Leadership

Transformational leadership, as developed by Burns (1978) and Bass (1985), is all about inspiring and motivating people to reach for a shared vision that goes beyond individual self-interest. Transformational leaders aim to lift their followers toward a collective purpose, whether that's an ambitious organizational goal or a broader mission. This style of leadership involves four key components:

- Idealized influence (acting as a role model),
- Inspirational motivation (energizing the team),
- Intellectual stimulation (encouraging creativity and critical thinking), and
- Individualized consideration (providing personalized support for each follower's growth).

Together, these elements help transformational leaders create environments where people feel empowered to question assumptions and push themselves toward meaningful development. Questioning assumptions and critical thinking also leads to learning from mistakes and growing as a team.

Studies and meta-analyses, like those by Judge & Piccolo (2004), link transformational leadership to higher productivity, greater job satisfaction, and lower turnover rates across different cultures, industries, and organizational levels. In addition to improving performance, transformational leaders are said to inspire a strong sense of commitment and trust, creating workplaces where people feel motivated to go above and beyond.

The effectiveness of this leadership style may vary depending on the situation. Factors such as followers' personalities, cultural expectations, and the physical proximity between leaders and their teams can all influence how well transformational leadership works in practice. It's worth exploring whether this approach is equally successful across all settings or if certain conditions are more conducive to its effectiveness.

Although there is no evidence that transformational leadership directly drives high performance, we can see aspects of it in Microsoft's transformation under Satya Nadella's leadership from a toxic winner-take-all culture to a collaborative, open-source one. This transformation included significant changes to the product portfolio, including the Azure cloud, AI, and the acquisitions of LinkedIn, GitHub, and Activision Blizzard. His calm and inclusive style and deep technical knowledge served him well as he led Microsoft.

Political leaders such as Abraham Lincoln, Nelson Mandela, Mustafa Kemal Ataturk and Mahatma Gandhi are also labeled as seminal transformational leaders who act as role models, inspire crowds, and encourage critical thinking.

Other standard leadership frameworks have characteristics similar to transformational leadership. They contain behaviors, values, and competencies under their common theme. A second example of transformational leadership is authentic leadership. It has self-awareness, transparency, integrity, and a strong moral compass as its defining headings.

Before we move on, we want to remind the reader that the efficacy of standard leadership approaches is not always scientifically proven. Servant leadership is linked to higher job satisfaction and a deeper sense of trust within organizations. However, the direct causality of performance increase is not proven. Hence, we invite everyone to have a healthy skepticism towards a new and trending leadership style in the market.

Moving beyond generic leadership frameworks, let's explore organization-specific leadership models. Many of these frameworks draw inspiration from the broader, more general approaches but are adapted to suit the unique needs and culture of individual organizations. By combining the most effective aspects of generic frameworks, these tailored leadership models aim to create a style that aligns with the company's values, goals, and structure.

Organization Specific Leadership Frameworks

Designing and implementing leadership frameworks is not easy, and not for every company either. For smaller companies, the leadership framework can be an email from the founder or CEO about the required behaviors, and that can easily become the leadership framework.

However, for larger organizations, the process has deliberate steps that need to be considered and followed through. It is common for leadership frameworks launched in large companies to remain PowerPoint slides, which challenges organizations to approach this topic intentionally.

A healthy leadership framework has three main stages: prerequisites, design, and deployment. It's critical to make sure the **prerequisites** are met, the framework is **designed** to fit the purpose, and to **deploy** the design with strategic actions and good communication.

1. Four Prerequisites of Leadership Frameworks

Three Phases of Leadership Framework

1. Prerequisites:	2. Design:	3. Deployment:
i. Timing ii. Purpose iii. Leadership Readiness iv. Cultural Alignment	i. Description of Wanted Behaviors ii. Headings to Group Behaviors	i. Strategic Actions in Multiple Domains ii. Communication iii. Monitor and Iterate

Although the standard leadership approaches help us understand different styles and types of leadership, organizations often require their own leadership framework.

When we discuss the organization-specific leadership frameworks, however, we have the liberty to have less scientifically proven frameworks than the standard leadership frameworks. Companies don't have the patience to do research experiments. "Let's try this leadership framework for one of our units and measure its impact against a control group for one year" is a healthy but unlikely scenario for companies.

In the absence of a scientific experiment, executive teams can put all their effort into understanding their underlying challenges and design a framework that is most likely to address those challenges while at the same time leveraging the strengths of the organizations. That is why they should pay more attention to prerequisites and design phases.

Four essential prerequisites need to be considered when developing a framework that will be embraced by leaders and create the desired impact: Timing, Purpose (Understanding the Why), Readiness and Culture Alignment.

i. Timing

The timing of a new leadership framework's rollout can make or break its success. Organizations tend to initiate major changes in times of challenge or even crises. Burning platforms, the danger of being redundant in the market, negative margins, and all the other scary elements usually set the context for change. Even though crises are good opportunities to make changes, at the same time, organizations should be aware of the challenges the crisis mode represents for behavior change.

When is NOT the Right Time

When things are not going well, the need to change becomes clearer for executives.

Imminent funding and cash difficulties, product portfolios underperforming, major fraud cases being discovered, and missing growth or profit targets are signs that "things are not going well". Seeing these symptoms, executive teams fall into crisis management mode, scrambling to address the most urgent issues, control the narrative, and minimize damage to the company's reputation and financials.

When companies face serious headwinds and underperformance, leadership teams often react in fire-fighting mode rather than proactively addressing root causes. The focus shifts to survival and damage control. Executives may need to renegotiate debt covenants, divest struggling business units, slash costs, lay off staff, and initiate internal investigations. Externally, they must manage investor and media scrutiny while working to restore confidence.

It is in that environment statements of "We are not innovative enough", "We work in silos", "We should work more end to end", "We need to do more with less", arise and end up with a culture change program, and a new leadership framework. Executives should resist committing to a long-term solution without the necessary mind space available.

> During crises, people often focus on immediate concerns, effectively "shrinking" their time horizon. Under stress and uncertainty, our cognitive resources narrow (sometimes called "tunnel vision"), leading us to discount long-term outcomes in favor of immediate survival or problem resolution. This is explained by temporal discounting in behavioral economics and observed in psychological studies on stress and decision-making.

Leadership framework and cultural change initiatives are best kept for calmer waters; three arguments why executives should wait for calmer times.

1. **Sustainable Change**: Effective change often aligns with long-term goals and involves engaging employees in a meaningful way. When changes are made proactively rather than reactively, organizations can avoid the pressures and resistance typically associated with crisis-driven changes. This approach allows for a more thoughtful and inclusive process (Ogbonna & Harris, 1998).

2. **Leadership and Employee Engagement**: Leaders who facilitate culture change during calm periods are more likely to achieve genuine buy-in from employees. This is contrasted with changes imposed during crises, which often result in compliance rather than true cultural shifts (Canato & Ravasi, 2015).

3. **Organizational Stability and Growth**: Companies that incorporate change as a part of their ongoing strategy rather than as a reaction to immediate threats tend to build more resilient and adaptable organizations. This proactive approach aligns with long-term strategic goals and fosters a stable environment conducive to growth and innovation (Gobble, 2015).

There is a value of a crisis in implementing changes. Behavior and culture changes are, however, longer interventions that require sustained attention. Organizations can use the momentum of a crisis to implement more instantaneous interventions, such as shutting down a product line or introducing a new pricing model. And once the imminent crisis is over, say after one or two quarters, companies can start working on a longer solution. Calmer waters do not mean a perfect calmness where everything runs smoothly, it is just calmer to allow mind space to execute.

When is the Right Time?

Change of a CEO.

The best time to implement a well-designed leadership framework is after a management change. The arrival of a new CEO is a critical enabler for changing culture and leadership practices, especially if the CEO comes from outside the company.

Alternatively, if the new CEO has a significantly different style from the former CEO, even if they are an internal appointment, this would also be a great time to implement change. The transition from Steve Ballmer to Satya Nadella at Microsoft is a good example. Also worth mentioning that when Microsoft transformed under Satya, they had good financials rather than a moment of crisis. Satya started in February 2014. The latest full-year result for Microsoft was the FY 2013 (July 2012 to June 2013), when sales were up 6% and operating profits were up 23%—hardly a crisis.

Let us be clear: Leadership frameworks and culture should not change with every new CEO. Well-established and successful companies should keep what is working. Jeff Bezos's handing over Amazon's CEO chair to Andy Jassy when things were going well for Amazon is a good example. Andy Jassy did not change behavioral expectations and stuck with Jeff Bezos's motto of "customer obsession."

Just before the new CEO gets appointed or right after the appointment, usually the "change is in the air". Six to eight months into a new CEO's tenure is an ideal time to initiate a leadership framework.

1. The CEO has had time to understand the internal culture and leadership practices and has a more informed opinion on what to change.

2. CEOs usually make changes to their executive team in the first year, and new executives enable further changes.
3. CEOs influence behavior through their expectations and actions. By the eighth month, employees had observed the new behaviors, and some had already adapted to them. Thus, the new leadership framework is not surprising.

If there are no imminent CEO changes, then leadership behavior changes should occur when the business is relatively stable. However, very few CEOs can pull off the trick of saying, "We have been working in a certain way for years together. Now things have changed, and I need you to work differently."

If that were the case, the CEO would need to replace at least 40% of the executive team, mostly in core business positions.

Case Study: Implementing a Leadership Framework with a New CEO

Typically, major leadership and culture transformations are best addressed after a crisis. However, organizations that lay the groundwork during the crisis can pivot much faster when stability returns. In rare cases, a highly capable talent team with deep executive trust can work behind the scenes to ensure the organization is ready to move when the moment is right, without losing valuable time.

At a global technology company facing executive turnover, compliance violations, and record-low engagement, the talent team recognized that poor leadership behaviors and outdated processes were reinforcing the very issues that led to the crisis. Due to the situation at hand, the board had decided to change the CEO, and a new leader was at the helm. Rather than waiting, the talent team worked side by side with the CEO and executive team, mapping the required leadership shifts and quietly redesigning key processes and a leadership framework in the background.

The ability to move forward in this way was possible because the CEO and executive team had deep trust in the talent leaders. This trust was built over time through a fact-based, research-driven approach that combined human behavior insights with strong business acumen. The talent team actively involved employees from the outset, collecting valuable feedback through carefully designed surveys and listening to their personal experiences.

When presented with the plan, the new CEO immediately saw the value in advancing the work, but with a deliberate approach. As he put it: "Let's move forward, but let's do it somewhat under the radar to avoid causing unnecessary strain on the organization."

For eight months, the talent team worked on the prerequisites, gathering data, building insights, and collaborating with the executive team while being mindful of their cognitive space. After eight months, the new leadership framework, consisting of five behaviors, was ready to be deployed. As the framework slogan read, they were "on the move."

The talent team managed to use the new CEO's momentum, strategically collected insights during the crisis, and worked with the executive team in the background to find a longer-term solution rather than forcing them to solve everything at once.

ii. Purpose (Understanding the "Why")

> "A problem well-stated is half-solved."
>
> Charles Kettering, Head of Research, General Motors 1920-1947

A well-designed leadership framework starts with a clear purpose, a strong understanding of why it is needed. This purpose should go beyond vague aspirations and address specific challenges or opportunities that the organization is facing.

The organization's real and unique needs are the most important input to the design of a new leadership framework. Before defining a new framework, the underlying reasons for challenges should be fully understood. Organizations sometimes make the mistake of rushing to conclusions and getting stuck addressing the symptoms with overused and generic leadership slogans like "Dare to Disrupt" or "Simplify to Innovate"—the fastest way to destroy the engagement.

A clear and accurate reason resonates more deeply with teams. It helps them see how the framework will positively impact their day-to-day work rather than feeling like an abstract initiative with no real impact.

The Importance of Critical Thinking

Leaders, especially executives, are inundated with information from various sources. This information can come from their own observations, leading to insights, or secondhand accounts that identify problems or successes. The ability to differentiate between noise and signal varies among executives. Skilled executives ask the right questions and thoroughly investigate issues; others may be less critical and interpret a larger portion of information as signal. Fatigue at the end of a meeting can also hinder an executive's ability to question information effectively. However, leaving aside the whole leadership framework topic, it is hard for a CEO to succeed in general without exceptional critical thinking abilities.

Unfortunately, executives tend to apply less critical thinking to talent-related topics compared to other issues. A CEO would typically pay close attention and question every detail when faced with declining product revenue, persistent product bugs, or increased costs. However, the same CEO is more likely to accept a statement like "Our employees received 37 thousand hours of training this year; we are developing our talent" without questioning the meaning behind the number, the relevance of the content, or the evidence of development.

The reason for highlighting executives' stance towards information, critical thinking, and particularly talent-related critical thinking is that when discussing the underlying reasons for challenges and how they relate to leadership behaviors, overarching statements like "we need more proactive leaders" often make common sense and receive a nod from the CEO. However, CEOs and executive teams need to be more inquisitive. Discussions such as "Why do you think we need more proactivity? What is the problem that you are trying to solve?" should be encouraged more frequently.

The Sources of Insight

There are four primary sources of valuable information for organizations: operational data, surveys, anecdotal experiences, and benchmarks. Academic sources and scientific research papers can also provide important theoretical frameworks to help interpret this information. Ideally, organizations should draw upon all these information sources as part of a robust decision-making process. Operational data backed by first-hand anecdotal experiences tend to be the most powerful and insightful, with surveys and benchmarks playing a secondary but still important role. Relevant scientific research, especially from the social and behavioral sciences, can shed light on the human elements at play.

Let's explore each of these information sources in more detail:

1. **Operational Data:**

   Operational data refers to real-time or near-real-time metrics and insights collected directly from the systems and tools used in daily business operations. It is generated as a byproduct of workflows, processes, and digital interactions and provides an objective, system-based view of an organization's activities.

   > In contrast to subjective perceptions or self-reported insights, operational data is system-recorded, measurable, and directly extractable from platforms where work happens.

   For example, in the context of meetings, the subjective opinion of a leadership team might be that everyone in the organization is experiencing a significant meeting load. However, operational data, such as the number, duration, participants, and frequency of meetings recorded within Microsoft Teams, reveals the reality. In this case, leaders had projected their own busy meeting schedules onto everyone, assuming a universal issue. Yet, the data showed that senior leaders attended an average of 30 meetings per week, while the average employee attended only 13, a significant contrast that only operational data could unearth.

Operational data is valuable for identifying trends, optimizing processes, and making evidence-based decisions. It eliminates biases and relies on actual system interactions rather than assumptions or anecdotal feedback.

These systems can be anywhere in the value chain. Platforms like Jira (an Atlassian project management tool), Salesforce (a customer relationship management system), or ServiceNow (a ticketing and IT service management platform) generate valuable operational data points.

When it comes to the actual system use, operational data almost always tells the truth.

2. Surveys and Perceived Reality:

Self-reported surveys are crucial information sources for every organization. They can be employee engagement surveys, customer satisfaction surveys, or various other employee satisfaction surveys. However, self-reported answers can be tricky and less reliable. The question style can easily manipulate the answers. Timing, the emotional state of the employee, social pressure, and many other variables impact how people answer surveys.

Therefore, survey insights should be scrutinized rigorously and verified with operational data. Organizations should determine whether there is an isolated problem or if the insights indicate symptoms of a larger underlying issue only after synthesizing both survey and operational data.

Some organizations suffer survey fatigue, and the root of this is failure to show any action. One could argue employees are not fatigued by surveys but rather enjoy sharing their views. The fatigue comes from a lack of follow-up. The number of surveys put in front of the employees without any decent follow up should be minimized.

3. Anecdotal Experiences:

In his podcast interview with Lex Fridman, Jeff Bezos said: "When the data and the anecdotes disagree, the anecdotes are usually right, it doesn't mean you just slavishly go follow the anecdotes. You go examine the data because it's usually not that the data is being improperly collected; it's usually that you're not measuring the right thing." As Bezos states, there is value in verifying insights from the sources above with real-life experiences. When we talk about anecdotal experience, we mean first-hand experiences rather than second-hand experiences that are heard from a colleague. It happens, hopefully not quite often, that leaders see positive indicators in Power-Point slides, where one or two actual experiences might tell a different story.

We have witnessed satisfaction surveys with stellar results, an average satisfaction score of 4.8 out of 5, and similar scores indicating extraordinary service, only to experience below-average service ourselves when we needed support.

The real world might differ from the averages presented to you. Anecdotal data will help you ask the right questions. "Is everyone answering the same questions?" "Are the answers anonymous?" "Might there be a trend that unsatisfied employees just avoid answering questions?".

On the other hand, if anecdotal experiences match operational data insights, then you know you have the truth.

4. Benchmarks:

Benchmarks are also sources of information that should be treated with care. We specifically mean industry benchmarks or other external benchmarks collected from the market. Every company is unique, and reducing the indicators to a common denominator is difficult.

For example, the benchmark indicator of "revenue per employee" can be misleading if one compares a company with all functions insourced to a company with 20% of the workforce outsourced, such as IT, customer support, and recruitment personnel.

Carefully conducted benchmarks have their merits, but we consider them to have low actionability.

Science and Research (for sense making):

Scientific research papers are reliable sources of theoretical information, at least in behavior and organizational psychology. Many papers can help companies understand customer and employee behavior. They contain proven truths with great potential to help companies, but unfortunately, they collect dust in academic libraries.

For example, it has been proven that individual and team performance does not follow a normal (Gaussian) distribution, which is mostly known as the bell curve. Only by understanding the research on human potential and performance, would we stop having policies based on that wrong assumption.

Unfortunately, there is a disconnect between the academic world and businesses. However, both worlds can learn much from each other. Utilizing the right science—by that, we mean relevant science with peer-reviewed and replicable research—is a big unlock for organizations. At the same time, the research could use a healthy dose of reality, such as what things look like in the real business world.

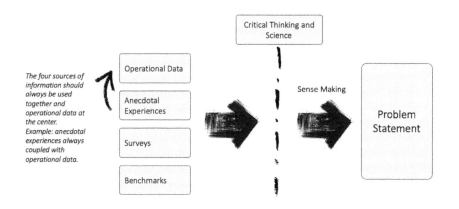

The search for problem statements should not overshadow the organization's successes. When things are not going well, we tend to focus on problems; however, the model above should also be used to scale successes. As David Coorperrider's Appreciative Inquiry[59] suggests,

---

59   About Appreciative Inquiry

finding those successes, understanding the conditions that exist for them, and scaling them is powerful for large organizations.

Understanding the underlying problems and success conditions is the key input for leadership framework design. This phase of exploration for purpose can take a few months, rather than weeks. It is wise to resist the need to rush.

iii. Leadership Readiness

Before introducing a new framework, it is essential to gauge whether the organization's leaders are ready for change.

- If leaders are already struggling with their own challenges or feel unsupported, they will be in survival mode. They may resist the new framework or fail to embody its principles. Successful adoption depends on leaders feeling psychologically prepared and engaged, they need to recognize themselves as part of the framework's development and success, not just as recipients of a new set of rules.
- There might be a fatigue of leadership initiatives in the organization. Frequent leadership interventions and fragmented messages can tire the leadership community.
- The maturity of leaders, on average, might not be adequate to understand the changes needed or their role. This might be because of the company's low average age and leadership tenure or the lack of historical good role models. A leadership framework can be used to develop the leadership community, and this disadvantage can become an opportunity. In this case, the framework should be more explicit about behaviors, and more resources should be allocated to get the leaders on board with the initiative.

Assessing the readiness of the leadership community at large becomes an important factor in implementing change. This assessment does not need to be formal. Subjective observations, understanding, and a survey can be good enough indications.

The readiness of the leadership community can influence the design and deployment of the leadership framework. Increasing sense-making maturity itself can be a purpose of the change and part of the framework's design. Addressing some of the leaders' basic needs before deploying a full-scale leadership framework will also be beneficial.

The second and higher level of readiness is the readiness of the executive team to design and implement the framework. A dysfunctional executive team with personal conflicts and a lack of collaboration will struggle to come together and design a leadership framework. The team's cohesiveness should be addressed before or during the leadership work. Again, a leadership framework can be a good opportunity to mend the team.

iv. Strategic and Cultural Alignment

A leadership framework should be tightly aligned with the organization's broader strategy and culture.

1. **Strategic Alignment**: The framework should reinforce the organization's vision, mission, and long-term goals. Leadership behaviors encouraged by the framework should actively support the company's strategic direction, helping move the organization toward its aspirations.

   If the strategy of an aging company is to maximize its assets and cash flow, the company's dire need will not be innovation.

2. **Cultural Fit**: It is equally important that the framework resonates with the organization's cultural values and existing leadership models. If the framework introduces leadership behaviors that clash with deeply ingrained cultural norms, it can create confusion and resistance. Instead, the goal should be to gradually shift the culture, and the framework should be designed to guide that evolution in a way that feels natural and organic.

> An aggressive sales culture with a culture of "everyone is on their own" will not handle a leadership framework of radical collaboration. The absorption of working together should be infused with leadership mottos like "winning together."
>
> A leadership community that has been trained to stick to detailed processes and central governance will not react well to a sudden "Be Innovative" slogan. Years of appointments and daily experience of "stick to the rules" will naturally breed a leadership community of good followers. Innovation will be an alien term.

The alignment is a prerequisite item, best visited when the problem statement is shaped and revisited during the design phase.

By ensuring that the framework aligns with both the organization's strategic objectives and its cultural values, leaders can create a sense of coherence. This alignment makes the framework feel authentic and relevant, rather than a top-down mandate that feels disconnected from the organization's identity.

> Sometimes, companies want to initiate a substantial culture change by radically changing their leadership behaviors. This can only be done by replacing part of the executive team and a meaningful portion of the leadership community.

The Role of Human Resources

Human resources professionals have a natural role of a moderator, coach, and enabler during the leadership framework process. It is a difficult role to play and requires in-depth experience in leadership science, good common sense, and critical thinking. It is usually beneficial to build an ecosystem of partners to support the process.

During the prerequisite stage HR's role is to:

- Ensure the correct data is collected and used. Design the surveys well, and pass on anecdotal data from the ground to the executive team.

- Provide the right scientific evidence and direction to make sense of the data. Invite experts and professors in the field for inspiration, development, etc.
- Assess the readiness and cultural fit of the leadership community objectively.
- Balance the selling eagerness of management consultant with rational and scientific facts. Utilize the ecosystem in a distributed way rather than depending on one source.
- Coach the CEO and the executive team towards being a cohesive team, prioritizing the broader company gains over their personal and unit gains.

The stages of design and deployment will be mainly under the facilitation of HR as well. CEOs must rely on a highly competent CHRO and an exceptional head of talent, anything less will result in failure. An HR team with high potential individuals can be developed during the journey if they lack the experience.

Designing a leadership framework is a complex but rewarding process. By carefully considering the timing, purpose, leadership readiness, and alignment with strategy and culture, organizations can build a framework that enhances leadership capabilities serving the organization's long-term goals. This thoughtful approach ensures that the framework is more than just a theoretical model; it becomes a practical, inspiring adoption and development.

2. Design of Leadership Framework

Three Phases of Leadership Framework

1. Prerequisites:	2. Design:	3. Deployment:
i. Timing ii. Purpose iii. Leadership Readiness iv. Cultural Alignment	i. Description of Wanted Behaviors ii. Headings to Group Behaviors	i. Strategic Actions in Multiple Domains ii. Communication iii. Monitor and Iterate

After thoughtfully considering the prerequisites, the executive team can move towards designing the leadership framework. The design phase involves laying out the desired behaviors going forward that will address the challenges and scale the successes. It is also about grouping those behaviors in a sensible way and simplifying the language so that the behaviors can become heuristics.

The design phase feeds mostly from the purpose work, where the executive team understands the underlying problems for the prevalent and future challenges, as well as the success factors of the wins. The insights and sense making throughout that purpose journey will naturally create conversations around "what do we really expect from our leaders". The design stage consolidates those ideas in a meaningful way and describes the expectations from leaders.

Other prerequisites are important inputs, too. For example, if leadership readiness and maturity are deemed low, the organization can design a leadership framework with more pragmatic behavior instructions. With high maturity and readiness, the leadership framework can truly be a framework of approaches rather than daily behaviors, and the interpretation of the frame is left to leaders.

Here is an example of how the flow through the stages will look like:

Initial Gut Feeling Statement:	Insights from purpose work (Prerequisite Stage):
"We are inefficient, we need to do more with less"	1. We ship "OK" product features with more bugs than industry average 2. Those features provide good enough end user experience not a real frictionless experience 3. We have too many developers working on the same things which causes slow down and inefficiency. 4. We hire too many average developers instead of a few exceptional ones. 5. Employees don't speak up when they see a mediocre result in fear of being ousted as a negative person. Leaders avoiding conflict with other leaders also choose to not mention poor quality. 6. Inefficiency of the buggy products and too many developers increase the cost and eventually our pricing 7. The mediocre user experience and high-cost result customers to churn to competition

The above work during the prerequisite stage will result in the underlying problem statement: "We produce mediocre product features with high cost because our leaders settle for mediocrity instead of demanding more". This work so far already inspires a list of new behaviors during the conversations. Consolidating them will look like this:

Problem Statement	Behaviors discussed to mitigate the problem:
"We produce mediocre product feature with high cost because our leaders settle down with mediocracy instead of demanding more"	1. Set higher standards from the get-go. 2. Establish trust in the team to tell when things are "lame." Demand participation by "listening" 3. Value critical thinking and questioning, don't allow toxic positivity 4. Don't hide behind "fail fast" 5. Collect radically honest feedback 6. Hire and keep a few exceptional people in the team 7. Hire and keep a few perfectionists to challenge the "lame" in the team

signals priority and resist the temptation to move on to "the next big thing."

- **Public Accountability**: Strong sponsors publicly own both successes and setbacks. They're willing to be measured against transformation goals and hold themselves accountable. This often involves personal risk-taking and vulnerability.

Unwavering sponsorship can be attained through ownership, having the executive team be part of the journey, and long conversations. HR leaders have an important role here. Instead of trying to get executives to wear the mantle of sponsorship, HR should make this a journey where executive team ownership occurs naturally. If the sponsor needs to be coaxed, you don't have the right sponsor.

i. Strategic Actions in Multiple Domains

Sustainable behavioral and leadership style changes cannot succeed through isolated actions. Training people or changing processes alone will not work. Organizations are complex systems where everything is connected. Meaningful organizational change requires simultaneous and coordinated adjustments to the "tangible" layers (like structures and systems) and the "intangible" layers (like behaviors and mindsets). These layers will be called domains, and actions, initiatives, and interventions are interchangeable concepts throughout this section.

The multiple domain actions are intended to create a web of reinforcing interventions that work together. For example, suppose you're trying to build a more innovative culture. In that case, you might need to simultaneously adjust your physical workspace, change how meetings are run, modify reward systems, develop new capabilities, and shift leadership behaviors. Each action supports and strengthens the others, creating a momentum that makes the change more likely to stick.

> This interconnected approach helps prevent the common scenario in which change initiatives fail because they don't address all the factors that influence how people work and behave in organizations. It is about creating an environment where the desired change becomes the natural way of working rather than something people must consciously maintain.

Behavior, leadership style, and culture change can only be deemed successful if they have changed the daily experience of employees. Take the example of an organization introducing "more empowerment and accountability" for their employees. If the organization fails to change the daily experience of an employee who must go through endless approvals for simple tasks, then the empowerment will not be part of the daily experience. "More empowerment" becomes a slogan on a slide. Eventually, the initiative will fail to deliver a real change in behavior and create cynicism in the organization.

Strategic actions should alter experiences or behaviors toward the preferred states. Eventually, those preferred experiences triggered by the actions will create preferred behaviors. A smooth procurement process with minimum approvals and a strong message of accountability will empower the manager.

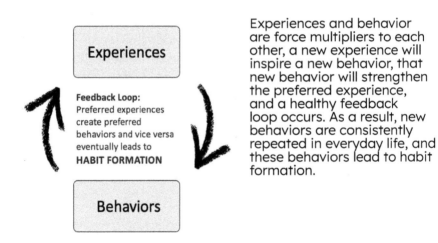

Experiences

Feedback Loop:
Preferred experiences create preferred behaviors and vice versa eventually leads to
HABIT FORMATION

Behaviors

Experiences and behavior are force multipliers to each other, a new experience will inspire a new behavior, that new behavior will strengthen the preferred experience, and a healthy feedback loop occurs. As a result, new behaviors are consistently repeated in everyday life, and these behaviors lead to habit formation.

There are five main domains for strategic action, ranging from strategic direction to the daily experiences of the physical workplace. These domains are grouped into two main categories: tangible and intangible. Any significant initiative should involve actions in multiple domains, preferably all of them. However, certain elements, such as process interventions and leadership capability interventions, are especially effective when utilized together.

The Five Domains of Strategic Action

This chapter focuses on the five domains and provides explanations and examples of strategic actions (or interventions). Organizations can choose to add to or remove domains from this model. Only multiple domain actions will provide daily experiences, and those experiences will enable the leadership framework to come to life and form habits, eventually shifting the culture.

These strategic actions require a strong project team to coordinate but not actively design and execute them. The interventions should be done by the "line organizations," every unit must make the necessary changes in its own mandate. The CEO and executive team should provide enough incentives and push for interventions, but it should never be the role of HR to push for interventions. Instead, HR should focus on its own accountability areas, like capability development or talent-related processes.

Companies might also choose to utilize change champions or thought leaders throughout their organizations.

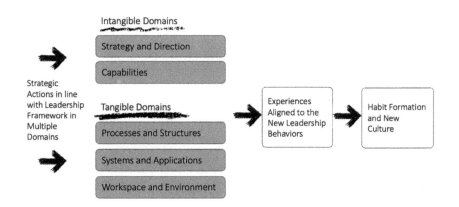

Strategy and Direction

The strategy and direction of any organization will give hints to behaviors that are expected from employees. The former Google chairman, Eric Schmidt, repeated his strategy as: "Product, product, product." This sets a tone about product development and R&D focus rather than a statement saying "Growth, growth, growth," which will then enforce sales focus. Those two directions inspire different sets of behaviors. A

237

similar change was observed during the transition from Steve Balmer to Satya Nadella at Microsoft, where, during Balmer's time, sales and competing for numbers was everything as opposed to Satya's product and curiosity emphasis.

A prominent technology company CEO requiring that the enterprise sales teams get the proposals right at the first submission rather than back and forth negotiations with the customer came up with the motto: "first time right". As a result, sales teams started taking longer turn-around times to prepare a proposal; they made countless iterations before going to the customer just to get to the "first time right". Meanwhile, Silicon Valley was moving at light speed with daily iterations with the customers involved, keeping the engagement high and moving to a common understanding faster. The repeated statement of "first time right" cost agility to the company and a few large deals. A leadership framework at that time, demanding agility, would not have withstood the strong direction of "first time right".

Apart from the formal strategy documentation, what we aim to articulate is the power of the CEO's tone. That tone would shape the behaviors of the executive team and send strong signals to the organization. Those signals are important catalysts that should be harnessed to demand certain behaviors.

Capabilities

When organizations expect a certain behavior, they should also give the required skills and capabilities to their leaders and employees. This is an intuitive logic that is often missed by the leadership initiatives.

In the example of "pride in our craft", the behavior of creating psychological safety is required. In that way teams will give and receive candid product feedback. The leaders might not have the capability to create a safe environment for their teams inherently. Or what they know might not be the correct way of doing things. It is unfair to expect a "pride in our craft" through candid feedback and not teach the leaders how to create that environment. At the same time, employees should be trained in handling a candid conversation and having a respectful discourse. A good leadership initiative must include psychological safety trainings for everyone, and good coaching sources for struggling leaders in place.

The same capability-building argument can be made for the leadership behavior of "fact-based decision-making." Not every leader is equipped with the analytical skills to demonstrate that behavior. Employees might not know how to prepare information and data analyses for fact-based decision-making or how to make those decisions themselves. Therefore, expecting fact-based decision-making must come with thoughtfully planned capability development for everyone.

Leveraging Processes and Structures

Processes and organizational structures define employees' daily experiences and, if used correctly, can significantly impact behavior change. They provide tangible evidence of change and nudge employees and leaders toward desired behaviors in a mechanical and structural way that limits misinterpretation.

Example: Designing for Accountability and Ownership

To create an environment of accountability and ownership for middle management, workflows and processes should be designed to give managers decision-making power. Questioning every dime spent and requiring multi-step approval for even the most minor expenditure while demanding ownership from leaders is unrealistic.

Consider a product manager designing a marketing campaign for a new product. If the senior director declines their request to hire a market research firm, even though it's within budget, and the development team dictates product specs while ignoring protests about recent feature quality, the product manager will not own any product failure. They can excuse themselves by saying, "I told the product team it wouldn't work," or "I didn't have the budget for market research, so we couldn't foresee market demand."

To expect a leadership style of accountability and ownership, the approval process should be redesigned to omit approvals within agreed-upon limits, and the development team should be structurally part of product management.

Aligning Reward and Recognition Processes

Reward and recognition processes are crucial. In our example of "pride in our craft," promotion criteria and processes should favor employees with the highest quality products in their portfolio. The best developers should be rewarded with generous bonuses and development opportunities. Without these interventions in processes and structures, creating the necessary on-the-ground experience of pride is difficult.

The Impact of Systems and Applications

Technology dictates behavior, and behavior shapes culture. As much as we try to downplay the impact of systems and applications on corporate culture (and society for that matter), the truth is obvious.

The Shift in Communication

The example of the plow at the beginning of the book is a stark illustration. Bringing it closer to corporate culture requires us to look more carefully at our systems. The increased capability of instant messaging tools at work has pushed many of us to leave emails behind. Our communication has become more frequent and concise, often just a few words. Our ability to read a long email is almost nonexistent. Work is constantly interrupted by instant messages demanding immediate responses, instead of the luxury of answering an email at our convenience. We've stopped walking over to our colleagues' desks, even when they're just a few meters away; a message is more convenient.

This is not a defense of emails, nor a yearning for the days when people would disrupt your work by walking to your desk. However, the effects of a new messaging application are deeper than we admit.

Leveraging Technology for Leadership Frameworks

Digital systems and applications comprise a significant portion of our daily experience, especially for knowledge workers. Leadership frameworks and behavior change initiatives can harness the power of technology to shape experiences.

Many organizations use Microsoft Office or MS 365 tools, 3.7 million as of 2024, to be exact. Google Docs is a humble competitor, significantly cheaper and much more focused on collaboration. The ease of co-creating documents has made Google Docs popular among students. These tools shape most of our daily experience; we read documents, send and receive emails, message colleagues, and hold meetings through them. An organization pushing its culture towards collaboration can utilize the power of changing from Microsoft to Google. It will create waves of reactions from frustration to indifference to relief. It will also send a message that the company aims to attract younger populations. Google Docs can make a difference with other collaborative leadership interventions and workflow designs.

Google is not sponsoring this book, unfortunately. And there might be other technological considerations for organizations when selecting Microsoft. The Google vs. Microsoft debate is not our focus here.

Designing Workspaces and Environments

The physical experience of an office inspires behavior. The entrance of a building, the warm work areas, thoughtful workspaces for collaborative or focused work, and sunlight-friendly seating all shape our daily work experience and subtly influence our behavior in office spaces.

The Science of Workspace Design

Unfortunately, enterprises do not widely use the science of physical spaces and their impact on human behavior. Despite mounting evidence, we continue to build large open offices instead of thoughtfully designing workplaces for different needs. An average organization usually chooses cheaper designs at the expense of productivity and employee health, likely a result of having most real estate functions under finance departments. Structures impact behavior.

Designing for Specific Behaviors

Workplaces can be designed to enforce behaviors. A seating plan based on product flow, from customer team initiation to development, production, pricing, marketing, and sales, can increase agility and collaboration.

Giving the corner office to the AI architect who develops critical AI model architecture emphasizes technical expertise over hierarchy. Even simpler interventions can send strong signals. For example, placing a large whiteboard in meeting rooms with outlined decision-making steps (problem definition, information gathering, alternative listing, etc.) will nudge meeting participants to consider rational decision-making processes.

The physical workspace is also a good place for executives to demonstrate the behaviors they expect from their leaders first hand. An executive requiring the leaders to be present in the office and accessible should be accessible themselves, by walking around the office often and having impromptu conversations at the coffee machines.

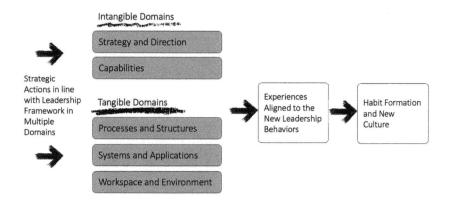

The strategic deployment of well-crafted interventions across multiple domains has the power to design transformative experiences. When seamless processes, clear leadership requirements, and intuitive software applications converge, they create a synergy that goes beyond the sum of its parts, a magical blend.

ii. Communication

Clear and well-timed communication, tailored to the audience and focused on what truly matters, can be the difference between success and failure. In fact, boring and generic communication content, using only emails or the intranet as the primary communication channels, and similar mistakes will turn the most well-designed frameworks into forgettable footnotes in an organization's history.

Authenticity is Crucial

Whatever the channel and audience segment strategies, the content must be authentic and sincere. If (because) the executive team creates the framework themselves, it is easier for them to discuss and explain it in their own words. Scripted, generic messages invite cynicism and resistance.

Although all communications professionals agree that authenticity is important, there are few good examples of authentic executives in the market. To ensure authenticity, internal communications should demand more from executives and involve external professional support, such as editors and consultants.

Additionally, executives should be encouraged to share personal developments, failures, and lessons related to the leadership framework. This can help humanize the message and make it more relatable.

Tone for Change and Transparency

A leadership framework often signals a shift in culture or priorities, and people need to understand why this change is happening and why now. The framework may be perfectly designed, but without clear communication, employees don't know where they are headed or why. Clear communication about the purpose keeps everyone informed and included.

"Pride in our craft" should be explained, creating a future vision of all team members being proud of what they have done. This, in turn, brings success to the company, a winning and proud team.

Transparent communication builds trust. While explaining the purpose at the start and updating about progress, the content must be honest and transparent. When leaders openly share what's happening, acknowledge challenges, and invite feedback, they create a sense of partnership. Employees feel like they are part of the journey, not just passengers. Moreover, leaders should be open about what they don't know and what they're still figuring out. This vulnerability can foster a culture of learning and experimentation.

It is interesting to observe that almost none of the failed leadership initiatives reported any failures until the very end, which is a sign of unhealthy governance and a lack of willingness to learn from mistakes.

Another big reason communication is crucial is adoption. A leadership framework only works if people use it consistently. Imagine trying to introduce a new system without explaining how it works or why it's valuable, confusion and frustration would be inevitable. Clear communication gives people the understanding and confidence to embrace new ways of working. To drive adoption, communication should also highlight the benefits of the leadership framework for individual employees, not just the organization as a whole.

Timing and Channel Matter

Trying to convey all messages at once is ineffective. Knowing the limits of their employees' absorption should set the limit for communication. Attention is scarce. It is important to explain "the why" first and then move forward with the plan. After that, it should be about key progress updates and early successes when they occur.

The choice of channel matters, different audience segments have different consumption habits. Not everyone checks the internal webpage for detailed news; some prefer emails, some will follow the news feed in their applications, and some would prefer short videos. More interested employees would prefer a long-format podcast conversation that goes deeper into the issues and underlying reasons.

A multi-channel customized approach is a must. Different channels will allow opportunities for two-way communication, such as Q&A sessions or forums where employees can ask questions and share their thoughts.

Feedback is Not Always Obvious

Communication needs to be flexible. The approach should be adjusted as people give feedback. Some content and channels are more suitable than others, and some content doesn't vibe with the specific audience. Listening to feedback and adapting the comms strategy make a huge difference in communication effectiveness.

Feedback is not always obvious but there is always a cue, whether it's verbal, nonverbal, behavioral, or situational. The key is to develop the ability to recognize and interpret these cues effectively. Receiving only three likes to an article from an audience of thousands should say something about the content or the channel. Channel and content might be perfect, but the audience is not interested. If the video you posted only gets one comment, there might be something you are missing there. If there are lots of comments under a post, listen to those, they are great feedback. It also means people are interested and want to know more. There is engagement.

If comms departments are open-minded and there is a safe environment for employees to say, "This communication didn't work out," then improvement and progress will come quickly. Employees give feedback in many forms.

Practical Tips to Consider

- Communication must be authentic and appropriate for the audience. Avoid using one tone and one channel, and most importantly, avoid generic, scripted formats. Lack of authenticity undermines leadership initiatives.
- Treat employees as competent adults who can see through corporate talk. This is a golden rule.
- Leaders usually need coaching to become effective communicators, and some leaders are not suited for stage performance. It is challenging to tell an executive that they are not effective on stage. Instead, communication experts should find the medium that the executive feels most comfortable with, whether it be a personal video shoot, a podcast, or serving as a silent sponsor.
- Celebrate milestones and recognize individuals or teams who exemplify the leadership framework in action, but only if their success is genuine. This reinforces the importance of the initiative and encourages others to follow suit. If the successes are half-baked and trivial, employees will understand that; remember, they are smart.
- Continuously evaluate the effectiveness of communication efforts and be willing to pivot if something isn't working. Use operational data here as well, click-through-rates, comments, digital engagement are good indicators. Employees always give feedback about communication, if you listen.
- The leadership framework communication strategy should evolve as the organization does. It is useful to handle communication in stages, launch stage for awareness, momentum for deployment, and sustained interests for long term execution, and conclusion can be four example phases.

Communication is a vast area. As with everything else, experts should lead the way. However, hiring external help can be valuable. In the end, introducing a leadership framework brings people together around a shared vision, gives them the tools and understanding to succeed, and builds trust along the way. Communication enables these. By prioritizing clear, thoughtful, and authentic communication, organizations can set their leadership frameworks up for success.

iii. Monitor and Iterate

As with any long-term strategic initiative, the impact of a leadership framework should be monitored closely. The complicated nature of intertwined interventions makes it necessary to track the organization's actual reaction.

Consistent Metrics

The best monitoring measures are the same variables used during the purpose stage. The operational data, surveys, benchmarks, and other metrics used during the problem statement investigation are also the right metrics to measure progress. While the emphasis should be on operational data, anecdotal experiences will also provide valuable insight into the extent to which changes are being adopted in the organization.

Organizations can be creative about the use of operational data. For example, the dedication to high-quality products expected with "pride in our craft" should be measured by the number of bugs, production ease, and user experience excellence from the operational systems.

Avoiding KPI Pitfalls

An important warning is not to use these metrics as KPIs for the initiative, referring to Goodhart's law: "when a measure becomes a target, it ceases to be a good measure." Setting KPIs for these initiatives will reduce a complex topic to simple measures and leave it vulnerable to target achievement manipulation. Executive teams should be mature enough to assess if they are progressing well or if there is a need to strengthen some of the messages.

Iterative Strategic Actions

Iterations of strategic actions can be decided depending on the results of continuous monitoring. By closely tracking the impact of the leadership framework and being willing to adapt as needed, organizations can ensure that their initiatives remain effective and relevant over time.

Conclusion: Effective Leadership Frameworks for Organizational Success

Throughout this section, we have explored the intricacies of leadership frameworks and their potential to drive meaningful change within organizations. Successful leadership frameworks are not merely a set of aspirational statements but rather a carefully crafted system that aligns with the organization's unique challenges, culture, and strategic objectives.

The journey begins with a deep understanding of the prerequisites: timing, purpose, readiness, and alignment. Only by thoroughly assessing these foundational elements can an organization ensure that its leadership framework resonates with its leaders and employees. The design phase then transforms these insights into a set of actionable behaviors and principles, tested and refined with real employee input.

However, even the most well-designed framework will fail without effective deployment. This is the true challenge. It requires unwavering executive sponsorship, resilience in the face of setbacks, and a multifaceted approach that touches every aspect of the organization's daily experience. From strategic direction to capability development, from processes and structures to technology and workspace design, each domain must be leveraged to create a web of reinforcing interventions.

Communication emerges as the critical thread that binds these efforts together. Authentic, transparent, and well-timed communication has the power to inspire buy-in, clarify expectations, and maintain momentum. It is the key to transforming a leadership framework from a static document into a living, breathing part of the organization's DNA.

Finally, the work does not end with deployment. Monitoring progress, learning from setbacks, and iterating based on feedback are essential to ensuring that the leadership framework remains relevant and impactful over time.

In conclusion, designing and implementing an effective leadership framework is a complex and challenging endeavor, but one with immense potential for driving organizational success. By approaching this process with rigor, authenticity, and a commitment to continuous improvement, organizations can unlock the full potential of their leaders and create a culture that thrives in the face of any challenge. The path may be difficult, but the rewards, a unified, adaptable, and high-performing organization, are well worth the effort.

Before we shift our focus to the Future of Leadership, a relevant case study will provide practical context for the theories we've explored.

Case Study: TechSphere International - The Journey of a Leadership Framework

This chapter covers a practical example of designing and deploying a leadership framework while remaining true to the theory. Whether you are a seasoned leader or a leadership practitioner, you will find practical insights and reusable terminology to build or enhance your framework.

> The case study is a deep dive and intended to give the full context of the organization. The reader can choose to skip the case study and move to the "future of leadership" chapter, if the length becomes too extensive.

The framework presented in the case serves as a strong foundation for organizations across various contexts. It is more of a broad framework than detailed behavior descriptions.

For easier reading, the case study will be through the lens of a fictitious company, TechSphere, and its fictional Chief People Officer, Sam. While the company and characters are fictional, the case, challenges, and changes are inspired by real events and a genuine context. The chapter has the structure of the model discussed earlier:

Three Phases of Leadership Framework

1. Prerequisites:	2. Design:	3. Deployment:
i. Timing ii. Purpose iii. Leadership Readiness iv. Cultural Alignment	i. Description of Wanted Behaviors ii. Headings to Group Behaviors	i. Strategic Actions in Multiple Domains ii. Communication iii. Monitor and Iterate

Prerequisites Timing (and the Context)

It had been less than a year since Sam joined TechSphere International as the Chief People Officer. The function used to be called human resources, but the name had been changed just before Sam got on board. TechSphere is a technology company, not one of the big ones like Google, but a more traditional infrastructure company like HP that serves both enterprise and individual customers. With roughly ten thousand employees and a geographical spread, they were doing well but probably below their true capacity.

TechSphere had a healthy business, albeit slow growth and no significant competition. Their competition landscape was mild and steady, with only one real competitor and almost equal market shares. The workforce was diverse in tenure and age. Some legacy units were aging and had high tenure. Newer technology units had younger generations, with an average tenure of a few years in the company.

There were, however, perceived problems in productivity and execution of tasks and projects. The level of output did not match the effort and resources they seem to put into the business.

Even though they knew that productivity issues were not present everywhere in the organization, there was an overall sentiment that some things restrained the organization from reaching its potential output. They could see that some simple product features were taking too long to develop. Once developed, some of those features could not pass the quality and security thresholds. The teams were working hard, but something was off. Everything took too much time and effort.

The Executive Team

The CEO and Sam invested significant energy in changing the team and hiring the best talent from the market, which was paying off. The team now had the intellectual capacity, the required experience, and the mental maturity to make a change. Sam called it "a rare constellation." They just needed to be a team: Rallying behind a common vision, relying on each other, and moving as one.

HR Team Capability

Although the people function had good, dedicated team members, its main occupation was administrative HR work. The talent management function, where culture and leadership related tasks are usually found, had good foundations but was not geared up to deploy a leadership framework.

In general, the organization lacked the expertise to design and deploy a leadership framework. There had been some attempts in the past to formulate the values of the organization, with varying success on the ground.

Timing and the Q3 Meeting

In Q3, the leadership team held a day-long meeting, and the year was not looking good. The agenda was packed with budget discussions and sales targets. The meeting also included an hour-long discussion about accountability. Conversations had suggested that the leaders lacked a sense of accountability. One executive had already invited the organization's "culture champion" to come and do a workshop.

They spent the first six hours of the meeting having difficult discussions about reducing the operating expense (OPEX) run rate. They debated cutting large budget items, reallocating resources to a few big sales deals, and delaying or canceling others. It was a tough day. At three o'clock in the afternoon, the "culture champion" arrived to talk about accountability and how to fix leadership.

He walked into an already tense atmosphere where everyone was focused on getting through the next four months. Sam slightly shifted in the chair with the opening line, "We have an accountability problem," and a text appeared in the team group chat: "No, we have an OPEX problem, and he is part of it."

That text revealed a lot. The group was just not ready to discuss leadership that day, and the approach didn't help. The team remained polite and engaged in a good conversation, as one does. The moment he left, they all returned to discussing OPEX savings. No one ever spoke about that session again.

Behavior and culture changes are tricky because they have little tolerance for failure. A meeting going south, like this one, can lead to a long-lasting cooling period before leadership topics can be approached again. The same holds true for failed culture initiatives and leadership framework launches; organizations often need years before attempting another initiative. The second attempt will face heftier resistance as the organization's immune system remembers how to resist the previous failed initiative.

TechSphere was lucky, they never had a failed culture initiative. Even though there were financial challenges, a few tweaks would get them back on track. They will not be performing at their best, but it wasn't a crisis. It gave enough sense of urgency to act, but not a full-blown crisis to overtake all activities. A few quarters later, once the crisis is dealt with, they could work on the underlying challenges and leadership.

Purpose: Understanding the Real Problem

Quarterly business reviews were important, it was where each executive presented their past quarter, their numbers, and plans for the next quarter. Those indicators were almost always positive. The slides always showed a world where everything went well; all charts were green.

However, on the ground, internal stakeholders were not satisfied with the level of output from their neighboring units. Even some grumbling voices could be heard during those quarterly meetings from the other executives. "You say everything is going well, but we had serious downtime in our systems last month," was a regular statement to dispel the magic of green indicators. Since it was a newly formed team, they were careful with each other, though nobody pushed too hard.

What Was Not Working

Some underlying problems and their symptoms were easy to pinpoint:

1. There was an obvious lack of collaborative work between major units. There were times when different teams in the same unit, looking after the same value chain, did not talk to each other. For example, a product feature that should have been cleared by the security unit went directly to production without their involvement. As a result, they had to put the product launch on hold for weeks.

2. There were clear signs of an unhealthy decision-making process. At times, the required parties were not involved in decision-making, resulting in decisions that were deemed irrelevant. Decisions pivoted rapidly and frequently, and management did not know the exact reasons.

3. Execution of agreed-upon actions or decisions was also not a given. Leaders and employees felt free not to follow commitments made, which created tension across the organization. Decisions and commitments did not carry too much weight.

4. They had a strong culture of "speak up," where everyone was free to state their opinions in any setting. That was a great advantage of the company; they could utilize the diversity of thoughts. However, that freedom to state one's opinion went a few steps too far, making decision-making impossible. Everyone's opinions mattered at the same level, whether you had a gut feeling about the topic or you were the top expert in the company. Your opinions had the same vote.

All these signals and sentiments needed to be tested with facts, starting with operational data and proceeding through the stack of anecdotal experiences, surveys, and benchmarks.

Operational Data

Execution Delays and Constant Re-scoping

> The project management tool revealed constant delays and rescoping in product feature development. The average delivery time for product features was getting longer. Decisions were

frequently changed, leading to time overruns. Explanations for delays often included accusations against other departments.

Customer Support Response Time

After new product launches, case resolution took days or weeks instead of hours, impacting customer satisfaction. The ticketing system confirmed concerns about the disconnect between sales and customer support.

Micromanagement and Lack of Trust

Microsoft's insights report showed managers attending excessive cross-functional meetings with their subordinates present, indicating potential micromanagement and tense meetings where managers defended their turf.

No Formal Processes in Place

Investigations revealed a lack of standardized processes and systems usage. For example, new hire approvals took weeks due to inconsistent approval processes. Similarly, selling enterprise solutions lacked proper technical department involvement and customer voice integration in planning.

The company relied on personal connections and historical practices rather than well-defined procedures. Sam was surprised by the extent of the lack of standardization.

Anecdotal Experiences

The executive team usually had senior management and experts attend their meetings and present progress in their areas. The topics included sales targets, compliance, product roadmaps, and future business opportunities. If the team asked the right questions, those conversations revealed a lot.

1. The sales departments have not vetted a few products for the enterprises. Product development and marketing have worked together to develop products and features without representing the customer through the sales account managers. Not being involved, sales was resistant to selling the new products and features. The disconnect was deep.

2. Compliance and digital security were involved in product development on paper, but when they voiced concerns, they were politely ignored. Real collaboration was missing.

3. Customer support was performing poorly. There were too many manual processes and complicated products, and sales were not preparing customer services for new product features.

4. When their decisions were questioned, senior leaders could not provide solid facts about why they made them. Faced with resistance, they were easily compelled to change their decisions.

5. Once there was a slight hiccup, leaders were quick to find excuses. Sometimes, it felt like listening to schoolchildren explain that their dog ate their homework.

TechSphere Employee Survey Results

Their employee survey indicated serious problems in execution, collaboration, and decision-making. The employees said that there was extreme bureaucracy and that getting things done was very difficult.

Key Challenges:

-   Process inefficiencies and excessive bureaucracy create significant operational barriers
-   Limited cross-departmental collaboration and siloed operations impede progress
-   Communication gaps between units and leadership lead to misaligned efforts
-   Slow management response time and unclear decision-making processes delay project execution

Organizational Strengths:

-   Strong professional environment
-   Excellent work-life balance
-   Positive evaluation of direct management

While TechSphere faced operational challenges, particularly in execution and collaboration, the organization maintains a strong foundation of professionalism and employee satisfaction to build upon for future improvements.

Benchmark

Like many of its peers, TechSphere was used to working with big consulting companies. It always sought help with organizational design and strategy setting from those partners. Naturally, it also required some benchmark data from one of the industry-leading consultancy firms. Benchmark reports also showed gaps in efficiency throughout the company's output rates. TechSphere had significantly higher costs than similar operations of similar size around the world.

Sensemaking and Synthesis

This information flow is an insight-rich place to start the design journey. All that data and insights require facilitation and a good level of sense making to arrive at the underlying problem statement.

The information came in waves, and the executive team held multiple meetings for each source. There were a few half-day sessions with the benchmarking company, a workshop for employee surveys, and so on. Toward the end, a few weeks into the journey of understanding the challenges, they consolidated all the data sources for final sensemaking. By that time, a project team of skilled analysts was working under Sam. The executive team used McKinsey's 7S model[60] strategy execution model. Strategy, structure, systems, style, staff, skills, and shared values, the 7S, gave a good sense of interdependencies for the necessary change, and made it visible that they needed a systems thinking rather than isolated interventions. Leadership was at the core of enabling those seven levers.

A paper by Joanna Radomska and Cyprian Kozyra called "Awareness of strategy execution barriers in the decision-making process: moderated mediation analysis," which came handy. It cemented the role of leadership. Strategy execution had many levers, but leadership was the most impactful of those, according to the paper. By focusing on leadership as the linchpin, they could tackle execution barriers holistically.

---

[60] Enduring Ideas: The 7-S Framework | McKinsey

Even though some of these concepts are not novel revelations, discussing them together as a team and having meaningful conversations about real-life experiences helped the team align their thinking about the root causes.

The Problem Statement

The performance during those first few conversations was a solid sign that the executive team could pull off a substantial change. The major challenges in the organization were now revealed through facts. Execution was a problem, but underneath lay collaboration and repeated change of decisions as core reasons. This conclusion was not easy to make, even though it was obvious when the pieces of the puzzle got together. The data gathering and sense making conversations primed the team for a deep understanding.

Finally, they found what they needed to fix: Collaboration and decision making. The actual delivery or tasks were in good shape.

Leadership Readiness

Executive Team Readiness

Making an organization-wide leadership intervention requires a cohesive executive team. Realizing this, the TechSphere executive team decided to focus on their internal dynamics first, before addressing broader leadership topics within the company. As the famous flight safety instruction advises, "Tend to yourself before tending to others."

Finding the right team coach was crucial. Sam and the CEO found an effective coach after a few conversations and good references. The coach worked with the team for about a year, shaping them into a more harmonious and effective unit.

The roles of the different parties during the process were:

- The CEO, being attentive, open-minded, and setting expectations.
- The HR leader, catalyze the process, coach the CEO and the team.
- The team members, being attentive and ready to change.
- The coach, anchoring the change and designing interventions.

A common methodology that team coaches follow is based on Patrick Lencioni's famous book The Five Dysfunctions of a Team. The standard starting point for intervention is to understand the team's level of trust and strengthen it with various vulnerability and relationship-building activities. The coach starts by building trust within the team. Then, they pursue impactful interventions that benefit team dynamics.

The Art of Listening

The first intervention focused on listening. The team used Otto Scharmer's Four Levels of Listening framework:

1. Downloading - reconfirming what we already know
2. Factual Listening - gathering new information with an open mind
3. Empathic Listening - connecting with the emotions and experiences of the speaker
4. Generative Listening - connecting with the highest future potential

The team worked on staying mostly at the Empathic Listening level. They also introduced a no-laptop policy during meetings and restructured their meetings to be more intentional. These changes led to more engaging and productive conversations.

Handling cynical team members required genuine conversations and the CEO's direct involvement to get them on board. It worked to have genuine conversations about "what would you have done, if you were me". More resistant executives, having been asked their opinion, felt more involved. A sincere but firm "I need your help to make this successful" from the CEO worked for them.

Usually, an intelligent design based on science with a credible team coach helps.

The Art of Intentional Dialogue

With better listening skills, the team moved on to mastering intentionality and clarity in their conversations. They aimed to make sense together and design solutions synergistically.

To be more synergistic, they ensured each person's comments advanced the conversation, either building upon or constructively challenging previous statements. The CEO called out tangents until this became a team habit.

They drew inspiration from the "Conversations for Action" framework to improve clarity, focusing on making clear requests and commitments.

Daniel Schmachtenberger, founding member of The Consilience Project, works primarily on improving public sensemaking and dialogue. Daniel Schmachtenberger's philosophy of synergistic truth-seeking was an inspiration. This philosophy emphasizes the importance of integrating diverse perspectives and a comprehensive understanding of reality.

Following that, TechSphere executives embraced a simple rule: they would always advance the conversation, either building on what someone had said or challenging a statement constructively so that the team could reach a higher level of truth.

Combined with good listening, that created an environment of collective intelligence and teamwork.

Broader Leadership Community Readiness

The readiness of the leadership community became a more subjective judgment of the executive team. They have used some facts like average managerial tenure they had in the organization, leadership behavior insights from employee engagement surveys, and some of the more formal assessments the leaders have gone through.

At the end of the day, the executive team decided that the organization had enough leadership capital and maturity to initiate a leadership framework. There was a good mix of senior leaders who knew what they were doing and some more junior ones who had the right potential. The team decided to have a broader framework description rather than specific behaviors that an organization would deploy when maturity was lacking.

At the same time, the leadership community was ready for what was coming; they were anticipating it and mostly eager for the opportunities ahead. After all, the executive team had some changes already, so the change was "in the air".

Moving to Design Phase

The TechSphere team had done thorough work that would ensure success in the coming steps. They had collected and evaluated all relevant insights, understood the purpose of the work they were about to do, and built their own readiness as a team.

This journey took roughly six months for the team. While working on the team dynamics and the quality of conversations, they also started to formulate solutions to repeating patterns using their new powers of listening and conversing. The initial understanding from the operational data and their anecdotal experiences was painfully accurate:

The organization needed to be more collaborative. The decision-making process and commitment to decisions also needed strengthening. The team was ready to start designing the leadership framework. With the groundwork done, the actual design would be easier and a more joyful experience.

Designing TechSphere Leadership Framework

While laying the groundwork in the prerequisites phase, the executive team was already doing much of the design work. During their meetings, conversations, and daily work, they discussed the behaviors that they wanted to see more of.

Statements like "OK, now we need to be decisive here" or "Can we please stick to the decisions we have taken? We are not executing as we agreed" were commonly used by the executive team. Behaviors started to shift even before they specifically named the direction. The executives even started using those words in their own teams, already setting expectations.

During one of the team meetings, the CEO presented a new concept that he had been discussing with Sam. He wanted the team to be more "generative." TechSphere leaders were quick to finger-point and state excuses, but the CEO wanted this to change, starting with his team.

Engineering-heavy organizations have the tendency to see what is not working. The CEO wanted to harness that ability toward the solution rather than only stating what was not working. He wanted his people to come up with alternative solutions when they saw a problem.

In one of those meetings, Sam then asked the CEO directly: "Given all our work together in the past months, how do you expect we should be relating to each other?" The answer came out very clear: "I want us to be generative and collaborative. As a third element, we also need to be decisive." People were nodding around the table; it was a silent but strong consensus. Sam was smiling as he wrote those three on the white board: Generative, Collaborative, and Decisive. They were designing the framework.

Describing the Three Capabilities: Generative, Collaborative, and Decisive

Time to write down definitions

When the team felt it was time to formally define their expectations for themselves and the organization, they decided to hold a structured workshop and seek external help. The goal was to align, fine-tune, and document the definitions of "Generative", "Collaborative", and "Decisive".

Sam had seen many times that the assumed common definition of words often derails the work before it has even started. He wanted to make sure everybody understood the same things from Generative, Collaborative, and Decisive.

So the executive team convened for a half-day workshop to align and articulate the expectations under the three headings. During the session, the team ironed out some surprising misalignments. It was an eye-opener; after months of conversations, still encountering differences of understanding made the workshop even more valuable.

- Some in the team thought "Collaborative" meant involving everyone, discussing things openly, and deciding together. However, what they really wanted was to involve only the necessary people and add them at the right time.
- "Generative" did not mean being positive about everything. As engineers, they valued critical thinking. False positivity would harm our business and culture. What we wanted was

a generative approach, solutions attached to challenges for a better tomorrow.
- "Decisive" did not imply making fast decisions. It meant that the decision-making process should be rational and fact-based. Once a decision was made, it was time to execute. Revisiting decisions and pivoting were acceptable, but only under significantly changed circumstances.

The Actual Definitions

These alignments were another wave of agreement and show camaraderie in the team. The team quickly came up with the following three descriptions:

——----------------------------

Being **generative** means we are solution-focused and bring new opportunities to life.

At TechSphere, we solve immediate problems and envision future possibilities. Whether facing challenges or identifying opportunities for innovation, we are focused on bringing ideas and solutions to reality. We believe in the power of ideas and creativity, and we combine this belief with an action orientation and resilience. We think first about what is possible, even if we might have to overcome challenges to get there.

Being **collaborative** means that we harness the right strengths at the right time of our teams.

At TechSphere, we develop and commit to common goals. We actively engage the right people with the right skills, value their contributions, and cultivate strong relationships to achieve these goals. Collaborative people build trust and utilize expertise, driving for collaborative execution.

Being **decisive** means making fact-based, thoughtful decisions and committing to their execution.

At TechSphere, we make thoughtful, timely decisions and are committed to their execution. This means considering all relevant information, balancing urgency with due diligence. Decisiveness also means a commitment to execution and agility—acting swiftly when possible while being willing to pause when necessary.

—-------------------------

The team chose not to delve into more detailed behavior descriptions than those provided above. After all, they wanted to leave some autonomy for the leaders. An important principle they always followed was the belief that their employees were smart adults with common sense. When trusted, they always delivered. Providing more detailed descriptions would confine them to a tight space. The team trusted that TechSphere people would understand the general direction and would know what needed to be done.

Even without deploying this framework, seeing the team at work in such a harmonious way made the CEO hopeful about the coming changes.

Deploying TechSphere Leadership Framework

Organizations often prefer formal launch events to introduce new values or leadership frameworks, creating momentum and awareness. These high-quality events and ambitious commitments lead to high employee expectations. However, if the implementation momentum doesn't match the initial launch, disappointment quickly follows.

For TechSphere, Sam and the CEO believed a more subtle launch was appropriate. The executive team consistently discussed the three capabilities, and during a quarterly all-staff meeting, they formally launched the definitions and interventions work. The CEO and executives firmly communicated their expectations and commitment to strong enablement through interventions. An internal marketing campaign with visuals and banners created awareness and buzz, but the humble tone acknowledged the real work ahead lay in implementation.

TechSphere Strategic Actions

TechSphere deployed a wave of actions across the five domains, as we will discuss below. This is not an exhaustive list but rather a representative list of actions.

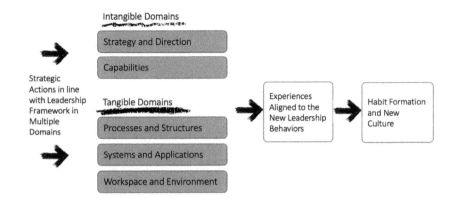

Strategy and Direction

For TechSphere, the CEO started using generative and collaborative language early on in all employee meetings. Although the three words were not used anywhere in the strategy document, they were constantly in the language of the CEO and the executives. Over time, they could see a softening of the organization's blaming tone.

Words, especially coming repeatedly and genuinely from the CEO, are powerful.

Capabilities

For TechSphere, when they expected the leaders to be more decisive, emphasizing fact-based decision-making, they needed to increase the leaders' capability to evaluate data and analyze.

They started with increasing the data literacy and fact-based decision-making skills of leaders and served as an ignition towards behavior change for leaders. Leaders were expected to question data and utilize critical thinking more. Those behaviors of critical thinking and attention to facts made the decision-making process much more diligent.

Similarly, working collaboratively requires specific skills. Some examples include facilitating inclusive meetings, creating a culture that values expertise over opinions, giving experts more space without alienating others, and managing stakeholders and relationships when decisions do not favor all stakeholders. All these daily tasks and actions require specific skills. Without formal development and enablement, leaders might feel unsupported and underequipped, even if they are willing to adopt new behaviors.

The people team (HR) were struggling to design all these interventions in leadership capabilities. There was also so much that the leaders could absorb. Sam's team needed to spread those capability interventions across quarters.

Even though they chose only three leadership headings for their framework, even those were difficult to deploy together. This was a decision the TechSphere team needed to take. One option is to approach this from a sequential perspective. They would do one leadership heading at a time and then move to the other. And within a year, they would cover all three. Alternatively, the second option would be to deploy all three and spread the interventions throughout the year. They chose the latter. They would do interventions in all three areas.

As a result, they have partnered with a learning content provider and designed rational decision making, inclusive meeting facilitation, data analytics, and critical thinking trainings. They all had two levels, for leaders and employees, or for experts and beginners, and consisted of in-class trainings, online trainings, and follow-up sessions. It was a big investment, a clear sign towards the organization.

Processes and Structure

Promotions

TechSphere put their three capabilities, Generative, Collaborative, and Decisive, in the selection criteria of their leadership roles. At first, they only put them as capabilities to explore the capabilities of the candidates. It was a pragmatic insertion of required behaviors in the job descriptions of leadership positions. Sam's team also added representative questions to ask during the interviews to inquire about those three capabilities. During the second year, they worked with a partner company to develop more formal assessments of their leadership candidates. At the end of the first eighteen months of the project, having demonstrated those three capabilities became a rule to be promoted to a visible leader¬ship role.

Some of the questions used in interviews:

- Generative, Scenario Exploration: "Imagine you just joined TechSphere, and your team is facing a complex problem with no clear solution. Walk me through your process for generating and evaluating new ideas." Evaluates the candidate's approach to ideation, creativity, and risk-taking.
- Generative, Opportunity Recognition: "If you saw a process that could be completely reimagined to create significant value for the company, how would you convince others it's worth exploring?" Tests how they champion new ideas and overcome potential resistance.
- Collaborative, Building Alignment: "How would you bring together people with different perspectives to define a shared vision for a project? What steps would you take to ensure everyone feels heard?" Reveals how they create mutual goals and trust among team members.
- Decisive, Decision Framework: "Suppose you have two competing strategies to achieve a critical goal. How would you approach making a decision within tight deadlines?" Evaluates how they balance urgency with the need for data and stakeholder input.
- Decisive, Executing Decisions: "Once a decision is made, what measures or processes do you put in place to ensure it gets implemented effectively?" Shows how they handle follow-through, accountability, and alignment to action.

Changing the Product Development Cycle

The tone is set by how the value chain operates and how tasks flow throughout the organization. A fast go-to-market flow within the company signals agility. The working style in the organization's core processes is a good place to start catalyzing change, but it is also the most difficult place to change radically.

The TechSphere products team identified that product feature development would often be vetoed toward the end of the project, causing development units to start over. For well-functioning teams, the average time to develop a product feature was around ninety days. If the development unit was not in good standing with the sales team, the time to develop a product feature averaged around a hundred and forty days. This was a significant difference.

Senior management of sales and product sat together and defined critical steps for collaborative design, decision-making, and execution. For the first time, they had a formal process and definitions for when to invite whom and what approval was needed. They kept the process light and empowered the leaders on the ground.

Alongside these process tweaks, the team also replaced a few critical leaders with more collaborative ones, which made the process changes effective. This highlights the importance of multilayer interventions.

The above change sent a shock wave for TechSphere, especially the change of the more non-collaborative leaders and the formalized mandates to the lower levels. The CEO was particularly proud of how his team worked on this and did not compromise on their purpose.

Identifying Collaborative Teams

A significant improvement that came with the advancement of HR analytics is the ability to monitor collaborative work in the organization through an organizational network analysis (ONA). ONA records and analyzes the interaction points, such as who talks to whom and at what frequency. This information is a good indicator of collaboration. Linking this information to project stages will give organizations further insights. At what stage of the project has the unit collaborated with which unit? In theory, one could see the communication activities at the product ideation phase.

Operational data from the communication tools in organizations makes this information accessible and accurate. It shows who emailed, had meetings with, or messages, and who is easy to reach.

For example, TechSphere could see which product managers emailed and had feature meetings with commercial units and their frequency of correspondence. They could pinpoint the units that worked closely with commercial units and follow up on the development time of the product feature and its commercial success.

Once the well-collaborating units are identified, product teams can replicate and scale the good practices. One of the factors of collaboration was the rotation of leaders. Whenever someone from the product teams was appointed as a leader in a commercial unit, the collaboration between those teams increased. TechSphere then put more emphasis on cross-functional appointments.

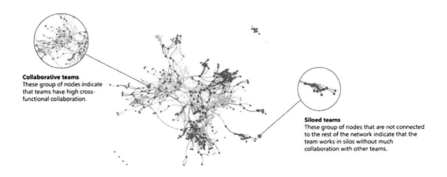

Collaborative teams
These group of nodes indicate that teams have high cross-functional collaboration.

Siloed teams
These group of nodes that are not connected to the rest of the network indicate that the team works in silos without much collaboration with other teams.

The above visual is from Deloitte's article "Harnessing Organization Network Analysis (ONA)" by Maya Bodan et al. It depicts a good example of ONA analysis, in which organizations can identify "what is going on" with operational data.

Systems and Applications

Interventions that design the digital experience to reinforce the preferred behavior are, therefore, impactful. Being a technology company, TechSphere aimed to utilize it.

Information Accessibility

If systemic enablement is in place, some behaviors can be introduced and monitored much more effectively. For example, consider the leadership capability "Decisive," which requires rational decision-making based on evaluating facts and data. TechSphere could not expect leaders to make decisions based on data if the relevant data wasn't available. This meant accurate data through dashboards and analytics should be implemented. Consumer insights, such as satisfaction scores, top-selling products by districts, and product feature usage data, became accessible in real-time dashboards.

In the past, it took time and effort to request additional information and review slides, and leaders made decisions based on incomplete data. With the newly created dashboards, everyone could slice and dice the information as they wanted. No intermediary analyses were needed. They could also see the impact of their decisions early in the process and course-correct when necessary.

The introduction of these dashboards and real-time data access was strengthened with data fluency training for employees, a new decision-making process, and a strong call for fact-based decision-making through the leadership framework. These multilayered interventions improved the decision-making process significantly in only two quarters.

Unfortunately, the idea of moving from Microsoft Office to Google Docs could never be seen in daylight.

Workplace and Environment

Simple Floor Swaps

TechSphere did not want to start a large real estate project. They had budget restrictions for the first year. However, there were low-hanging fruits. For example, the units that needed to work together the most were occupying different floors in the same building. This meant that they never got together by the coffee machine. TechSphere shuffled the floor seating plans and got the product and commercial units together on the same floors. The organization's value chain from product development to marketing, pricing, and sales was now co-located on the same floor. The seating of those smaller teams was designed literally to match the flow in the value chain.

This physical move, combined with the changes to the product development process mentioned in the previous chapter, had an amplifying effect.

Communication

The TechSphere executive team started by applying the Generative, Collaborative, and Decisive qualities to themselves. They consistently formulated the message as "we want to show up as Generative, Collaborative, and Decisive" rather than positioning these as demands from leaders. This was an appreciated inclusion; they were all subject to the same standards in the organization.

The communication team utilized different channels, from simple emails to long-format podcasts with executives, to one-minute short mobile videos about the successes and billboards in the building. The tone was not intrusive and was rather in the flow of daily work. The "faces" of change were selected carefully to reflect everyday employees and executives as sponsors. There were highly appreciated expert talks about being decisive and collaborative a few times every quarter.

The communication team partnered with a stellar agency that handled content creation and channel optimization. Their expertise enhanced the team's abilities.

End of TechSphere Case Study

A leadership framework is a long-term investment that should be approached with care and thought and within the right context. Rushed work can have long-lasting damaging effects. TechSphere took its time, was intentional, and allowed the framework to emerge through thoughtful discussions over a period of time.

Even if the result is not a formal leadership framework, the thoughtful conversations, efforts to improve team cohesiveness, and collective sensemaking will have a tremendous positive impact on your business and people. The journey itself is rewarding.

TechSphere's leadership framework, Generative, Collaborative, and Decisive, emerged through discussions of "how do we want to show up for our organization and team." Their aim was to create a set of guiding principles about how the executives expect themselves as individuals and as a team to show up. Some final benefits and summary of the three capabilities, Generative, Collaborative, and Decisive, are:

1. There were only three of them. Simple and relevant. Any leadership framework with more than five headings will be very challenging to implement.

2. Generative, Collaborative, and Decisive attitudes and styles were broad enough to be relevant to any situation in our

context. In the end, they were not only for leaders but also for employees.

3. They were inclusive. Everyone could be Generative, Collaborative, and Decisive. These were not leadership skills that companies assessed against and had the leaders pass or fail. They were attitudes that, with some training and enablement, every leader could demonstrate.

We hope this section gave enough practical insights to inspire further conversations in your organizations.

A Glimpse into The Future of Leadership

The COVID-19 pandemic has changed how we view leadership. It has made the humane side more visible, increasing our attention to developing more empathetic and humane leaders.

With generative AI, advancing in its ability to understand, interpret, and reason in human language, the concept of leadership is poised for significant transformation, one that we argue will lead to a better future.

The changes will be drastic in two areas: Interpreting behavior data and coaching.

Interpreting Behavior Data with AI

Artificial Intelligence (AI) is revolutionizing the way organizations gather, consolidate, and interpret behavior data. As AI becomes increasingly integrated into all platforms, it can collect vast amounts of data from various sources, such as meeting transcripts, emails, group chats, interactions with enterprise content, and work habits throughout the day. This wealth of information flows into a centralized database, where AI can analyze it and build detailed profiles of actual behaviors.

The key advantage of AI-driven behavior analysis lies in its objectivity. Traditional methods like assessments and engagement surveys rely heavily on subjective observations and reporting, leading to limited accuracy and detail. In contrast, AI can draw conclusions based on situational behavior data from the original source, significantly enhancing the objectivity of the insights.

A typical 360 assessment will transform traditional surveys based on subjective observation "She is a democratic leader"

Unlike traditional surveys that might yield simplistic results like 'She is a democratic leader,' generative AI can provide more contextual and accurate insights. Here is an example:

> "Sarah asks for opinions before making an important decision. She puts the proper emphasis on expertise and avoids listening to all voices.
>
> When she is stressed, she switches to autocratic decision-making even though she gives everyone enough time to express themselves.
>
> Afternoons are the best time for her to listen and consider others' opinions; in the mornings, her mind is less focused on others. After her check-ins with her manager, she tends to be more open to new ideas.
>
> Sarah listens to Kate the most on her team. When Sarah needs to decide, Kate's ideas have an implementation rate of 25%. However, Sarah ignores Bruce most of the time, even though she is respectful and hears him out. Bruce, who has a 2% idea implementation rate, is likely looking for a new job.
>
> Sarah is ranked in the top 10% of leaders in Democratic Leadership style."

AI-powered behavior analysis not only provides insights into individual leadership styles but also reveals overall organizational trends. With a comprehensive view, organizations can better understand the climate in selected units and geographies. These trend insights can range from identifying parts of the organization with talent-developing leaders to areas where employees struggle with non-collaborative managers.

Moreover, AI can go beyond merely analyzing behavior data and actively contribute to leadership development. By leveraging the scientific knowledge of human psychology and organizational behavior, AI can provide personalized coaching to leaders. It can identify areas for improvement, suggest strategies to enhance leadership skills, and offer real-time guidance based on the leader's specific behavioral patterns.

While the scenario of AI gathering and analyzing behavior data is not yet a reality, technological advancements and the address of data governance and privacy concerns will make it increasingly feasible. The ability to access and interpret factual information at this level will transform the way organizations understand and develop their leaders.

As we embrace the potential of AI in interpreting behavior data, it is crucial to ensure that it is used ethically and responsibly. Organizations must establish clear guidelines and safeguards to protect employee privacy and prevent misuse of the collected data. Transparency, consent, and security should be at the forefront of any AI-driven behavior analysis initiative.

In conclusion, integrating AI into interpreting behavior data holds immense promise for organizations. By providing objective insights, identifying organizational trends, and offering personalized coaching, AI has the potential to revolutionize leadership development. As we navigate this exciting frontier, it is essential to strike a balance between leveraging the power of AI and upholding ethical standards to create a thriving and empowering workplace culture.

Coaching

Conversational AI already has consumer use cases for therapy and coaching. Character.ai, an AI conversational chatbot platform, already has 475 psychologist bots and has facilitated 78 million conversations in one year[61], mostly with younger generations.

There are already startups offering AI coaching services to enterprises. While those solutions are not yet fully proven, they have won over large-scale customers. Soon, companies will seek to implement enterprise-branded AI coaches responsible for mentoring and coaching employees and leaders based on the latest science and the preferred behaviors dictated by the organization. TechSphere, for example, could fine-tune future AI coaches to detect non-collaborative leaders

---

[61]   The Rise of AI Therapy Bots: Character.ai's Psychologist Dominates the Digital Mental Health Landscape

and coach them to work better with other departments without being overly intrusive.

The significant advantage of AI coaches is their ability to provide real-time support to leaders in need. These coaches are anticipated to be integrated into the daily workflow via the messaging and meeting platforms used by the company, such as Slack or Microsoft Teams. This integration will enable the AI to support leaders during stressful meetings, offering encouragement or prompting them to take a calming breath. Immediately following the meeting, the AI coach would debrief the leader, highlighting strengths and areas for improvement.

Access to real-time, knowledgeable, and cost-effective coaching will provide organizations with a notable competitive edge. It is also foreseen that these AI coaches will soon be integrated into overarching platforms like Microsoft Copilot, which already possess behavioral data on employees and leaders, facilitating the implementation of AI coaching.

However, significant risks must be acknowledged and carefully considered:

1. Observation could easily transition into surveillance, potentially leading to a dystopian future where companies demote leaders based on AI coach assessments. This could result in leaders becoming overly cautious and aware of their actions and words, diminishing authenticity and fostering a culture of fear-based leadership.

2. The guidance provided by AI coaches may eventually create homogeneous, generic leaders. Encouraging all leaders to adhere to a standardized form of collaboration could ultimately reduce behavioral deviations, which often serve as the wellspring of genuine diversity of thought and creativity.

These risks, along with numerous related security and privacy concerns, warrant careful examination. Nevertheless, access to real-time improvement and learning opportunities is believed to yield a net positive impact.

Real-time coaching may evolve into augmented leadership, with AI coaches collaborating with human leaders and gradually assuming certain leadership responsibilities. The AI coach may begin allocating tasks, drafting initial budgets, attending less critical meetings armed with the knowledge gained from the leader, and so on.

Ultimately, it is conceivable that AI will, and perhaps should, perform leadership within organizations. There will likely come a time when AI capabilities surpass those of human leaders. At that juncture, AI will be equipped to lead, coach, and develop humans, serving as an objective, all-good, endlessly patient leader that everyone requires. There is also a possibility that with AI assuming leadership roles, unnecessary politics and competition within organizations will be eliminated. AI, as the ultimate fair manager, could create a more enjoyable work environment.

With this thought, we conclude our exploration of leadership by looking to the horizon with immense optimism, eagerly anticipating the substantial quality improvements AI will bring to the experience of being led in the emerging landscape.

———————————————————————————————————

SECTION 5

Introduction to Skills and Skill-Based Organization

Starting with the late 2010, the human resources world became more interested in utilizing skills and capabilities and put them at the center of their talent practices. COVID accelerated this trend when some skills became urgently in demand, and some skills became irrelevant overnight. Utilizing the skills people have in the relevant role where they are needed became a demand.

The obvious advantage of skills-based talent practices is that they help make promotions, development, and hiring fairer and more rational. Using a well-designed skills framework serves two major purposes:

1. The pace at which new technologies are introduced and the deeper expertise required to implement them strengthen executives' concerns about future readiness. Organizations need to better understand and quantify their capability needs and be proactive about acquiring those capabilities.

2. Employee surveys consistently identify a lack of development and career progression as the reason for retention and engagement issues. Skills-based talent practices are proposed to help with employee development and career opportunities. According to Korn Ferry, skills-based organizations are 107% more likely to place talent effectively and 98% more likely to retain high performers[62].

---

[62] Redefining a Skills-Based Organization

The Broader Shift

Beyond the two major but more obvious purposes above, a skills-based organization points towards a perspective change in work design. Employees and their skills become equally important as tasks when designing the work and formulating jobs.

In smaller organizations like startups, we can see that the jobs evolve based on the skills of the individuals. A startup with only twelve employees will add new tasks and responsibilities to individuals' work depending on what they are good at. A large multinational company of a hundred thousand people will be more likely to stick with job descriptions with a set of standard tasks. However, a recent Deloitte survey found that 63% of current work being performed falls outside of people's core job descriptions[63]. The standard job description of large companies does not work in real life.

Noticing that, organizations are adopting a natural shift towards having a broader description of roles, especially with highly skilled employees. A brilliant product manager who should only look after brand management tasks is also involved in mobile application user interfaces, web design, pricing, and vendor management. The job description of a product manager then becomes broader and more like a frame than a list of tasks.

The evolution towards broader responsibility frames can use individuals' skill sets to decide on frames. Organizations can accelerate this flexibility in work design by using skills initiatives as the driving force. These flexible frames will unlock the potential of their employees' unused skills.

Skills-based organization means more than implementing a successful skills framework and applications; it means seeing work through the lens of capabilities people have and shaping the work to utilize those skills to the maximum—a profound change in how we see work, teams, hierarchy, and organizations at large.

AI is already causing a major disruption in work design. With the skills of individuals waiting to be unlocked and AI taking over the majority of mundane tasks, the future of work can be more enjoyable and productive for everyone.

---

[63]   Skills-based organizations | Deloitte Global

This chapter will focus more on the mechanical and expertise-required aspects of the skills framework. However, the mindset shift is an equally important project to design and implement.

Understanding the Drivers Will Inform Solutions

One major catalyst for our discussion of Skills is that HR technology platforms have advanced to the point where they can enable the measurement and storage of skills information across the organization.

It is useful to understand in detail the emergence of skills-based work (or skills-based organizations) and the drivers behind it so that we know what problems we are solving. This will then help us design the solutions we need. In this section, we will address both topics: why organizations need skills and what talent applications will satisfy those needs.

Skill-based work and a comprehensive skills framework are not for every organization. Creating a skills framework is not easy, and not all initiatives return the investment. These chapters are more cautionary, with a rational business needs mindset at the center.

The skills topic requires clarification of terminology. We will focus on the key definitions in this area before discussing organizational needs and solutions.

Definitions

Before embarking on the journey of becoming a skills-based organization, it is useful to agree on the core definitions of skills-related terms and the nuances between them. Pragmatic and simple terminology will be used throughout the book. However, assumptions about simplifications will be outlined beforehand here. The reader can easily skip this section of definitions wholly or skip parts of it when the jargon becomes too technical.

Skills, Competencies, and Capabilities

Understandably, there is significant confusion regarding what the terms skills, competencies, and capabilities mean. Even human resources practitioners are not aligned and might be confused about these terms. Here, I will be slightly simplistic and make some assumptions about interchangeable concepts, even though this may frustrate some experts.

Let's take a look at these primary concepts, along with their definitions.

1. Skills, in the organizational context, refer to specific learned abilities required to perform certain tasks. Examples include proficiency in Java or Python, pricing for enterprise software sales, operating production machinery, etc. Skills are core and more granular than competencies or capabilities.

2. Competencies encompass a broader set of knowledge, experience, behaviors, and skills that enable someone to perform effectively in a job or situation. These often include problem-solving, leadership, and emotional intelligence. Competencies

are less about what you can do and more about how you do it. Crisis management is a good example of a competency. It requires specific skills like effective communication, stakeholder management, decision-making, etc. We can say crisis management is the competency to use the necessary skills effectively, relying on relevant experience.

Competencies were an overused term in leadership development in the mid-2000s. Many organizations developed leadership competency models or competency dictionaries to describe the behaviors and knowledge they expected from their leaders. Driving for results, building partnerships, and strategic thinking were examples of leadership competencies.

3. Capabilities represent the overall capacity of an organization or individual to achieve their objectives, combining skills, competencies, resources, and strategies. In practical terms, a company might have capabilities in areas like innovation, customer service, or agile methodologies. An individual has the capability to develop an end-to-end mobile application.

In short, the term skills really refers to a subset of competencies, and competencies are a subset of capabilities.

Skills: Core Element

Set of Skills + Experience = Competencies

Competencies + Resources + Strategies = Capabilities

The first major simplification is to avoid using the term competencies throughout the book and focus on skills and capabilities. Competencies and capabilities will be, at times, interchangeable, but the compromise of the accuracy of used terms will pay off as simplicity and easier understanding.

At times, certain skills might blur the line with competencies. That's okay; a bit of gray area is acceptable if it helps us stay practical and grounded in evidence.

My strong suggestion to human resource practitioners and talent experts is to use the two terms skills and capabilities, with a strong focus on skills. Otherwise, we risk confusing business leaders with unnecessary jargon. The fastest way to lose a room full of senior leaders is to try to explain the difference between skills, competence, and capability.

Now that we have cleared the fundamental definitions, we can move on to the next level of definitions.

Skills Taxonomy, Skills Ontology, and Skills Inventory

During skill initiatives, you'll encounter different terms often used interchangeably, though not always intentionally. There are, however, differences that an HR practitioner should know. It is better to avoid disclosing the level of jargon below to business leaders.

Skills Taxonomy

Think of this as a structured list that organizes skills into clear categories. For example, under "Sales Skills," you might have subcategories like relationship management, pricing, and offer configuration. This arrangement is tidy and makes skills easy to find and use.

Skills Ontology

This goes beyond a taxonomy by connecting related skills to show how they interact. For example, imagine a web where Python and R programming are linked because they are both tools for data visualization. Ontologies help you see how skills work together, making it easier to navigate and understand skill networks.

Skills Inventory

A skills inventory is simply a database of all the skills within an organization. It includes details about who has what skills and how proficient they are. A skills inventory is like taking stock of your workforce's abilities to better plan training, development, and hiring.

Although the above nuances might be useful, it is best to avoid disclosing them to business leaders. Nobody wants to sound like an arrogant HR professional. The ideal and user-friendly title to adopt is *Skills Inventory.*

Technical Skills and Power Skills

Technical skills refer to the abilities and knowledge needed to perform particular tasks or operate specific tools, such as coding in Python, machine operation, or financial forecasting. Technical skills don't need to be only about computers. Functional and industry-related knowledge are also technical skills. These skills are often tangible and can be quantified or certified through tests and performance evaluations.

On the other hand, power skills (also known as soft skills) encompass a broader range of capabilities that enable individuals to navigate the workplace and interact effectively with others. These include critical thinking, communication, adaptability, and systems thinking. Unlike technical skills, power skills are less about technical proficiency and more about how one engages with and influences others or situations.

The value of technical skills is undeniable, especially in industries that rely heavily on specialized knowledge and expertise. They are the backbone of an employee's ability to contribute to specific, technical aspects of a job.

The integration of power skills with technical expertise often leads to better outcomes. For example, teams that communicate well and adapt quickly to new information or market changes can more effectively leverage their technical skills. Being adaptive and a good communicator are two powerful skills that will amplify technical skills.

Organizations find impactful power skills like critical thinking difficult to define, assess, and develop. That difficulty might push some organizations to adopt shortcuts and prefer easier skills to emphasize. Presentation skills and empathy are two examples that have been crowding the power skill inventories. They are not less valuable, but there should be enough rigor to tackle the difficult ones too.

Power skills are assessed through contextual behaviors in daily work life. Soon, AI in the form of LLMs will be able to detect patterns of behavior and accurately assess power skills. The section will cover AI-enabled assessments further.

Finally, our definitions chapter will conclude with the skill-based organization.

What is a skill-based work and a skill-based organization?

Skill-based work involves defining roles based on the specific skills required for success. It provides a systematic answer to the questions: "What skills are essential for success in this role?" and "What level of proficiency is needed in those skills?" A skills framework then serves as the structured synthesis of this information for all relevant roles. Skills framework has skills and proficiency levels for relevant roles.

Currently organizations describe work based on the required outcomes and the responsibility areas. Even though there are suggestions to have work defined only based on skills needed, the healthier approach is to have a complimentary description of the outcomes, responsibilities, and skills.

A skill-based organization defines work and manages all aspects of talent practices based on the skills framework. Some organizations go to the extreme of building every human resources process based on skills, from reward systems to performance management and promotions. This approach has disadvantages that we will discuss further in this section. For now, understanding the definition of a skill-based organization is enough.

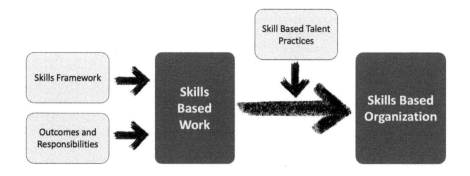

Implementing a skills framework sounds great in HR strategy meetings, but few leaders grasp the massive resources it demands or the market's low success rate.

The foundational piece above, the skills framework, is extremely difficult to put in place. In this chapter, I will argue that it is not entirely necessary for every organization either. There are too many HR strategy conversations where the statement pops up as "we need to implement skills" and the following argument about how it will enable internal talent mobility.

Without careful consideration, there is a risk that "skills implementation" will be included in the HR strategy slides, causing the wheels of corporate strategy execution to start turning. The details of designing and deploying a skills framework and related talent practices are meant to provide leaders with a clear understanding of what it entails to execute a skills implementation, leading to better decision-making about whether to begin this work. Alternatively, if you have already decided to transition to a skills-based organization, these details will guide you through the challenging execution path. This concludes the core definitions that are needed for the skills topic and the heads-up warning about the difficulty of implementation. Now, we will answer the question, *"Why do we need to be a skills-based organization?"*

The Purpose of Skill-Based Organization

The primary goal of a skill-based organization is to enhance employee development and ensure organizational readiness. Skills also allow for fairer talent processes and help with employee retention and engagement. We touched upon these objectives in the introduction.

Repeating the purpose and being specific about what problems we are solving can be beneficial, especially when we are dealing with major changes like switching to a skill-based organization. Problem statements help us focus on the necessary solutions and prevent initiatives from becoming unnecessarily big and complicated. Skills initiatives tend to be unnecessarily big and complicated.

If done right, the skills definitions and assessments of employees against those skills will create a platform for employee development decisions. Those development decisions will then be intentional and align with the organization's capability needs. Skills will also allow the leaders to be intentional about individual employee development, targeting the right employees for the right skill development.

It's important to recognize that while skill-based organizations can address many talent-related challenges, they do not solve all talent and capability challenges. Overemphasizing the outcome of a skills program as an overall solution will be misleading.

We will cover the organizations' needs that catalyze Skills conversations first in detail and then move to solutions.

1. Capability Readiness of Organizations

There's no shortage of doomsday prophets screaming about the skills gap, but a little cynicism can cut through the noise and reveal where the real problems lie.

The half-life of skills is reported to be decreased significantly. In the context of skills, "half-life" refers to the period during which a skill remains relevant before it becomes outdated due to changes in technology, industry practices, or knowledge. For example, if a certain programming language like Java has a half-life of 6 years, it means that in 6 years, only half of the original knowledge and proficiency in that language will still be relevant and applicable.

"Some 40 years ago, developing a skill had a "half-life" of at least 10 years until it was time for a refresher. Today, that half-life has shrunk to about four years — and keeps shrinking", says Kian Katanforoosh, lecturer at Stanford University, and CEO/founder of Workera, speaking on CXOTalk with host Michael Krigsman[64]. "With digital technology and artificial intelligence skills in demand, that half-life may be about two years at most until a refresh is needed", he adds. This indicates new skills will be highly sought after. This then forces the organizations to be more adaptive and intentional in addressing the current and future capability needs of the organization.

There is a catch. The faster half-life statement is more relevant for technology-related skills. There are more durable skills related to processes, crafts, and tools—the kind of skills that financial controllers, procurement specialists, pricing managers, and project managers have.

Executives also have skills on their agenda 77% of the CEOs we surveyed voiced concern that skills shortages could hinder their organization's growth[65]. These surveys also need to be interpreted carefully. There are two types of gaps under the umbrella of "skills gap." When it comes to technical skills, the scarcity usually lies in a few key and specific areas: Data engineers, front-end developers, or AI developers. However, companies also experience a scarcity of "top talent", who are driven and high-performing individuals. Executives tend to put

---

[64]   Demystifying AI: From Deep Learning to Workforce Transformation | CXOTalk
[65]   4 concerns that keep CEOs awake at night | World Economic Forum

those two in the same basket and confuse their ambition to have a higher performing unit with a specific skill set of, for example, "data engineering."

This is an important distinction to make, as the solutions to those two differing problems require different interventions.

1. The lack of technology skills is more about the skills framework and an upskilling or hiring conversation.

2. The lack of performance and top-quality output can be one of the wide range of conversations of leadership, hiring, or engagement.

We can make this clearer with real-life examples.

1. The company TechSphere wants to deploy AI conversational chatbots. However, they don't have anyone in the company who understands from foundation models and have done a complex conversion of product knowledge to an AI chatbot before. TechSphere relies on consultancy companies to put this chatbot in place, but doesn't know if they are managing the service providers in the right direction or not. This is a clear lack of capability.

2. The company TechSphere wants to build a mobile application so that consumers can find and purchase their products directly from that platform. TechSphere needs great mobile developers and front-end developers, etc. They do have all those developers in the organization who have built similar applications before. However, the TechSphere application becomes difficult to use, badly designed, creating a buggy mobile application. This is more of a performance issue than a skills gap. We can also argue that the development leaders and user experience experts did not know their stuff enough, but in the end, it is a capability gap due to low-performing teams and individuals. After all, tech companies like Meta and Google made statements towards a productivity difference of 8x to 25x between an average developer and a top talent developer.

Organizations must grasp these gaps and recognize their overarching impact on the company. As Charles Kettering, the pioneering head of research at General Motors from 1920 to 1947, aptly put it, "A problem well stated is half solved." This profound insight underlines the importance of clarity in identifying challenges.

It is essential to go beyond the buzzwords "skills half-life" and "skills gap." Major consulting and learning companies often emphasize the extent of the skills gap, creating a significant demand for services related to skill development. However, it is wise to look past this hype. While their claims may be somewhat valid, a more balanced perspective will ultimately serve everyone better.

Future readiness is a major challenge, and while a skills framework can clarify what's needed for strategy execution, organizations can often achieve the same results with simpler, role-based capability planning—sometimes, less is more.

On the other hand, future readiness is a serious challenge for the majority of companies. Organizations rarely break down their three-year strategies to required capabilities. Strategy execution requires a set of leadership and technical skills, making them explicit helps organizations to decide whether they should develop those capabilities or hire them. This is basically what strategic workforce planning stands for. A skills framework is a powerful tool to make the necessary skills for strategy execution explicit. Again, to be on the cautious side, a skills framework is not an absolute must, but only a good tool.

Organizations can clearly state their future capability needs in terms of broad roles instead of formulating them in complicated skills frameworks. For example, a future readiness plan can easily look like "we need to have at least 5 to 8 senior cloud architects specialized in our vendor tech stack." Alternatively, a skills framework can help the company break it down into detailed lists: 2 Senior Engineers with Expert Cloud Architecture AWS skills and 3 Senior Engineers with Proficient Cloud Architecture Microsoft Azure.

Usually, simplicity works better, but a skills framework can also be helpful in getting leaders to think about future capabilities in a more structured way. Even that on its own is a value add.

2. Employee Retention and Engagement

Right after organizational readiness, retention and engagement are areas where skills can help organizations address challenges. A skills framework brings intentionality to employee development, hiring, and promotions. In this context, intentionality means employees receive development based on their relevant skills or get hired based on relevant skills. Relevant means relevant to the organization's capability needs and relevant to the employee aspirations. If those conditions are met, the organization builds the capability it needs, and the employees get the growth they want.

Promotions, hiring, and development based on skills will also bring fairness to those processes. There is a distinction to be made here: development, hiring, and promotions can't be solely based on skills. There will be other factors, such as personality traits and behavior. Some positions require conscientious and curious people. Even though one has the skills to do the job, the hiring manager might decide on someone with curiosity and drive for development. Skills are not everything; however, a good supportive lens to make the processes more intentional and fairer.

The intentionality and fairness, in turn, will increase employee retention and engagement. At least, that is the hypothesis of the proponents of the skills approach. A brief double click on retention and engagement can explain further the impact of skills.

Retention

Retention of talent is a complicated topic. There are hundreds of surveys that list reasons why employees leave their companies. Quick research would list major elements as lack of fair compensation, development, career growth, good company culture, good leadership, recognition, and work-life balance. These are all big topics, and they cover almost all talent areas together. Two reasons to approach these retention-related survey results:

1. "Employees are leaving because they don't feel recognized" is a difficult problem statement to understand and act on. Recognition might mean different things to different employees. It can be monetary, a promotion, or deserved praise in front of the team. Some require cultural and leadership solutions, some require a fairer promotion approach, and some require a new compensation system. These are not easy fixes.

2. Even within a company, the reasons for talent leaving can differ from one division to another or from one geography to another. The reasons can be idiosyncratic to every employee. Averaging out survey results and finding blanket solutions might not be the cure for employee attrition.

Given these considerations, it is unrealistic to expect a single talent practice intervention to significantly reduce employee attrition. Retention issues often have multiple contributing factors, and no single measure, other than addressing a toxic manager, offers a complete solution.

The same line of arguments can be used for employee engagement as well.

Engagement

Gallup surveys rank development as one of the key five drivers of employee engagement[66]. Although this topic is the most discussed among human resources communities, relevant scientific research on employee engagement and employee development relationships is difficult to find.

However, there is evidence that development and career opportunities have an impact on employee engagement. It is better to build on that fact rather than delving into the rabbit hole of employee engagement truths. Given the assumption above, it is only natural that organizations intentionally invest in their people's skills and career development to create a more engaged workforce.

A skills framework will provide a foundation for development and career models. It is a good start. Personal and career growth will help retain talent and increase engagement; there is no question about it. However, for a skills framework to be impactful, it needs to be designed and implemented exceptionally well. Even then, it is just the beginning of the journey of linking skills to talent practices. And even that will not be the answer if employees are disengaged or leaving the company.

Even though skills have positive impact on retention and engagement; organization readiness is the main benefit to the organization. Now,

---

[66] How to Improve Employee Engagement in the Workplace - Gallup

we will go ahead and look at how these skills frameworks are woven into organizations' readiness.

How Exactly Skills Framework Supports Organization Readiness

A good skills framework serves in three main ways.

1. Organizations will create transparency and a sense of fairness by defining the required skills and proficiency levels for roles and creating career paths based on those skills. A clear and fair career path will boost employee belief and help organizations hire or promote the right people, which will have a huge positive impact on engagement and the organization's capability needs.

2. By accurately assessing the skill proficiency of employees, organizations will know their current capabilities across units. This will create valuable insights into the capability-building strategy of the organization. "Which capabilities do we need in the short, mid, and the long term?" and "Do we build the capability by developing our people, do we buy the capability by hiring the right skills, or do we borrow the skills from our ecosystem as consultants?" The answers to those strategic questions can then become much more informed, knowing the skills inventory of the current organization.

3. By knowing the capability needs and accurately assessing the proficiency levels of the employees, the organization can deploy much more intentional development programs that are personalized and customized for each employee's needs. This, in turn, will make the development much more effective, helping to solve the original two organizational challenges.

These three main areas will support the readiness of organizations, put a framework in place for assessing the gaps and strengths, and take action accordingly.

Further in the section, there is a detailed walkthrough on how to design and implement these frameworks. Before we go there, skills initiatives require a good sense of the organization's challenges and what the skills framework can really provide. The next chapter contains relevant inquiries that CEOs and executives should make. Companies should consider the questions carefully and should not shy away from postponing or rescheduling skills initiatives.

What Should Business Leaders Expect

Setting the right expectations is a critical success factor in implementing a skills framework or any talent initiative. Without clearly defining business needs and specific outcome expectations, vague purposes and broad agreements on concepts will have negative downstream effects. To ensure a healthy start, business leaders should ask the right questions and set precise expectations for a skills framework.

The natural first step for any business leader is to clearly understand the problem statements. Two major problem statements, readiness and employee engagement, are discussed earlier in this chapter. While these are relevant for most organizations, it is essential to understand the detailed symptoms and specific challenges unique to each organization. This understanding will shape the design.

Do We Have a Skills Gap or Performance Problem?

We have seen that performance problems can seem like skills gaps and vice versa. There will be pockets of skills gaps and performance issues in an organization, determining which will lead to the right solution. There might be blurry cases where required skills and performance are missing. Handling the performance issue first and then attending to the skills gap results in better outcomes.

Effective leaders can recognize when employees are deeply engaged but still struggle to produce the required features and outcomes; this frequently signals a skills gap. There is a marked distinction between an IT generalist attempting to navigate data architecture and a specialized data architect addressing the same challenge. Executive teams must scrutinize these symptoms and trust that frontline leaders can differentiate between performance issues and genuine skills deficiencies. This exercise helps organizations pinpoint the real skill gaps in the units, and identifying these areas is key to the success of any organization.

Questions for Defining the Scope and Readiness

Given you have arrived at the conclusion that you have skill gaps for today and for the future, the questions below will help good leaders understand the need for a skill initiative and set the right expectations for a tailored initiative:

1. What is the scope of the skill gap for the current business and the future? Is the gap a natural lag of new technology adoption, or is there a big capability gap that requires a big intervention?

    Hint: Any skills gap that is around 3-5% of the headcount is a minor, business-as-usual gap; anything that corresponds to 20% of the headcount requires a serious intervention.

2. Does the scope justify a full skills initiative, or can that be handled more organically by leader initiative and a good hiring and development follow-up?

    Hint: If the gaps involve the same skills repeated but fragmented in the organization, a structural company-wide skills framework might be needed. If the gaps are specific to units and isolated, it is better to address them with the leaders.

3. Are the current training and development plans intentional toward the needs of the organization, or are they sporadic and based on individual aspirations and on-the-spot decisions?

    Hint: If there is a good competency gap analysis with specific skills in the units, and the trainings are focused on the gaps, it is a good sign. If the competence gaps are generic, like AI, Analytics, or Leadership, the first step should be increasing the quality of the competence gap analyses, not a full-fledged skills initiative.

4. Do we want detailed insight about all the skills available, even for administrative roles, or mainstream skills, or do we want to limit the knowledge to critical skills only?

Hint: This decision will define the success or failure of the skills initiative. Defining the scope as focused as possible at first will be beneficial. Leaving generic skills out of scope helps.

5. Can we start with one part of the organization and see the use cases and return on investment?

    Hint: It is always useful to start with a pilot unit and scale from there, unless the organization has fewer than a few thousand people. In that case, it makes more sense to do it in one phase.

6. Do we have the right competence to drive a skills initiative like this?

    Hint: A capable HR function, both in skills and in program management, is a must. A good technical HR infrastructure is a prerequisite as well. Lacking any one of these should put the initiative on hold or decline.

7. What does success look like?

    Hint: Avoiding the generic KPIs, the executive team and human resources should be able to define specific success measures. If they struggle to define those specific targets, then it is likely the problem can be solved without a major skills initiative.

These conversations should be open-minded and critical, and the questions above should be discussed rigorously. Executive teams are more inclined to say yes to a talent initiative if the monetary cost is not too high. Sometimes, we mistake the amount of money we pay to a consultancy for the real cost that the organization will pay. We omit the hours spent and managerial energy cost of those initiatives.

Questions for Defining the Real Cost

A skills initiative should be considered a big investment. Just like entering a new market, starting a new talent initiative should also be carefully evaluated and interrogated. The above questions will help create an environment of critical thinking and a thorough conversation of "Do we really need this?"

Some additional questions to understand the cost:

- What is the amount of managerial time this will consume? On top of the other ongoing talent-related initiatives and activities?
- Is this the right time to do this? Or should we wait a few more years to test out the real need?
- What are the expectations we will create in the organization? What is the risk of not meeting that expectation?

One often overlooked aspect of talent initiatives is the Cost of loss of trust when they fail to deliver. These initiatives usually come with promises to employees about their development and career progression, including fair and skill-based internal hiring, diverse career options, and significant development opportunities. When these promises are not met, it fundamentally damages the organization's credibility, potentially harming employee belonging and engagement.

The topics outlined in this chapter cover the essential inquiries of the skills initiative in terms of real need, scope, risks, resources, and governance. They will facilitate a good decision-making conversation and a healthy start to any skills or talent initiative.

Implementing a Skill-Based Organization

An organization is "skills-based" when the majority of talent practices are based on skills. It is a journey starting with a skills framework and continuing with basing that framework on other talent applications like internal and external hiring, promotions, workforce planning, and employee development.

Every organization cannot fully embark on that journey; a skills framework and skills-based organization require careful design and good deployment. A skills initiative will be overkill for any company with fewer than a few thousand employees.

The concept of a "skill-based organization" is unlikely to be widely adopted in most workplaces. Instead, jobs and employees will continue to be assessed, compensated, and promoted primarily based on their performance outputs. Although skills are crucial for attaining these outputs and achieving success, the prevailing paradigm is expected to focus on job roles rather than skills.

Skills are vital for the systematic development of an organization's capabilities and people, directly contributing to organization's success. However, skills can be utilized while avoiding a too-complicated HR system. The chapters to follow will contain key elements for keeping skills as a pragmatic system.

Here are four essential elements of a skill-based organization. I suggest that organizations begin by implementing a skills framework along with one or two talent use cases, and then expand to other talent applications. I will prioritize these talent applications in an order that will provide the greatest benefit for organizations.

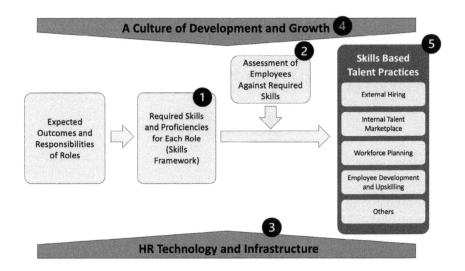

The four elements that make skills-based talent practices possible are:

1. Design and deployment of a skills framework based on the required skills and proficiencies for each role
2. Assessment of employees against the required skills they occupy or against the skills that they aspire to
3. Human resources technology platform and infrastructure
4. A company culture of development and growth

As the fifth element becomes the cluster of skills-based talent practices, we will examine the main ones, such as hiring, talent marketplace, workforce planning, and upskilling. Once those practices are at the heart of the company, the shift toward a skills-based organization is mostly complete.

We will explore each element further in this section, starting with the skills framework.

1. Design and Deployment of Skills Framework

A skills framework provides standard definitions of critical skills required for roles within a specific organization and describes proficiency levels for each skill. This is the most substantial part of skills initiatives, serving as the foundation upon which all other talent applications are built. The quality of the framework will determine the success of the talent applications and the overall business impact of the initiative.

The skills framework has two main parts:

1. Definition of the skills for each role
2. Definition of the proficiency levels required for those skills

The table below represents two skills and required proficiency levels based on the description of a front-end developer role. In this section, we will discuss how to define the skills and proficiency levels.

Role Description	Example Skill	Proficiency Level
A Front-End Developer is responsible for implementing the visual and interactive elements of a website or application, ensuring a seamless user experience. They translate UI/UX designs into code using HTML, CSS, and JavaScript frameworks, collaborating with designers and back-end developers to integrate functionality.	Proficiency in HTML, CSS, and JavaScript – foundational for building and styling user interfaces.	Required Level: 4 (Expert)
	Experience with frameworks like React – for efficient and dynamic development.	Required Level: 3 (Advanced)

Caution 1: Please note that the proposal is to avoid defining all skills for each role. Skills frameworks are much simpler and more efficient if they only contain critical skills. Collaboration is a soft skill that every front-end developer needs to have, but it is a hygiene factor for almost all roles, and there is no added value to include it in the list. The same argument is valid for presentation skills and Microsoft Office proficiency. Focusing on the critical skills that will make the individuals successful will prevent having a taxonomy of thousands of skills.

Caution 2: A prerequisite for any skills framework is to have an understanding of who holds what role in the organization. If you don't know exactly who your front-end developers are, you cannot allocate the skills to them. A job architecture then becomes a prerequisite to a skills framework.

Defining Skills

This step covers allocating critical skills to the roles and defining the skill descriptions. The aggregation of all the skill definitions creates a meaningful skills taxonomy.

Establishing the Scope

The last thing you want is a three-year project that requires 16.000 skills, is impossible to maintain, and is already out of date by the time it is launched.

The scope of implementation is often what distinguishes a successful project from a protracted, mediocre one. Organizations frequently attempt to define skills for every role on their payroll, resulting in hundreds of roles and thousands of skills. This approach typically complicates and prolongs the implementation process.

Here are some scope considerations:

Scope of Roles: Select Roles vs Every Role

Organizations should strategically select which roles to include in a skills initiative. Attempting to cover all roles simultaneously is a common pitfall.

Focus on the roles with large headcount: The top 20 to 30 job roles typically represent 80% of the workforce. Focusing on these roles first can markedly speed up completion and simplify the process. The remaining 20% of employees, often in diverse roles, can significantly extend the workload.

Focus on roles with critical competence impact: Some positions are at the heart of an organization's capability gap, or they play a crucial role in executing strategy. Although they may have a small number of employees, it is essential to include them in the scope. For instance, there may only be a few dozen data scientists or senior market analysts within an organization, yet critical capability gaps might still exist.

The skills framework should incorporate them. The limited scope above can also be seen as the first phase of a skills framework. Focusing on the critical and large headcount roles. The rest of the roles can be rolled out in the second phase. It is important to note that the organizations can choose to skip the second phase and stick to the initial scope. The tradeoffs will be clearer during the talent applications chapter.

Exclusion of Line Managers: Line management roles, which are usually unique and should comprise under 20% of employees, should be excluded from the first phase. This applies unless there is a significant cohort of similar roles, such as "Delivery Managers," which can be standardized. Otherwise, "Head of Procurement" should not be in the initial scope.

Scope of Skills: All Skills vs Critical Skills

Once the key roles are identified, concentrate on the critical skills that set apart an average performer from an exceptional one. Limit the scope to 8 to 10 essential skills for each role. The 11th skill is likely to be considered non-critical.

It is prudent to exclude leadership skills in the initial phase, but if there is a need within the organization, you can address those skills in relation to the reporting level. First-level line managers require a distinct skill set and proficiency, and leaders of leaders or senior leaders require a different skill set.

There are several pitfalls in defining the skills, as illustrated by another role example.

Skills Definitions and Risks to Avoid

A second example, following the front-end developer, is a data engineer, who has been a core foundational role in analytics.

Data engineer short role description:

A data engineer is responsible for designing, building, and maintaining the infrastructure and systems that enable the collection, storage, and analysis of large volumes of data. They develop data pipelines, ensure data quality, and optimize data workflows to support analytics and business intelligence efforts.

Skills needed for data engineer role:

- Programming (Python, Java),
- Database management (Knowledge of SQL and NoSQL),
- Data warehousing solutions,
- Big data technologies,
- Cloud platforms (AWS, Azure, GCP),
- DevOps practices
- Analytical Skills

Please note that this list only outlines the critical skills of a data engineer, not all the skills needed for that role.

The list above can easily be obtained through a large language model (LLM) like ChatGPT and then fine-tuned via a short conversation with one of the data engineering managers. However, the job is not done. We need descriptions of each skill, preferably short and concise, for an organization-wide structure.

For example, Data Warehousing Solutions: Designing and managing data warehousing solutions, including cloud platforms (Snowflake, Redshift) and traditional systems, focusing on ETL pipelines, schema design, and query optimization.

Additionally, in the list above, there are some uncertainties that we need to avoid. Here are the risks:

Risk One: Bundling skills will create confusion

The item "Programming (Python, Java)" combines two programming languages required for data engineers. What about HTML, which is required for front-end developers? What about React, a JavaScript library used for building user interfaces? A front-end developer should know Java, HTML, and React; a data engineer, on the other hand, should know Python and Java.

The questions is, should we leave the skill "Programming Python and Java" and have a separate one called "Programming Java and HTML" for front-end developers? Eventually, we will define all programming languages separately as individual skills: Python, JavaScript, HTML, etc. This will also create clarity when designing personalized development plans for developers.

You can now understand that adding roles to the scope can exponentially increase the number of skills you will have to define and allocate.

Risk Two: Lack of clear skill definitions will allow interpretations

Another problem with the skills allocated to data engineers above is that some headings are too vague: analytical thinking and DevOps practices. These headings require specific and concise definitions to avoid false interpretations of those skills and wrong allocation to irrelevant roles. As mentioned above, DevOps Practices bundle a few practices and create confusion.

Similar to the data warehousing solutions we have described above, analytical skills are also open to interpretation and hence require a definition like the one below.

"Analytical skills refer to the ability to collect, analyze, and interpret data and information to solve problems, make decisions, and understand complex issues. This involves logical thinking, critical assessment, and the ability to break down complex information into manageable parts to find patterns, draw conclusions, and generate insights."

As you will see in the next section, the analytical skill level required of a data engineer and an HR generalist is different. A data engineer must have the in-depth ability to break down complex information and find patterns. In contrast, an HR generalist only needs to be able to understand presented trends and insights.

Precisely defining each skill and correctly allocating those skills to the right roles can quickly become a complicated and extensive task. This is where scoping becomes the critical success factor of any skills initiative.

Risk Three: Customized Definitions

Whenever possible, employ standardized skills and descriptions that are common in the market. You can use your partners and vendors to obtain market-relevant standard definitions. If no vendor partnership exists, advanced AI models like ChatGPT provide a robust foundation for defining skills.

Standardization helps align with market trends and streamlines practices such as hiring and external skill development. Once the organization has most of the skills defined in a standard way, it is easier to map those skills with candidate search platforms and other benchmark tools.

Relying on standard market definitions for skills will also reduce the time and effort spent on discussions about simple wording. The moment you start writing definitions, a natural series of discussions about words will emerge. Should we use the statement "collect, analyze, and interpret data" or should we add "consolidate' to the definition as well?" After all, data engineers consolidate data. It's a detailed conversation that you don't want to spend time on.

Defining The Proficiency Levels

Once organizations have identified the necessary skills for their roles, following the prioritized scope outlined previously, the next step is to define the proficiency levels for each skill. Every skill that is identified in the initial step should have clearly defined proficiency levels to support accurate assessment and development within the organization.

Proficiency levels are standard descriptions of the different expertise levels. A simple example could be three levels for each skill: "beginner, proficient, and expert." While being simplistic, this example should give an idea of the extra layer of complexity the proficiency levels will add to the picture.

Assume that we aim for the top 30 populated jobs as the initial scope and that every job has roughly 10 skills. For the initial phase, we will be looking at roughly 300 skills. Let's also assume that some jobs will have common skills, and we will end up with 200 unique skills.

We need to define proficiency levels for 200 skills. This makes the next decision strategic: Should we have standard proficiency levels for each skill or specific expertise levels for each skill?

Given the tone so far in the book, you already know the answer to the question above. However, here is a breakdown of the two alternatives.

Proficiency levels can be defined in two main ways:

Alternative 1: Standard levels and standard definitions for every skill

Standard definitions for each skill and brief generic descriptions provide a broad idea for the assessor but do not specify the exact differences between skill levels. A commonly used example is a five-level system: beginner, intermediate, advanced, expert, and master. Below is an illustration of how an organization can establish a standard five-level description for each skill that is sufficiently descriptive but does not provide the exact wording associated with the skill itself

- **Beginner**: Possesses basic knowledge and limited practical experience with the skill. Can perform simple tasks under direct supervision and requires substantial guidance to complete most activities related to the skill.
- **Intermediate**: Has a moderate understanding and practical experience. Can perform tasks independently in familiar contexts and requires minimal assistance. Begins to apply the skill in more complex situations but might still need support for advanced challenges.
- **Advanced**: Demonstrates comprehensive knowledge and proficiency. Can perform complex tasks independently and effectively uses the skill in varied situations. Often assists others and contributes to problem-solving within this scope.
- **Expert**: Possesses deep, specialized knowledge and extensive experience. Can lead projects and innovate solutions using the skill. Routinely handles complex and unprecedented situations effectively and can mentor others to develop their capabilities.
- **Master**: Exemplifies the highest level of expertise and mastery over the skill with significant experience and recognition in the field. Influences broad application and development of the skill, sets standards, and leads strategic initiatives. Acts as a key resource for strategic decision-making and development in the organization.

Selecting a similar standard proficiency description set will significantly simplify your project and give it the needed speed boost. However, it will sacrifice specificity.

Alternative 2: Customized level descriptions for each skill

The second alternative is to write customized levels for each skill. Please note that the number of levels should stay the same across the organization. One major mistake would be to select four proficiency levels for one skill and five proficiency levels for another. No infrastructure will support this customization, which will create confusion throughout the organization.

Customized definitions for each skill make it easier for the line manager to assess the proficiency level of the individual and explain the outcome to them. Here is an example of how customized levels would look:

Database Management Skill:

- **Beginner**: Basic understanding of database concepts. Able to perform simple queries and manage small databases.
- **Intermediate**: Proficient in SQL and capable of designing and implementing relational database schemas. Can handle database normalization and basic performance tuning.
- **Advanced**: Skilled in complex SQL queries and optimization. Experienced in managing large-scale databases and implementing security measures.
- **Expert**: Expertise in multiple database systems, such as SQL and NoSQL. Able to design and implement high availability and disaster recovery strategies.
- **Master**: Recognized authority and thought leader in database management. Leads innovations and mentors others in advanced database technologies and architecture.

The more straightforward approach, Alternative 1 in this case, should be chosen in this critical decision-making juncture. There are many of these junctures and decision points throughout a skills initiative. And even though these decisions seem like isolated topics, they compound the complexity of the initiative. Choosing only the heavily populated roles, critical skills, and standard proficiency level descriptions results in a completely different skills framework initiative than choosing to include all roles and all skills and have customized proficiency descriptions for each skill. The latter initiative is more complicated than the former by an order of magnitude. Even though isolated choices seem manageable on their own, two choices for the complicated alternative can make a difference of months or a year in implementation.

Now we have covered the definitions of skills and levels. Once implemented, those are the skills framework, the foundation of all skills-based applications.

Summary of the suggestions:

1. The best deployment practice is to design and deploy the skills framework in two phases: the first phase for the heavily populated roles and the second phase for the long tail.

2. Another important success factor is to deploy the first phase in a sizable unit as a pilot. Then, observe and note what went right and what needs to improve. Try out one or two use cases in that pilot unit, and then complete phase one with the rest of the organization. Iterating the ways of working and revisiting some of the critical decisions in light of real-world applications is priceless. A good size for a pilot phase one would be around 800 - 1000 employees and 20 roles.

3. Stick to the market standards when defining the skills. It will make life easier afterward.

4. The proficiency levels must be standard and stick with the same five levels throughout the whole organization.

2. Assessing Employee Skills

Once organizations have a skills framework, the next step is assessing current employees against the skills and levels required for their roles. This exercise is necessary if organizations want to inventory current capabilities and possible gaps. However, it is not easy.

Many organizations skip assessing their employees and only deploy a skills framework. They use the framework to clarify role requirements and use it either only for hiring or individual development plans. Even though this approach doesn't give the organization any capability status, it is still a good use of skills. Please remember that the full-fledged skills approach is not for every organization, and as we argued previously, most organizations are better off without one.

Back to the scenario of assessing employees. Assessment methodologies depend on how accurate organizations want to be and what type of skills they want to assess. For example, technical skills will require different tools to assess than power skills.

This section covers different approaches and tools. It is also important to note that AI will soon disrupt these methodologies.

There are fundamentally four ways to assess skills:

1. Using specialized tools and certification: Technical skills, such as proficiency in programming languages or specific technology platforms, can be assessed using tools and certificates. Certifications from the vendors themselves, like Microsoft Azure certifications, are usually good references. Other testing tools, especially those for programming, can be less accurate as references.

   The suggestion with all assessment tools is to have a layer of human verification with them. For example, a coding assessment done by a testing platform should be reviewed by a senior coder.

2. Self-assessment: A pragmatic way is to ask the incumbent to assess their proficiency in given skills. Simply giving the proficiency level descriptions and asking where they see themselves is a good start. Self-assessments are usually biased[67], and as with the above tool verification, the results should be verified.

3. Crowdsourcing perceptions: Organizations can ask their stakeholders and peers for an individual's proficiency levels, gathering data from people who would see the assessed employee using those skills in action.

4. Line Manager assessment: Asking the line manager is a common way to assess an employee's skills. Line managers are eventually responsible for their teams' capability inventory, and evaluating their employees will give them a good view of the current and future gaps. This method has the advantage of putting more accountability on the line manager.

---

[67] The Talent Strategy Group - 5 Reasons to Eliminate the Self-Review

The simplest and best way to assess employees' proficiency levels is for them to self-assess their skills and levels, and then have the line manager verify those assessments. Good communication that emphasizes the purpose of this work as the development of employees will give managers a better foundation on which to challenge any biased evaluations from employees.

Examples of Market Applications

Hiring platforms offering a mixture of community assessments and surveys:

LinkedIn is one of the platforms that has invested in skills and skill assessment for a while now. The platform is starting to provide candidate rankings to the recruiters based on the skills match of the candidate and the position for the last few years. The skill assessments are mostly binary, whether the person has the skill or not. Those skill assessments don't have proficiency levels yet. Someone with an HR background might have "talent management" as a skill based on the nominations from the LinkedIn connections. And any role that requires talent management skills then shows up as a match.

The LinkedIn platform offers a feature where users can take a 15-question survey, but the quality of the surveys is questionable.

This is a blend of self-assessment, crowdsourcing, and utilizing a simple tool. The reliability for now is limited but signals a future focus.

CV Scrapping and HR Data Harnessing:

A few new-generation skills platforms use AI algorithms to detect skills from CVs and HR data, such as job titles. These smaller companies usually work with organizations and connect their algorithms to the organizations' HR systems. The algorithm then gets information about individuals, their CVs, job titles, and project assignments. With their algorithm, these platforms allocate skills to employees.

The ad for these platforms will say that their "AI-driven Skill Engine extracts, interprets, and contextualizes skills from unstructured data such as project reports, digital footprints, and other work-related documents. This process ensures a comprehensive and unbiased overview of the workforce's skills, providing 100% coverage that manual methods cannot achieve."

These AI algorithms are not generative AI. Organizations should be careful about these platforms' capabilities. After all, these platforms and their algorithms interpret the available data in HR systems, and the data quality in those systems is usually not great.

A utility for those vendors in the market is to use their generic skills frameworks. Without having to formulate what kind of skills are needed for a data engineer and other standard roles, the skills library of these companies can be used. Then again, a good ChatGPT user can also achieve the same results.

Learning Platforms and Certifications

There are good learning experience platforms in the market that provide well-curated content to employees. Degreed, Coursera, Udemy, and Pluralsight are good examples. Organizations that partner with these learning companies will offer their employees a vast online library. These learning platforms track the training employees consume and give them certifications and badges, which can be used as skills indicators.

These learning platforms also provide short tests to measure skills and proficiency levels.

A credible certification outside of these learning platforms is one of the most reliable sources of knowledge. The credibility of the certification methodology and provider is critical. Examples include a cloud architecture certification from Amazon Web Services (AWS), the famous Cisco Networking certifications, or a change management Prosci certification.

Online learning or even certifications are not real-life experiences. Gaining skills requires on-the-job practice and going through a week of change management theory training is not the same as leading major changes in organizations. Ideally, a base of theory and good practice is an ideal skill acquisition. The assessment of that level of skill is only possible by the line manager or stakeholders.

Summary of practicalities:

1. The strong suggestion is to keep the steps as simple as possible. Skills initiatives have numerous steps, and complexity accumulates quickly.
2. For assessments: Compromising on the accuracy if it brings significant simplification is logical.
3. Self-assessment and line manager approval are pragmatic and signal the right level of accountability to the leaders and an agency to the employees.
4. Assessment should be transparent and focused on development and communicated clearly as such.
5. Technology is improving, and skill assessment tools are improving. However, for now, they can only be complementary data points; their results should be verified by humans.

3. Technology Platforms and Infrastructure

Skills architecture requires a solid technology platform. Any skills initiative should be considered without including IT's corresponding technology counterparts. The success of the skills applications depends on the platform's capability and integration, as well as its user-friendliness.

A robust technology infrastructure is essential for establishing a skills framework and subsequently developing skills-based applications. Manual documentation and lists cannot be used to design or maintain a skills framework. It is also valuable to outline the platform's requirements. We suggest starting with basic functionalities and then moving to advanced ones. The selected platform should already have the capabilities for advanced functionality; turning on those functionalities depends on the adoption strategy.

As usual, the suggestion is to stick with the skills module of the current Human Capital Management (HCM) system in your organization. In layman's terms, don't buy an extra platform; instead, try to use the module of the HR system you already have. This approach will be beneficial for integration and data architecture. Although these modules often lack advanced functionalities, they can serve as a solid starting point without requiring a significant technology investment. With generative AI on the horizon in the HR world, the landscape will change drastically. It is wise to wait for AI capabilities to be rolled out before investing in a new platform. Here are the functionalities that organizations should be looking for:

Basic Functionality

The basic purpose of the platform would be to store the skills framework and make it available to the organization in a user-friendly way. The admins should be able to add skills comfortably, and line managers and employees should see the relevant skills and proficiency levels easily. The simple process of employees self-assessing their own skills and sending those for approval to their line managers. All these transactions and, eventually, the skills of employees should be stored in a good data architecture.

With its basic functionalities, this platform should also be integrated into the main HR system. When consolidated information is requested for an employee, compensation, demographics, past roles, past performance appraisals, and skills and skills development should be available.

Advanced Functionality

The advanced functionalities of these platforms would enable internal marketplaces and help with career modeling. This requires an algorithm to understand employees' aspirations and match their skills and aspirations for future roles based on general career paths in the organization.

Imagine a software engineer who aspires to become a cloud architect. The platform is expected to outline the missing skills that the engineer should develop, help with possible training, and alert the employee when an architect role is open in the organization.

Another important feature of an advanced platform is that it should support skills assessment. It can be in the form of a few survey questions when the employee is having a self-evaluation, or a more technical test that can be utilized.

The Near Future Functionality

AI is rapidly entering this area. Once AI has access to all the tasks and projects the employees have completed, skill assessments will be more accurate. Generative AI can make sense of that big data and list the employees' skills.

With the potential of the employee and their aspirations in mind, AI will coach employees toward their goals, provide them with training alternatives, or tutor them.

The technology and the user interfaces that it will provide will be important for the adoption and daily use of the skills framework. On the other hand, the integration and good data architecture in the background will enable companies to understand the skills development of the workforce and capability gaps in a systematic way. The basic functionalities mentioned above are not too difficult to come by. Still, they do need to be planned and implemented intentionally, preferably by experts in user experience (UX) design and data architecture. Those profiles will add value to the project team.

4. A Culture of Development and Growth

Cultivating a culture of growth and prioritizing development is the key to successfully adopting skills frameworks and other skills-based initiatives. These tools bring focus and purpose to personal growth, shaping development efforts toward relevant skills and helping both individuals and organizations discover the most effective ways to advance.

A Culture of Growth

Unfortunately, few companies have this kind of personal growth culture, and the signs are easy to spot. You will find active online forums about new technologies, employees frequently changing roles, people eagerly consuming and sharing valuable insights, and cross-functional teams working together voluntarily to create real impact. In such environments, leaders, especially CEOs, personally engage with the latest trends, delving deep to stay informed. These organizations value expertise and rational decision-making, setting the stage for growth. Promotions are based on merit and expertise. There are usually equally high-paying and prestigious expert roles as senior leadership roles.

Skills-based applications act as a catalyst for an already thriving development culture. Organizations with this foundation experience quicker and more widespread benefits. When the culture supports and drives the adoption of skills-based practices, companies can rapidly expand these frameworks to encompass all roles, even in the early stages of implementation.

A Culture of Stagnation

On the other hand, there are companies whose culture feels stuck. Here, opinions often hold weight because of relationships, not expertise. Employees stay in the same roles for years, promotions are based on visibility rather than skill or knowledge, and succession plans remain empty. In these environments, executives rely on surface-level knowledge from presentations rather than truly understanding emerging technologies. Organizations at this stage, often in their lifecycle's maturity phase, are at greater risk of stagnation.

This is where adopting a skills framework can face resistance. The silver lining? A skills initiative can also act as a spark for cultural transformation. However, this change must be approached holistically—it is not just about implementing a new tool but reshaping the organization's mindset. Leaders must model desired behaviors, promotion criteria need revision, and development budgets should reflect this priority. For more on leadership interventions, check out the Leadership section of this book.

Even the best-designed skills framework will fail to gain traction without the right cultural support. Assessing the organization's cultural readiness is crucial before launching any major initiative. Earlier sections of this book outline key questions to guide this evaluation.

Once the skills framework is designed and implemented, the foundation for skills-based applications is in place. Yet, this is often the moment when many organizations run out of steam.

Effective program management can define skills, levels, and employee assessments within six to eight months for midsize companies and eight to twelve months for larger firms. If your process takes two years, it may be overly complex, but you are not alone.

Many organizations pause when implementing skills and assessments due to excessive effort and time, which is risky. The true value lies in applying these skills, and companies should prioritize employee development quickly.

5. Talent Applications of Skills:

Skills in Hiring

Skill-based hiring is one of the most relevant use cases of skills. Skills are increasingly used in external and internal hiring. Recruitment processes are being fine-tuned to evaluate candidates based on their skills in a more structured way.

Skill-based hiring has existed for a long time; recruiters and hiring managers have always assessed candidates based on the necessary skills. The skills framework adds more structure. The definitions of skills and levels provide clarity and standardization for all hiring managers. This standardization also enables hiring platforms to match candidates to jobs based on their skills automatically. Modern applicant tracking systems (ATS), which are essentially hiring platforms, already claim to find candidates based on their skills and rank applicants according to their skills compatibility.

This feature of ranking candidates based on skills requires a healthy skills assessment in place for the candidate. In most cases, the skill proficiency assessments are not that reliable. That is the weak link for those algorithmic candidate matches. Based on LinkedIn self-reported skills, everyone's an expert at change management! Good luck ranking people based on that.

As a result, organizations end up with a stack ranking that somewhat makes sense but is far from trustworthy. On the other hand, the assessment methodologies will evolve, and those rankings will be more accurate in time.

The future of hiring also lies in GenAI, especially with models that can understand the roles and have conversations with candidates. GenAI will take over the hiring process, which will then translate into a better skills assessment by the AI agent and the storage of that candidate data.

To address the concerns, nothing is more human than wanting to be evaluated by a fair and unbiased person. That person is AI, which will not judge you by your accent, gender, and nationality but only by your values, experience, and skills.

Can companies still do external hiring based on skills without a big skills initiative and a skills framework? Yes. The hiring manager can briefly define the skills needed for a job, and the recruiter can then start working with those. A systemic skills framework is good for automatically defining skills for roles, but it is not a requirement. Internal hiring processes benefit from a skills framework more, as skills help build a fair internal talent market.

Internal Talent Marketplace:

Internal Talent Marketplace (or Talent Marketplace) is an exciting innovation in skill-based hiring. It leverages platforms to match internal candidates with new opportunities based on their skills and aspirations. These opportunities can range from full-time roles to part-time, project-based, or temporary assignments. The particularly transformative aspect of this approach is that it normalizes part-time or short-term assignments, greatly benefiting both employees and organizations.

The foundation of a talent marketplace is twofold: understanding an employee's current skill set and their future role aspirations. By defining roles in terms of the skills required and matching employees with those skills, organizations can unlock hidden potential.

Example: Imagine Sarah, a finance controller with proven project management skills. She could be matched with a part-time program management opportunity in the Mergers and Acquisitions (M&A) unit. Sarah's financial acumen and project management expertise make her an excellent fit. The platform could notify Sarah and encourage her to apply, enabling her to develop additional skills like culture change, product portfolio design, or organizational strategy, all while contributing to the M&A team's success.

For such scenarios to materialize, the talent marketplace platform needs comprehensive data on Sarah's skills, aspirations, and the requirements of the M&A role. A well-structured skills framework provides this critical information.

Why Talent Marketplaces Matter

Talent marketplaces empower organizations to:

1. **Increase Talent Fluidity**: Encourage internal mobility and, thus, collaboration between units. Internal mobility is a powerful tool for personal growth, employee engagement, and retention. However, moving employees with the right skills to relevant roles will most likely increase overall organization capability and readiness.

2. **Promote on-the-job Skill Development**: Normalize part-time gigs for skills growth. Organizations can market part-time needs and create flexibility for employees to work on them. These part-time gigs, which allow employees to learn by doing alongside their colleagues, will be powerful, just like Sarah in the example above.

3. **Enhance Networking**: Facilitating connections across the organization. The talent movements and part-time gigs will expose employees to units and leaders that they would not normally have. If those internal assignments are done at scale, say 10% of the organization every year, at the end of the third year, the organization would have significantly larger connections across the units.

Advanced platforms like Gloat, Fuel50, and Eightfold facilitate this process with user-friendly interfaces and matching algorithms. Meanwhile, many Human Capital Management (HCM) systems are developing their own marketplace modules—the competitive landscape and innovation pressure organizations to implement skills inventories and assessments.

Practical Considerations

1. **Organizational Scale**: Talent marketplaces are most effective for larger organizations. For companies with fewer than 5,000 employees, the investment may outweigh the benefits.

2. **Cost**: These platforms often involve substantial subscription fees and require significant integration and maintenance efforts. Organizations should not underestimate the hard and

soft costs of integration, which usually are downplayed by the vendors.

3. **ROI Evaluation**: Before adopting such systems, leadership must carefully assess the total cost of ownership and potential return on investment. Maintaining relevance and usability over time demands ongoing commitment.

Upskilling and Development:

The goal of any skills initiative is to empower employees and strengthen organizational capabilities. Skills inventories and standardized definitions, often housed in HCM systems, enable organizations to:

1. Identify current strengths.
2. Develop targeted learning programs to close capability gaps.

With a capable learning and development unit, organizations can be intentional about who and how they develop. Who in the organization has the base skills and aspirations to be developed for future capability needs? Together with the internal marketplace above, the intentional development of employees can be very powerful.

Example: If data modeling is identified as a critical skill for data engineers, the organization needs expert-level engineers (level four on a scale of five). A learning program could then be designed to elevate engineers from level three to four within six months by placing them in training programs and assigning them more complex projects.

While this example simplifies and idealizes the use of skills inventories, it closely mirrors reality, provided organizations avoid the common pitfall of defining all skills for everyone.

Workforce Planning for Future Readiness

Workforce planning is an essential process for ensuring that an organization has the right talent to meet its goals. It can be approached at different levels of detail, each offering its own advantages and challenges.

Traditional Headcount Planning

Most organizations start with basic headcount planning, which focuses on forecasting the total number of employees needed for the upcoming years. This approach is often tied to financial forecasts and budgeting. For example, a company currently has 380 employees, and it might plan to have 400 employees next year due to its product portfolio and revenue growth.

Role-Based Workforce Planning

A more detailed approach is role-based planning. Instead of a single number, organizations allocate headcount across specific roles. For instance, the same 400 employees might be broken down into 150 developers, 30 support staff, 45 sales representatives, and other roles. This helps organizations better understand and plan for the distribution of their workforce.

Skills-Based Workforce Planning

Skills-based planning integrates the specific skills required for each role. For example, among the 150 developers, the plan might specify that 45 should be front-end developers with experience in iOS and Android app development. This level of planning enables a much more precise understanding of workforce needs.

The advantage of a skills initiative is that the organization has a better view of the AS IS capabilities. Given the organization has defined the critical skills for the majority of roles and has assessed the current employees against the required proficiencies in the roles, the skills inventory would give a sound overview of the capabilities of the organization. From that "AS-IS" status, based on the mid and long-term business strategies, the organization can start planning for future capabilities.

While skills-based planning can be done without a structured skills framework, having such a framework speeds up the process and ensures consistency. However, organizations should be cautious not to overcomplicate the process. Introducing a skills framework into workforce planning can sometimes create unnecessary complexity. Instead, it's often more practical to focus on identifying critical skills and roles without fully embedding a skills framework into the planning process.

Steps for Success:

1. Define Key Skills: Engage business leaders to identify critical skills for mid- and long-term strategies. For instance, a company focusing on digitization might prioritize cloud development skills for platforms like Azure or Google Cloud. Outcome: "We need 5-10 Cloud Architects for Google Cloud and 30-35 developers with cloud application experience by the end of next year."

   The above outcome can be gathered from leaders without a skills framework as well if the leaders know exactly what capabilities they have today.

   After having identified the need for cloud architects and developers, the organization can work on the sourcing strategies for those skills.

2. Apply 'Build, Buy, Borrow' Tactics:

   - Build: Upskill existing employees with adjacent competencies.
   - Buy: Recruit new talent with critical skills.
   - Borrow: Partner with contractors or other businesses to temporarily fill gaps.

Having a skills framework can help you make decisions about building, buying, or borrowing talent more structured and actionable. For example, employees with skills adjacent to cloud architecture can be identified for upskilling through targeted training and project assignments. Alternatively, hiring teams can focus their search and build pipelines for candidates with the right skills.

Workforce planning is often more discussed than effectively implemented. A practical, cautious approach is key. Overly complicated, skills-based workforce planning can create significant issues. Leaders may become disengaged, relying heavily on forms, templates, and approval processes. This can shift core responsibilities, such as building competent teams, to HR, which is a situation no organization desires.

Rethinking Compensation for Skills

Should compensation be tied to skills? The short answer is no.

While skills are a driver of outcomes, compensating for skills alone can be problematic. Employees might accumulate skills without translating them into meaningful contributions. Compensation should primarily reflect individual impact.

Key Considerations:

1. Scarce skills, like advanced AI expertise, often command market premiums. However, due to rapid upskilling trends, these premiums are often temporary. Skill-based compensation policies rarely catch up to that rapid market speed.
2. Skills are fluid and difficult to assess precisely, making skill-based pay risky.

While skill-based compensation may work in specific contexts, organizations should approach such models cautiously, ensuring they align with broader performance and impact metrics.

The five major talent applications of the skills framework discussed here will transform an organization into a skills-based one. Most of the applications, except for a full talent marketplace, can also be put in place without a detailed skills framework. A reminder that will have come up often in this section.

Summary and Main Takeaways

What is realistic and what is hype:

1. Jobs Will Always Have Outcomes: Jobs will never be defined solely by skills. Expected outcomes will always be a key descriptor, providing broader frames rather than detailed job description bullets. Let's remain realistic about the role of skills.

2. The shift towards people and their skills and making a person's available skills part of the work design is good for employees and employers. Organizations are getting rid of rigid task-based job descriptions, and the skills topic contributes to the flexibility of work design.

3. Skepticism Towards Vendor AI: Don't rely entirely on the AI capabilities of vendors or black-box algorithms to fix your skills inventory or find the right candidate with the right skills. You still need to do the heavy lifting of defining and assessing skills. GenAI or Large Language Models (LLM) will evolve fast and be a significant enabler.

Checklist for Skills

- Make sure the CEO and executive team understand the costs and return on investment. Use the questions covered earlier in the section to ensure that everyone understands the invisible costs included.
- Focus on Key Roles and Skills: Avoid defining every skill for every job in your organization. Instead, focus on the top 20-30 roles that encompass 80% of your workforce and define only

the critical skills needed for those jobs. For example, don't include "presentation skills" for a front-end developer.

-   Use Standard Skill Definitions: Most of your roles will be standard in the industry. If you can use standard skill definitions, there is no need to reinvent skills for a Finance Controller. Standard skills will enable your organization to do benchmarks and make candidate skill matching easier.
-   Use Standard Level Definitions: Defining necessary skills is challenging, but defining proficiency levels and assessing individuals' proficiency is even tougher. Opt for standard level descriptions, four or five standard proficiency levels for each skill.
-   Simplify Skill Assessments: Use line manager-verified self-assessments, which may sacrifice some accuracy but offer significant simplicity and speed. They also send the right signals to the organization.
-   Manage Executive Expectations: Avoid overpromising to executives. Your initial skills solution will likely not be perfect. Under-promise and overdeliver to manage expectations effectively.
-   Velocity Is Your Friend: Avoid spending 18 months on a skills initiative. By deciding on the right scope, involving business representatives at the right time, and assembling a strong project team, you should aim to see initial results by the end of the sixth month. Prolonging the process beyond this can risk tiring the organization.
-   Reserve energy for skills-based talent applications. The skills framework is only the foundation. Focus on employee development and internal mobility as the initial applications.

The skills approach will center work design on humans and their capabilities, particularly for knowledge workers with niche skill sets. When used wisely, skills-based applications can help develop employees and create new opportunities for those seeking growth. By following the suggestions in this section, organizations can effectively avoid getting trapped in a complex skills initiative. They can implement pragmatic and dynamic solutions that foster a culture of development and growth, which will ideally extend to society as well.

Generative AI will disrupt this field with its ability to accurately assess skills from operational data and by being an excellent tutor for skill development. Skill software, learning platforms, and talent market-place applications will soon be replaced by one AI solution.

www.ingramcontent.com/pod-product-compliance
Lightning Source LLC
LaVergne TN
LVHW011803070326
832902LV00032B/4653